The Wildlife of New England

The
WILDLIFE
of NEW ENGLAND

A VIEWER'S GUIDE

John S. Burk

UNIVERSITY OF NEW HAMPSHIRE PRESS

Durham, New Hampshire

UNIVERSITY OF NEW HAMPSHIRE PRESS

An imprint of University Press of New England

www.upne.com

© 2011 University of New Hampshire

All rights reserved

Manufactured in the United States of America

Designed by Eric M. Brooks

Typeset in Arnhem and Fresco Sans by Passumpsic Publishing

Unless otherwise specified, all photographs were taken by the author.

Maps courtesy of Virginia Dickinson and Michelle Grald.

University Press of New England is a member of the Green Press
Initiative. The paper used in this book meets their minimum
requirement for recycled paper.

For permission to reproduce any of the material in this book, contact
Permissions, University Press of New England, One Court Street,
Suite 250, Lebanon NH 03766; or visit www.upne.com

Library of Congress Cataloging-in-Publication Data appear on the
last printed page of this book.

5 4 3 2 1

CONTENTS

Color images follow page 100

ACKNOWLEDGMENTS

Thanks are due a number of people whose assistance was of great benefit to this project. For information about specific places, thanks to Jody Anastasio of the Cape Cod National Seashore, Beth Bazler, Jan Beckett of the Friends of the Sunkhaze Meadows National Wildlife Refuge, Chris Eaton of the Massachusetts Audubon Society, Chris Ellison, Karen Flabin, David Govatski of the Friends of Pondicherry National Wildlife Refuge, Anne Harding, Brian Hall, Andy Haskell of Lily Bay State Park, René Laubach of the Pleasant Valley Wildlife Sanctuary, Kendall Marden of the Steve Powell Wildlife Management Area, Bob Mayer, the New England Basking Shark Project, Dawn Osborne and Kim Miedema of the Sharon Audubon Center, Polly Pillsbury, Tom Pirro, the volunteers and webmaster of romepointseals.org, Jay Sullivan of the Great Bay National Estuarine Research Reserve, Tom Wansleben, Kate Walker of the Green Mountain National Forest, Laurie Wunder of the Umbagog National Wildlife Refuge, the White River Partnership, Rachel from the Willard Pond Audubon Sanctuary, and the rangers at Baxter State Park, Beavertail State Park, Franconia Notch State Park, the Monomoy National Wildlife Refuge.

For leading informative field trips and tours, thanks to the Cape Cod Museum of Natural History, Sue and Ron Cloutier, Larry and Joan Duprey, Jeff Johnstone, Carl Kamp, John McCarter, the Northfield Mountain Recreational Center, Norton's of Jonesport, Maine, Dave Small, Mark Taylor, Paul Wanta, Nick Wisnewski and Valerie Major of the Walnut Hill Tracking School, and Linda Woodard of Maine Audubon.

For tracking down and providing a variety of useful sources and other resources, thanks to the Athol Public Library, the Harvard Forest, the Petersham Memorial Library, and the Woods Memorial Library.

Special thanks to Brooks Mathewson for contributing several excellent photographs and sharing sighting reports from several locales, and to Tony D'Amato and Elizabeth Farnsworth for feedback on potential sites and continuous encouragement.

Special thanks as well to my editor Richard Pult for encouragement, feedback, and the opportunity to pursue this project, and Amanda Dupuis, copy editor Glenn Novak, and the rest of the staff of the University Press of New England for their work throughout the publication process.

Thanks to my parents John and Lale Burk and brother Nicholas for their encouragement in learning about and exploring the outdoors over the years, and accompanying me on some of the site visits.

INTRODUCTION

Nestled in an especially picturesque setting beneath Mount Katahdin and neighboring South Turner Mountain, Maine's Sandy Stream Pond offers an ideal combination of scenery and wildlife viewing opportunities. As I followed a trail along its west shores on one sunny late June morning, a solitary cow moose was just exiting the water after a breakfast of aquatic plants. Over the next hour, there was plenty to observe: a white-tailed buck made a brief appearance to take a drink at the pond's outlet, a group of red-breasted mergansers cruised back and forth across the shallow water, two belted kingfishers staged a whirling territorial duel, and darner dragonflies hovered above the vegetation along the shore.

Around midmorning, two female moose with calves appeared on opposite edges of the pond. One of the youngsters, whose newborn status was evident by its light tan coat and unsteady legs, dropped out of sight into the vegetation and rocks along the shoreline, while the other tentatively followed its mother into the water. Soon a young bull, whose stubby antlers had a coating of velvet, emerged from the woods and began working his way around the pond. The calf that had been drinking returned quickly to the shore, while his enraged mother chased the bull three-quarters of the way across the pond. When the mother returned, she couldn't find her calf and waded over to the other female, who was now with her own offspring, and the two engaged in a tense stare-down for several minutes. By morning's end, no fewer than 11 moose, including a large bull and a pair of female yearlings, had made appearances to escape the summer heat and ubiquitous insects.

Several weeks later, I rode in a small tour boat as it navigated the sandbars of Monomoy Point at Cape Cod's elbow amid groups of basking gray and harbor seals. Just a matter of hours from central Maine, this was an altogether different environment of mudflats, salt marshes, tidal creeks, and gentle topography where elevations of a few feet changed the natural communities. We then landed on one of the islands, where there were large colonies of terns and gulls. The late-summer migrations were well under way, and mixed groups of shorebirds joined uncommon residents such as American oystercatchers in feeding forays along the tidal flats.

It's indeed an exciting time to be a wildlife watcher in the Northeast, as many species have recently rebounded to levels unseen in previous centuries and decades. Today, sightings of moose, white-tailed deer, beavers, great blue herons, wild turkeys, humpback whales, and gray and harbor seals are commonplace, but these encounters aren't to be taken for granted. Indeed, only a matter of decades ago one could travel throughout much of the region and have little or no chance of seeing these and other iconic species.

New England's wildlife populations have undergone a remarkable series of changes over the past 400 years, reflecting the change in the region's landscape. In the period prior to European settlement, the region was largely forested, with abundant wildlife and inhabited by a variety of Native peoples, some of whom practiced agriculture by rotating fields on cycles. When colonists arrived from the seventeenth century onward, they rapidly transformed this landscape by clearing extensive areas for permanent agricultural use. At the height of this activity, it is estimated, roughly three-quarters of the region was cleared, especially in the southern and central regions. Though farming wasn't as widespread in the rugged north woods, much of the area was logged, and very little virgin forest remains today. As a result, many species were deprived of their food and cover source.

At the same time, unregulated hunting and trapping, motivated by markets (beavers and whales, for example), predator control (wolves and mountain lions), subsistence (deer and wild turkeys), or merely sport, further decimated populations of many species, to the point that many were greatly reduced or entirely eliminated.

As the nineteenth century progressed and then drew toward a close, many New England farms were abandoned, and the region's forests and wildlife began to gradually recover. However, during the mid-twentieth century, the widespread use of pesticides such as DDT had devastating consequences for bald eagles, peregrine falcons, osprey, and other species. The one benefit from this unfortunate episode was that it triggered studies and conservation efforts that were part of an increased environmental awareness.

Thanks to the regrowth of the woodlands and many successful reintroduction projects, many species are again thriving. Two notable exceptions are eastern timber wolves and mountain lions, whose continued absence has had a lasting effect on the food chain. The possible presence of both species in New England has been a subject of substantial intrigue and debate, and recent evidence indicates that these large predators may again roam isolated areas of the region. With the return of forests has come the

Nesting boxes and open fields, such as those at the Sharon Audubon Center in Connecticut, provide homes and habitat for eastern bluebirds and other grassland species.

loss of open and brushy habitats, and species that favor these areas such as eastern bluebirds, bobolinks, meadowlarks, and New England cottontails have inevitably declined in recent decades.

While New England's wildlife populations are again thriving, several concerns remain. Increased suburban and shoreline development reduces productive habitat for many species, exposes wildlife to conflicts with humans, domestic animals, and predators such as coyotes, raccoons, and seagulls that thrive in these areas, and can disrupt travel corridors to vernal pools and other breeding habitats. The forests are continually stressed by pests and diseases, such as the chestnut blight, which effectively eliminated one of the Northeast's most important wildlife trees during the early twentieth century, and the hemlock woolly adelgid, an insect that has infested and killed large groves of eastern hemlocks in areas of southern New England. Individual species are vulnerable to diseases, such as the brain worm that is fatal to moose, and white-nose syndrome, a fungus that has decimated wintering brown bat colonies in the Northeast in recent years.

MANAGEMENT AND DIVERSITY

In order to provide habitats that benefit a wide variety of wildlife, many conservation agencies manage their land by maintaining fields, meadows, brushy thickets, old orchards, and freshwater impoundments. "Edges," or areas where different habitat types meet, are especially significant zones that offer multiple benefits for wildlife, including food, cover, drinking water, and breeding habitat. Clearings replicate to a certain degree the effect of forest fires, which were once part of the natural cycle but have been largely suppressed by modern technology.

Some species, including moose and snowshoe hares (which in turn are a food source for predators such as Canada lynx), also benefit from timber cutting, which creates a food source of young hardwood sprouts. Other human interventions that have benefited wildlife include the construction of artificial reservoirs and flood control lakes; the construction of the Quabbin and Wachusett reservoirs in central Massachusetts provided prime habitat for common loons and bald eagles.

VIEWING TIPS

With the return of all these creatures have come wonderfully diverse viewing opportunities. The most important rule for wildlife watchers is to respect the animals and their habitats. Collecting wildlife is illegal, causes the animal considerable stress, and displaces it from its familiar surroundings; if an animal remains motionless and seemingly tame, it is obeying a defensive instinct. Leave baby animals alone; even if they appear to be helpless, their mother is often in the area. Never feed wild animals, as this conditions them to behave unnaturally and potentially aggressively around humans. Use binoculars, spotting scopes, and telephoto lenses for close-up views. In winter, it's especially important to keep a distance from moose, deer, and other animals, in order to not stress their already limited energy reserves.

The best way to ensure a successful viewing trip is to simply know the basic life histories of the various species, especially their habitats and migration patterns, if applicable. You're unlikely to see harlequin ducks, snow geese, or snowy owls during the summer, a monarch butterfly in spring, a bluebird or indigo bunting in the deep woods, or a black bear, puffin, humpback whale, or turtle in the dead of winter; but in the right season and habitat, sightings of many of these creatures are almost guaranteed. Even resident species that are active and present year-round, such as moose and seals, have favored areas that change by the season.

Blending into the surrounding landscape significantly increases the odds of glimpsing or photographing an elusive creature. Camouflage, after all, enables most species to survive and hunt successfully. Hunters and photographers often wait silently in full-body camouflage or blinds for the right look at a subject. Even if you don't go to this extreme, simply wearing neutral colors makes a difference. Automobiles often are effective as blinds, as many animals will tolerate their presence but quickly disappear as soon as a door opens.

When on the trail, walk at a relaxed, quiet pace, and make frequent stops to look in all directions and listen for sounds and sign. Unlike traditional hiking, where there is usually a defined main goal such as a scenic vista or waterfall, wildlife sightings and encounters may occur at any time, and a successful trip doesn't necessarily require completing a trail in its entirety.

Timing is crucial, both on a seasonal and daily basis. The odds of seeing most mammals and birds are greatest as the light changes in the early morning and evening. The periods before and after a passing storm can also be productive. Other creatures, such as butterflies, dragonflies, reptiles, and amphibians, are visible in the middle of the day.

Once you do find a subject to watch, take note of its movements and activities and the surrounding habitat. Veteran bird-watchers can distinguish certain species by their flight patterns alone. Keeping an informal nature journal is a great way to document your sightings and may even be of use for wildlife studies as the populations and ranges of many animals continue to change. Items worth recording include date, place, time of day, weather conditions, and feeding behavior.

Finally, have patience. Though there are many fairly reliable viewing opportunities, wildlife watching can be notoriously fickle, even for the most experienced naturalists and outdoorsperson. It's entirely possible to spend hours outside without seeing anything, then have an animal walk through your backyard or motel parking lot. It's not uncommon for photographers and bird-watchers to spend hours or even days staking out a particular area for brief glimpses of a subject. Enjoy the species you do see, and with a bit of field time you'll have plenty of stories for your friends.

TRACKING

You can easily spend months or even years outdoors without actually seeing a fisher, coyote, or bobcat in the wild, but during the course of a single short winter walk in the right place, you may well uncover evidence of these and many other animals. Options for trackers range from simply identifying the various prints while walking a particular area (your backyard is a fine place to start) to a more involved excursion following an animal's

Tracks of bobcat (left) and river otter (right) along the edge of a frozen lake in winter.

prints through the backcountry. If doing the latter, be prepared to negotiate obstacles such as dense tangles of shrubs and tree saplings and wet areas; a map and compass are strongly recommended. If unsure about your location, backtrack along your own trail to the starting point. It's also a good idea to check the rules of the place you're visiting, as some landowners don't allow travel off designated footpaths.While it's helpful to be able to identify each individual print, trail patterns are an equally important, and often more interesting, part of the learning process. Each animal has a different stride length and walking pattern, and following trails is perhaps the most exciting part of tracking, as paths reveal travel patterns, hunting activities, and rest areas. Fishers and river otters are among the most interesting species to follow, as they routinely travel long distances and leave evidence of a variety of intriguing behaviors. Because some animals, such as Canada lynx, fishers, and moose, are still expanding or reclaiming historic ranges in portions of New England or are altogether uncommon, tracks offer an important resource for wildlife researchers.

Though tracking is most easily done during winter, plenty of clues are available for careful observers in all seasons, including prints in mud and sand, browsed vegetation, claw and antler rubs on trees, and scat and droppings.

BIRD CALLS

Another great way to enhance viewing skills is to learn birdsongs, which allow observers to locate and identify birds otherwise hidden in tall trees and shrubby thickets. From the melodious, flutelike song of wood and hermit thrushes to the deep-throated gurgle of American bitterns, each species has a distinctive, recognizable call, and with a little field time you'll soon know where and when to expect them. One method is to start listening for calls as individual species return from migrations, and gradually build a knowledge base as spring progresses. Relating calls to specific sounds and inflections, such as the "squeaky wheel" of black and white warblers, the *drink-your-tea* of rufous-sided towhees, and the laughing "Woody Woodpecker" sound of pileated woodpeckers, is an especially effective technique for learning individual calls. Recordings are available on CDs and Internet sites such as that of the Cornell Lab of Ornithology.

Birdsong peaks in late spring and early summer, when the dawn chorus of songbirds reaches its height. Many birds are most active in the early morning and evening, though some, such as red-eyed vireos, ovenbirds, and black-throated green warblers, sing throughout the day. The songs gradually taper off around mid-July, and by early to mid-August most areas go largely quiet. Though the various songs are popularly associated as a harmonious harbinger of spring, they are in fact territorial calls that are part of a competitive scramble for mates and nest sites, and individuals often engage in fierce dueling acrobatics when their interests overlap.

While birds are the most conspicuous noisemakers, there are many other sounds in nature, including nocturnal howls and wails of coyotes, the territorial chatter of red squirrels, grunts of alarmed white-tailed deer, mating sounds of courting moose, barking river otters, a beaver's tail-slap, and the various calls and choruses of frogs.

ENCOUNTERS IN THE WILD

All told, wildlife watching in New England is fairly benign compared to the American West and other regions of the world, though there are a handful of circumstances to be aware of. In northern New England, it's not a question of if but when you'll encounter moose, and they are increasingly common in the central and southern regions as well. Though moose often will flee from humans and in some areas may even seem tolerant and approachable, they should be observed at a distance, especially when mother is with her young or when a bull is encountered during the autumn mating

Be alert for moose and other wildlife along New England's roads and highways, especially at dawn and dusk.

season. Signs that a moose is agitated include raised hairs and ears swiveled toward the perceived threat.

The greatest threat that moose pose to humans is road collisions, and hundreds of moose-vehicle collisions occur in New England annually. Moose have dark coats with little reflectivity, are often attracted to grassy margins and wetlands bordering highways (especially when leftover road salt is present in spring), and, as short-sighted creatures, often freeze in the middle of the road as a vehicle approaches. When driving in moose country, reduce your speed, be able to stop well within the range of your headlights, and watch the road edges carefully, especially at dawn and dusk.

Though black bears are elusive in the wilderness, encounters often occur at campgrounds, picnic areas, and backyards, where they have easy access to food and human garbage. Campers should secure food by raising it high out of the reach of potential raiders (10 to 12 feet is recommended), and avoid leaving edible items in vehicles for extended periods. A variety of advice has traditionally been given in regard to bear encounters, but a recommended course of action is to back off slowly and not abandon food if possible (doing so may encourage return visits and harassment of other humans), making noise with pots and pans or a whistle if available.

The odds of encountering a poisonous rattlesnake or copperhead snake in New England by chance are very low, as they generally inhabit isolated outcroppings and avoid humans. Should you come across one, hold still and let it back off, then carefully move away. In the extremely unlikely event of a bite, victims should remain as still as possible while keeping the afflicted area closely below heart level to avoid circulating the venom. If walking to help is necessary, move slowly, exerting the bitten area as little as possible. While bites are rarely fatal, medical help should be immediately sought.

If you encounter a raccoon, fox, coyote, bobcat, skunk, or other mammal behaving in a seemingly friendly, aggressive, or lethargic manner, get away from it as quickly as possible and contact the police or animal control. These are symptoms of rabies, a disease spread by bite that is potentially fatal if not immediately treated by a series of injections.

During the warm months, be prepared for biting insects such as black flies and deerflies, mosquitoes, and ticks, which are anything but rare and uncommon in New England. Head nets and long-sleeved garments offer the best protection. Choices of repellents range from skin- and family-friendly products to sprays that contain high concentrations of diethyl-meta-toluamide (commonly known as DEET), which are most effective but present potential health issues, especially when regularly applied to bare skin.

While most bites are little more than a temporary nuisance, those made by tiny deer ticks (whose 1/16-inch size is half that of wood ticks) can result in serious complications if undetected. Early symptoms include weakness and fatigue, joint pain, fever, dizziness, sore throat, and swollen lymph nodes, and within a month a telltale circular red rash often appears at the bite location. If any of these signs appear, contact a doctor immediately, as the disease can easily be treated in its early stages. When extracting the tick, save as much of it as possible, as it may serve as an important part of the diagnosis.

Finally, be aware of human hunters, particularly in late autumn, early winter, and certain spring weeks. It's best to avoid active areas altogether, especially early and late in the day; if you do go out, wear plenty of blaze orange and stay on marked trails. Wildlife sanctuaries that prohibit hunting are good options during this time, though sportsmen may be present on adjacent properties. The presence of parked vehicles along road edges is a reliable indicator of hunting in a particular area.

"VAGRANTS"

One of the neatest aspects of wildlife watching is its unpredictability. In 1996 an ivory gull, a resident of the high Arctic that rarely ventures south of the Canadian maritime provinces, made a visit to the waterfront of Portland, Maine. Two years later a harbor seal made its way up the Connecticut River to Holyoke, Massachusetts, where it was something of a local celebrity for several days; and in 2009 a number of great white sharks suddenly appeared at the Monomoy Point area of Cape Cod. Other accidental and vagrant birds that have been recorded in New England include magnificent frigate birds, brown and white pelicans, wood storks, purple gallinules, painted buntings, and mountain bluebirds. The most likely areas to find species well outside their normal ranges are coastal "traps" where storms often blow in long-distance travelers, such as Maine's Monhegan Island, Plum Island in Massachusetts, and Hammonasset Beach in Connecticut.

BACKYARD WILDLIFE

A great starting point for wildlife viewers of all ages is your own backyard. Among the many creatures that are often present are birds, butterflies, dragonflies, fireflies, squirrels, rabbits, foxes, and milk and garter snakes. Maintaining your backyard for wildlife is not only an excellent way to observe your wild neighbors, but it also provides crucial habitat to balance areas that are lost to development on a daily basis. When planning a garden, some basic considerations include reducing open lawn space, which has minimal value for wildlife, maintaining trees and shrubs with varied heights and open travel corridors, using native plants, and having a water source available. Many books are available with specific information about plantings and design.

VIEWING WITH CHILDREN

Wildlife viewing is an excellent way to introduce children to the natural world, as many youngsters gravitate to animals. Family trips offer opportunities to appreciate the familiar species that are often taken for granted, such as robins and blue jays, squirrels and chipmunks, swallowtail butterflies, and bullfrogs and painted turtles. It's unrealistic to expect children, or many adults for that matter, to have the patience to stake out a pond for hours or find a rare warbler in a tall tree, but there are more than enough common species worthy of their attention. Many of the sites detailed in this guide include visitor centers with informative and interactive exhibits and stores.

When on the trail, be sure to select routes that are age appropriate, and allow for plenty of rest breaks. Make frequent stops so that children can look around with binoculars and magnifying glasses, and let them become actively involved by leading a search for a favorite animal. It's also a good idea to have snacks available, as this adds a positive reinforcement to the experience.

Some hands-on activities at home include helping assemble and erect a nesting box, maintaining bird feeders, and encouraging children to draw or write down creatures that they've seen.

EQUIPMENT

Binoculars and spotting scopes are invaluable tools for wildlife watchers, as they allow identification and viewing of elusive subjects such as songbirds in tall trees, seabirds and marine mammals on the open ocean, and hidden wading birds and muskrats in marshes. Prices run the gamut, from inexpensive pocket-size pairs to thousands of dollars for top-line models that offer features such as image stabilization and watertight construction. The large, bulkier models with wider lenses offer the sharpest views and best performance in low light, while pocket pairs are ideal for distance hikers and photographers looking to save weight and space.

Spotting scopes offer much higher magnification than binoculars and are especially useful in areas with long fields of view, including hawkwatch sites, marshes, mudflats and beaches, and open water. Some considerations to make when evaluating a purchase include ease in carrying over distances, lens diameter and performance in low light, type of glass, and comfort for eyeglass wearers.

Wildlife photography is a challenging but rewarding pastime that has become increasingly popular and practical with recent advances in technology. All the aforementioned viewing tips apply to being in the right place at the right time for the right shot. Adequate shutter speed is crucial when photographing animate subjects. Even with a tripod, it's best to operate at no less than $\frac{1}{125}$ second, though slower speeds can work if the subject pauses. Whether you have a digital or film camera, use the lowest possible ISO setting. Though some cameras and films offer reasonable quality at the faster speeds (ISO 400 and above), these images hold less detail and have more "noise" than the lower levels.

For versatility in the field, ease in carrying over distances, or a low-cost starter, telephoto zoom lens with focal lengths of 70–100 mm to 300–500 mm are a good option. With minimum apertures of f4.5 to f6.3, these are a level slower than professional lenses but are workable in most conditions. Those that start at f8 or f11 are much more limited and useful only in bright light. Fixed-length lenses of 500 mm and above are much more expensive.

Teleconverters are an inexpensive option for increasing the working power of a lens by 1.4 to 2 times, though they create slower shutter speeds and can cause distortion and reduced image quality. If your main interest is birds, it's best to have an outfit with at least 500 mm of focal length. Tripods are especially important when using telephoto lenses, which amplify even the slightest movement; monopods and shoulder stocks offer additional flexibility.

Macro lenses and related accessories such as extension tubes and diopters are used for close-ups of insects and amphibians; a lens with at least 100 mm focal length allows some working distance from the subject. While many photographers concentrate on close-up views, don't overlook wide-angle possibilities that show subjects in their natural habitat, such as moose in a pond or shorebirds along a beach. Even if no wildlife are present, there will likely be plenty of subtle sign, such as tracks in snow, mud, and sand, browsed vegetation, and trees that have been clawed or rubbed.

In the field it's essential to be able to operate your equipment quickly, so have the settings ready at the start of your outing. One useful mode that simplifies shooting is "aperture priority" (AV), where you set the aperture, and the camera automatically provides the correct shutter speed. Though it's always best to be as selective as possible, throwaway shots are inevitable with animate subjects, and the more you take, the better the odds of a good image.

If possible, try to avoid "bull's-eyeing" or centering the subject, as off-center images are generally more effective and appealing.

USING THIS GUIDE

This book details some of the best places in each of New England's six states to view wildlife. These include areas with reliable spectacles, such as moose in the Connecticut Lakes, the snow goose migration in upstate Vermont, and the seals at Rome Point in Rhode Island, as well as examples of New England's many diverse habitats, such as the alpine ridge of the Presidential Range, the boreal bogs and forests of Vermont's Northeast Kingdom, and the marshes at the mouth of the Connecticut River. The description of each site includes an overview of its habitats and features. "Viewing" includes information on representative species and the best times, seasons, and places to see them. Access to each preserve is detailed in the "Getting Around" section, which includes information about trails, automobile and boat access, hours, and recommended hikes that are especially suited to wildlife viewing. Driving directions, stewardship, and closest towns are also provided. Please note that trail conditions, fees, visitor center hours, and land ownership are subject to change. Call ahead or visit the location's website before your visit.

Following this information, you will find profiles of more than 55 of New England's unique or significant species, arranged by their primary habitats. These include iconic wilderness symbols such as moose, common loons, and bald eagles; familiar creatures that are often easily visible in the wild, including red efts, green tiger beetles, and painted turtles; and animals with especially unusual physical attributes or behaviors, such as hermit crabs, swordfish, and Virginia opossums. In many instances histories of population changes over time are presented.

The Wildlife of New England

CONNECTICUT

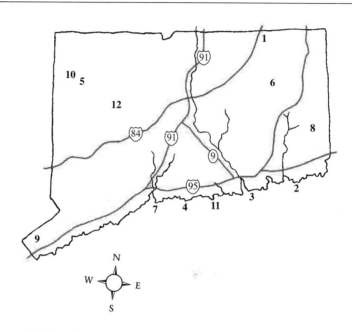

1. Bigelow Hollow State Park and Nipmuck State Forest
2. Bluff Point State Park and Coastal Reserve
3. Connecticut River Estuary
4. Hammonasset Beach State Reservation
5. Housatonic Meadows State Park
6. James L. Goodwin State Forest
7. Lighthouse Point Park
8. Pachaug State Forest
9. Quaker Ridge, Audubon Greenwich
10. Sharon Audubon Center
11. Stewart B. McKinney National Wildlife Refuge: Salt Meadow Unit
12. White Memorial Foundation Conservation Center

CONNECTICUT

Bigelow Hollow State Park and Nipmuck State Forest

Connecticut Department of Forests and Parks, 860-928-9200,
www.ct.gov/dep

CLOSEST TOWN: Union

DIRECTIONS: From Interstate 84 in Union, a short distance south of its junction
with the Massachusetts Turnpike, take exit 3 and follow CT 171 east for 1.4
miles. At the junction with CT 190 turn left and continue on CT 171 for another
1.3 miles and follow signs for the state park. After passing a view of Bigelow
Pond, look for the entrance on the north side of the road. There is no fee
on weekdays; $9 (Connecticut residents) or $15 (out of state) is charged on
weekends and holidays.

Northeastern Connecticut's "Quiet Corner" region is a pleasant mix of
rolling hills, forests, numerous ponds and streams, and classic New England
villages. One of its most wild and scenic areas lies within the bounds
of the contiguous Bigelow Hollow State Park and Nipmuck State Forest,
which encompass nearly 10,000 combined acres. Established in 1905,
Nipmuck is the state's second-oldest state forest and today is actively managed to promote a diverse woodland ecosystem, with groves of oak, birch,
maple, white pine, and hemlock.

The preserve's attractions include a trio of picturesque ponds, including
finger-shaped Breakneck Pond, which extends north for more than a mile
and a half to Sturbridge, Massachusetts, where its northern tip protrudes a
few hundred feet across the state line. Free from any evidence of development and bordered by the extensive forests, the pond is home to a variety
of wildlife and some of the state's finest hiking trails.

Bordering the southwest corner of the preserve is popular Mashapaug
Pond, which is privately owned but accessible to boaters and swimmers
from the state forest boat launch on its south shore. Next to the park entrance is the smaller Bigelow Pond, which is home to a nature trail, picnic
areas, a boat launch, and a fishing platform. A recently restored wildlife
marsh is also visible from the park road.

VIEWING

This is one of the best places in Connecticut to check for moose and
their signs, as neighboring Worcester County in Massachusetts hosts a
healthy and rapidly growing population that has been steadily expanding
southward throughout the past quarter century. Watch for large piles of

droppings that are an inch or more in diameter, much larger than those of white-tailed deer. In 1914 the state's first reintroduced beavers were released in this area, and over the past century they have rapidly reclaimed their former range, as evidenced by the wetlands and lodges along the trail to the pond. Black bears, bobcats, fishers, porcupines, striped skunks, red squirrels, and red and gray foxes all inhabit these woodlands; mink, river otters, raccoons, and Virginia opossums favor areas near wetlands.

The low vegetation along the pond edges offers abundant habitat for odenates—dragonflies and damselflies. Some common dragonflies to watch for are lancet clubtails, common whitetails, and widow and slaty skimmers. Their smaller damselfly relatives include black-bodied aurora damsels, colorful eastern forktails, slender spreadwings, ebony jewelwings, and several similar species of bluets. Some woodland butterflies to watch for along the trails are mourning cloaks, red-spotted purples, viceroys, and tiger and spicebush swallowtails. The latter are most often seen in deciduous woods, swamps, and parks and fields.

On sunny warm-weather days, watch for painted turtles basking on exposed rocks and fallen logs in the ponds. Much less common are spotted turtles, aptly named for the flecks of yellow spots across their black shells. They are among the first turtles to emerge from winter hibernation and may be glimpsed around vernal pools before leaves come out on the trees. Familiar amphibians here include bull, greed, wood, tree, and pickerel frogs. Fish found throughout the ponds include bluegill, yellow perch, chain pickerel, large and smallmouth bass, green sunfish, and brown and rainbow trout.

Feeding on these fine stores are belted kingfishers and wading birds such as great blue and green herons. Eastern wood peewees, black-throated green warblers, American redstarts, and other migratory songbirds arrive during spring; eastern kingbirds and tree swallows hunt insects over the wetlands.

GETTING AROUND

More than 25 miles of recreational trails are distributed throughout this area, which is popular with a variety of users. From the park entrance on Route 171, the 1.1-mile park auto road leads to the boat launch at Bigelow Pond at 0.2 mile, the picnic area and trailheads for the Breakneck and Bigelow Pond trails at 0.6 mile, and ends at the boat launch for Mashapaug Pond.

The 6.5-mile circuit around Breakneck Pond is a long but especially interesting and pleasant hike, with numerous scenic views of the pond from a variety of perspectives. From the parking area that also provides access to Bigelow Pond, the white-blazed East Ridge Trail leads past a beaver wetland and continues in the woods for 1.1 miles to a junction at the pond's southern tip, where the loop begins. Here hikers have the option of bearing right on the Nipmuck Trail, which follows the east shore for 2 miles, or left on the Pond View Trail, which traverses the rockier, rolling terrain along the west side; both routes meet again at the northern tip on the Massachusetts state line. Allow four to five hours to complete the round-trip. For a shorter walk, you can simply follow the East Ridge Trail to viewpoints along the south shores, then backtrack to the trailhead for a round-trip of 2.4 miles.

The 2-mile loop that circles Bigelow Pond may be accessed from the same parking area, or at the picnic area pullouts along the park road near the entrance. This yellow-blazed footpath follows rolling terrain past a series of glacial boulders along the base of the rocky hill along the west shore. At the pond's outlet it briefly follows a short path that parallels Route 171 adjacent to the park entrance, then turns north along the east shore. After passing a fisherman's platform with fine views across the water, it crosses two wood bridges over streams along the pond's north shore.

Another long-distance option is the 5-mile-long Mashapaug View Trail, which winds along the south shores of Mashapaug Pond before making a long loop through the woodlands, hills, and streams in the reservation's southwest corner.

 ## Bluff Point State Park and Coastal Reserve

Connecticut Forest and Parks, 860-424-3200, www.ct.gov/dep
CLOSEST TOWN: Groton
DIRECTIONS: From Interstate 95 in Groton take exit 88 and follow CT 117 south
   to the junction with US 1. Turn right on US 1 south, then left at the first
   light onto Depot Road. Bear right at the entrance to the Amtrak station and
   continue another 0.3 mile to the park entrance at the road's end.

In colonial times, John Winthrop, who served as Connecticut's first governor from 1698 to 1707, was so enamored with the promontory south of Groton known as Bluff Point that he established his mansion there. Nearly three centuries later the state continued to recognize the value of this area by designating the bulk of the point as a coastal reserve in 1975, protecting

The crescent-shaped barrier beach at Bluff Point State Park offers views of wintering waterfowl, shorebirds, crabs, mussels, and other marine wildlife.

the last remaining largely undeveloped tract of land along the state's densely populated coast.

This 800-acre peninsula juts into Long Island Sound, bordered by the Poquonock River to the west and Mumford Cove on the east. Within its bounds are a fine variety of habitats, including maritime oak-hickory woodlands, open grasslands, salt marshes, tidal flats, a narrow barrier beach, eelgrass beds, and dunes. The 40-foot-high rocky bluffs for which the reservation is named offer fine views of Long Island Sound, Fishers Island, the Thames River, and New London harbor. Because a walk of more than a mile is necessary to reach the mile-long barrier beach adjacent to the point, the crowds here are much smaller than at more accessible areas.

VIEWING

Thanks to this diversity, more than 200 bird species have been documented here throughout the various seasons. Check the muddy edges of the river and the barrier beach for black-bellied plovers, ruddy turnstones, spotted sandpipers, common and least terns, and regionally uncommon species and vagrants such as American oystercatchers, black skimmers, Iceland gulls, and roseate terns. In winter, hike to the bluffs and scan Long Island Sound for waterfowl such as buffleheads, common goldeneyes, red-necked and horned grebes, black, common, and surf scoters, common and red-throated loons, canvasbacks, and large flocks of greater and lesser scaups. The upland forests and dense thickets that cover most of the point host migratory songbirds such as rose-breasted grosbeaks, magnolia warblers, and northern parulas, while eastern kingbirds, willow flycatchers, eastern bluebirds, and mockingbirds nest along the edges of open fields.

Eastern coyotes and red and gray foxes and their tracks are most often found in fields and openings near woodland edges. Their prey includes abundant eastern cottontails, which can often be seen feeding along the grassy margins of trails, and field mice and voles. Raccoons and Virginia opossums are most active at night; the latter is North America's only marsupial, or mammal where the female carries her young in a pouch. Like many other areas of the coast, the point is home to a large white-tailed deer population that has significantly impacted the vegetation in certain areas; controlled hunts were conducted during the 1990s to bring the population toward the statewide average.

Look for a variety of marine invertebrates along the beach and in tide pools, including green, hermit, sand, fiddler, and blue crabs. The latter, named for the light blue coloration on its legs, has flat hind legs that allow it to swim rapidly in all directions. Horseshoe crabs, mussels, and clams are other familiar inhabitants of this estuary.

GETTING AROUND

The preserve, which is open from 8 AM to sunset year-round, includes approximately seven miles of easy trails, most of which are gravel roads. From the entrance gate, the main gravel road leads south for 0.1 mile to a junction, where a loop begins. Here the route on the right follows the east bank of the Poquonock River and its associated marshes for roughly half a mile; side trails and vistas on the right offer good viewing from the banks. At 1.2 miles, it reaches the edge of the barrier beach, where you have the option of walking this narrow strip for as far as 1.1 miles (one way) to Bushy Point. The main route continues for another 0.3 mile to the overlook atop the bluffs, 1.5 miles from the trailhead.

Walkers have the option of backtracking from this point, or continuing the circuit by following the path as it curves past Sunset Rock along the edge of the natural area preserve, then leads due north through the peninsula's interior woodlands to the grasslands and the Winthrop home foundation. From the house site it's another 0.9 mile back to the entrance. The loop distance is 3.7 miles, or 5.9 miles if the barrier beach is walked in its entirety. A car-top boat launch at the main entrance provides easy access to the Poquonock River.

 Connecticut River Estuary

Connecticut Department of Environmental Protection, 860-424-3000, www.lisrc.uconn.edu/coastalaccess

CLOSEST TOWNS: Lyme, Old Saybrook

DIRECTIONS: For Ferry Landing Park, from Interstate 95 in Old Saybrook take exit 70 and follow CT 156 south for 0.3 mile to a right (west) turn on Ferry Road, marked by a sign for the Department of Environmental Protection Marine Headquarters. Follow Ferry Road for 0.5 mile to its end at the headquarters parking lot. To reach the boat launches, take exit 70 and follow directions as detailed below.

Given the extent of development along New England's south coast, it's remarkable that no major city encompasses the mouth of the Connecticut River, the region's largest and most celebrated waterway. The river is simply too shallow at this point to accommodate large vessels, and as a result the area never developed into a large port and trade center. The fortuitous result is a large, relatively pristine estuary of considerable ecological significance. The salt marshes, wading birds, and sea turtles here offer a marked contrast to the moose, boreal birds, and spruce-fir groves characteristic of the river's headwaters in the Connecticut Lakes, some 400 miles to the north. The estuary was designated as one of the hemisphere's 40 "Last Great Places" by the Nature Conservancy in 1993.

Along the east bank of the mouth, and separated from the mainland by the narrow channel of the Back River, are 588 acres of tidal marshes collectively known as Great Island. The Roger Tory Peterson Wildlife Management Area, named for the preeminent ornithologist who lived in nearby Old Lyme, protects this unique, fragile complex, where tiny islands of trees grow atop rocky outcroppings. As part of a restoration project, mosquito control ditches, which had degraded soil quality and drained open-water pools, were removed in 2002. There are good views of, and access to, the estuary from a series of boat launches along the east bank and at Ferry Landing Park. The park provides access to a boardwalk and elevated observation platform near the state's Department of Environmental Protection marine headquarters.

VIEWING

The boardwalk and tower near Ferry Landing Park provide fine views of the marshes at the confluence of the Lieutenant and Connecticut rivers, where bald eagles, osprey, chattering marsh wrens, red-winged blackbirds, and yellow and chestnut-sided warblers all reside. Roger Tory Peterson once wrote, "For sheer drama, the tornadoes of tree swallows eclipsed any avian spectacle I have ever seen," and during autumn migrations, great flocks of these common but beautiful birds gather along the banks of the river. Watch for fiddler crabs popping in and out of narrow den holes in the exposed mud along the riverbanks.

The estuaries, salt marshes, and tidal creeks along the southern New England coast, particularly from the Connecticut River to the west, are the domain of diamondback terrapins, North America's only turtle that lives in brackish water (water with lower levels of salt than the ocean). A resident of the Atlantic coast from Cape Cod south to North Carolina, terrapins suffered population declines due to widespread development of salt marshes and human hunting during the early twentieth century. They feed on snails, crabs, mollusks, worms, and small fish during the warm months and burrow beneath muddy tidal creeks to hibernate in winter.

At the Great Island state boat launch, scan the area beyond the fence to the south for good views of ospreys and their nests. Their abundance is a legacy of Roger Tory Peterson, who noted their decline during the mid-twentieth century and spearheaded recovery efforts here during the mid-1970s.

Diving ducks present in the estuary during the winter include buffle-heads, greater and lesser scaups, common and Barrow's goldeneyes, and scoters. The marsh restoration project has allowed breeding black ducks, mallards, and green-winged teal to return. Mute swans are abundant here; large flocks are easily viewed near the harbor at Old Saybrook. The presence of these nonnatives is a recent phenomenon, as individuals were first introduced to the area during the early twentieth century. Short-eared owls and northern harriers hunt meadow voles and shrews in the marsh grass; other mammals present include muskrats, white-tailed deer, red foxes, and eastern coyotes.

Four species of healthy-size sea turtles call the waters of Long Island

Sound home. Loggerheads and green sea turtles weigh roughly 500 pounds, which is a mere one-third of the giant leatherbacks. The smallest and most endangered is the Kemp's ridley, which at 100 pounds is still considerably larger than the region's freshwater turtles (large snappers generally top out at around 75 pounds).

GETTING AROUND

From the parking area at Ferry Landing Park the boardwalk leads beneath the railroad drawbridge and follows the east bank of the estuary for 0.2 mile to its end at the wooden observation platform. Unimproved access for car-top boats is also available here.

Other launches along and off Route 156 with unimproved ramps for car-top boats include Pilgrim Landing at the junction of Route 156 and Pilgrim Landing Road, 0.7 mile north of exit 70. The Lieutenant River put-in is 0.4 mile south of the exit; from the put-in it's roughly a mile south to the confluence with the Connecticut River just below the railroad bridge near Ferry Landing Park. To reach the Smith Neck town landing, from exit 70 follow Route 156 south for 1.7 miles to a right on Smith Neck Road, then bear right at a fork to reach the landing.

The Great Island state boat launch is located at the end of Smith Neck Road, 0.6 mile from the fork to the town landing. It offers an improved ramp for all boats and includes a large parking area and observation deck with views from the Back River channel and the Great Island marshes to Long Island and the distant Lynde Point and Saybrook Breakwater lighthouses.

Both the Smith Neck and Great Island launches provide access to the Back River channel adjoining the Great Island marshes; downstream is the Black Hall River and Griswold Point. The round-trip to Griswold Point and back from here takes approximately three hours for most paddlers. Paddlers should be alert for potentially rough water, winds, and powerboats along the open Connecticut River.

 Hammonasset Beach State Reservation

Connecticut Department of Forests and Parks, 203-245-2785,
www.ct.gov/dep
CLOSEST TOWN: Madison
DIRECTIONS: From Interstate 95 east of New Haven take exit 62 and follow
the well-marked connecting highway south for 1 mile to the park entrance.

To reach the nature center and trails bear left and continue 1.5 miles to the nature center and 1.7 miles to the Moraine Trail. A $10 fee (out of state) or $7 (residents) is collected from late April through mid-September during working hours; this increases to $15 or $10 on weekends from Memorial Day through Labor Day.

Originally inhabited by Native Americans who bestowed the name "Hamonasseet," or "where we dug holes in the ground," the Hammonasset Beach State Reservation is Connecticut's largest coastal preserve, a 919-acre oasis of protected land a short distance east of the greater New Haven area. The park was established in 1920 and, like many current coastal preserves, served as a military reservation during World War II. Today, more than a million human visitors come to Hammonasset annually, mostly to enjoy three miles of sandy beach and the cooling waters of Long Island Sound in summer.

Roughly half the reservation is composed of salt marshes that are nestled between the beach and the mouth of the Hammonasset River. In recent years the state Department of Environmental Protection has completed several projects to restore these natural communities, including removing an old dike, mosquito control ditches, and colonies of *Phragmites* (common reed), and restoring pools and tidal creeks. Other habitats include open grasslands, maritime oak–hickory–black-cherry forests, shrubby thickets, and ponds. Much of the area north of the park road is set aside as a nature preserve, where access is by permit only. Near the southern boundary are the Meigs Point Nature Center and several short trails that explore the marsh, thickets, and other habitats.

VIEWING
Nourished by tides twice daily, the salt marshes are remarkably productive ecosystems and an integral part of the marine food web. These communities provide habitats and serve as nurseries for blue, green, lady, and fiddler crabs, horseshoe crabs, clam worms, ribbed and blue mussels, clams, mollusks, shrimp, small fishes, and lobsters, as well as insects such as greenhead flies and salt marsh mosquitoes. In turn, these creatures are an abundant food source for the next levels of the chain.

The reservation's size and variety make it one of New England's finest bird-watching destinations in all seasons, with more than 260 recorded species, including vagrants such as white pelicans and tricolored herons. Great egrets, which are threatened in Connecticut and are locally common

The popular Hammonasset Beach State Reservation offers many close-up views of saltwater marshes.

breeders along the southern New England coast, are regularly seen here, along with great blue, green, and black-crowned night herons. Black ducks and other waterfowl frequent the small shallow pools within the marsh known as "pannes." Other birds that specifically favor salt marshes, and therefore are especially susceptible to disturbances of these fragile environments, are seaside and saltmarsh sparrows and clapper rails. The latter, which is also rare to uncommon in New England, periodically overwinters in this area and makes grassy nests amid low shrubs and vegetation along salt marshes and tidal creeks.

Exposed bird nests are vulnerable to predation by raccoons, which are common residents of both salt and freshwater wetlands, and mink, which inhabit freshwater shores. Rare, state-listed diamondback terrapin turtles, which are near the northern limit of their range here, inhabit small creeks within the wetlands.

Thickets of bayberry, black cherry, red maple, and red cedar serve as rest stops for migrating songbirds during the spring and fall, when large flocks of warblers, vireos, and thrushes pause during their long journeys to and from the tropics. Sharp-shinned hawks, merlins, peregrine falcons, and other birds of prey hunt the songbirds and small mammals such as eastern cottontails, mice, and voles during these crowded times, while resident ospreys dive in search of small fish. Check the cedar trees along the trails and entrance road for state-listed short-eared, saw-whet, barn, and long-eared owls. Adjoining the nature center are a butterfly garden and a small pond frequented by red-spotted purples, red admirals, tiger swallowtails, and other insects, and two purple martin houses. In the early morning and evening, watch for eastern coyotes and red foxes stalking these open edges.

During winter, check the beaches and the exposed rocks near the end of the Moraine Trail for basking harbor seals. In May and June, horseshoe crabs breed and lay eggs above the tide line on the beach; after two weeks the hatchlings are washed into the sound, where they spend their youth burrowed in the sandy bottom. Piping plovers and least terns, which share beaches throughout New England's coast, nest along these sands as well. Shorebirds include American oystercatchers, whimbrels, willets, and Hudsonian and marbled godwits.

GETTING AROUND

The reservation is open year-round from 8 AM until sunset. Though off-limits to public access, the salt marshes are easily viewed from the auto road and two nature trails that begin near the picnic shelter behind the nature center. The mile-long Willard's Island Trail begins at a yellow gate on the left-hand side of the shelter and follows an old road lined with cedars across the marsh, then forks into a short loop around the small island, which was once the site of a farm. At post 9/10, an observation platform offers a fine view across the marsh. After closing the loop, return to the trailhead via the causeway. A shorter path behind the shelter leads east for 0.3 mile, crossing a bridge over the marsh en route to another platform with a panoramic view of the marsh-sound interface.

The Meigs Point area in the reservation's southeast corner is explored by the 0.6-mile (one way) Moraine Trail, which begins at the fishermen's and car-top boat parking area at the end of the auto road, 0.2 mile from the nature center. From the marked trailhead at the edge of the beach, just beyond the "No parking beyond this point" sign, it rises through rose thickets and large boulders that mark a geologic ridge, to a wooden observation platform with a good view of the sound, then descends to cross a beach of shells and rocks. After continuing through more thickets and wildflowers above the rocky shore, it ends at the edge of the sound and estuary, with fine views in all directions.

There are numerous access points to the beach, which is crowded during summer days but less so in the early morning and evening, when wildlife viewing is often best.

 ## Housatonic Meadows State Park

Connecticut Department of Forests and Parks, 860-927-3238,
www.ct.gov/dep
CLOSEST TOWNS: Sharon, Kent
DIRECTIONS: From US 7 at the covered bridge in West Cornwall drive south
for 2.7 miles to the campground, 3.2 miles to the Pine Knob parking area
and trailhead, and 4 miles to the picnic area. The latter is just north of the
junction of US 7 and CT 4.

As the Housatonic River meanders south from headwaters in the central Berkshire Hills of Massachusetts toward Long Island Sound, it carves a narrow valley through the rolling hills of northwestern Connecticut's highlands. Located along an especially scenic portion of the river between the villages of West Cornwall and Kent, the 450-acre Housatonic Meadows State Park offers a variety of options for explorers: here one can navigate challenging rapids by canoe or kayak, hike the valley slopes to overlooks with long views, enjoy fine catch-and-release fly fishing, or simply relax at the roadside picnic area and campground. For wildlife watchers the park offers easy access to river, upland forest, and ridgetop habitats. The valley is one of the region's prime migratory corridors and as such offers especially productive viewing during spring and early autumn.

VIEWING
A visit to the park during the height of the spring songbird migration in May and June may reveal as many as 60 to 80 species of these colorful long-distance travelers in a single morning. The extensive woodlands of the valley hills provide cover and rest areas for yellowthroats, chestnut-sided, and yellow warblers; less common species include blackburnian warblers and warbling and yellow-throated vireos.

Along the river itself, look for common and hooded mergansers, osprey, and mallard and black ducks; colorful wood ducks use the tall mature trees that border the river as nest sites. Belted kingfishers dive off of vegetated perches while hunting fish, insects, and amphibians. One of the few species where the female is more colorful than the male, these long-billed, territorial birds are easily located and identified by their chattering call. Waders such as great blue and less conspicuous green herons hunt the edge of the river. Both wildlife and fly fishermen enjoy fine stores of brown and rainbow trout and smallmouth bass.

During September and October days with a wind from the north, hike up to the Pine Knob lookout and watch for broad-winged hawks, osprey, American kestrels, bald eagles, and other raptors migrating south along the valley. These hills also provide habitat for breeding turkey vultures, red-shouldered hawks, and great horned and barred owls, some of which may pass quite close by the vantage points while on hunting dives.

Large and midsize mammals such as white-tailed deer, red foxes, fishers, bobcats, black bears, and porcupines all inhabit these woodlands. Sign of the latter, which compensates for its rather slow gait with hundreds of barbed quills, includes piles of droppings outside rocky cavelike openings and piles of chewed hemlock branches on the ground.

GETTING AROUND

The river is easily accessed and viewed from parking areas at the picnic area and campground, as well as pullouts along US 7. From the entrance to the picnic area near the park's southern boundary there is an especially nice upstream view of the valley.

Perhaps the best way to experience the river is by boat; the five-mile stretch of the river from the historic red covered bridge at West Cornwall downstream to the state park is especially popular with kayakers and canoeists, as it is home to several class II and III rapids and offers fine views of the surrounding hills. Several independent operators offer boat tours and trips here; contact the park for more information.

For an altogether different perspective, the Pine Knob Trail and the Appalachian Trail explore the moderately steep slopes of the valley. The former begins at a trailhead on the west side of Route 7 and makes a steady mile-long ascent along a hemlock-lined stream to a 1,120-foot-high ridge, gaining 700 feet from the trailhead. Here it meets the Appalachian Trail, which it follows for roughly half a mile before branching off to complete the loop with an easterly descent back to the parking area. Several partially open lookouts offer views to the south and east across the narrow, wooded valley and the surrounding Litchfield Hills. The loop is 2.5 miles and takes an hour and a half to two hours to complete.

 James L. Goodwin State Forest

Connecticut Department of Forests and Parks, 860-424-3200,
www.ct.gov/dep

CLOSEST TOWN: Hampton

DIRECTIONS: From the junction of US 6 and CT 198 two miles south of Chaplin
village follow US 6 east for 3 miles, then turn left on Potter Road at a sign for
the conservation center. The entrance and parking area at Pine Acres Pond
are just north of the junction.

With its mosaic of forests, fields, and wetlands, the James L. Goodwin
State Forest offers 2,170 acres of prime wildlife habitat in the heart of the
northeastern Connecticut hills. The preserve is named for James Goodwin,
a conservationist who purchased land here to practice forestry during the
early twentieth century. In addition to establishing many forest plantations, in 1933 he built the dam that formed 135-acre Pine Acres Pond. In
1964 Goodwin donated his land to the state of Connecticut. The property
is part of another large conservation corridor in eastern Connecticut, as it
abuts the 12,900-acre Natchaug State Forest.

Much of the preserve is forested with stands of oak, hickory, birch, and
maple, where examples of common forestry practices may be observed.
The woods are interspersed with open fields and old spruce and pine plantations and apple orchards that are holdovers from Goodwin's work. The
largest water body is Pine Acres Pond, whose shallow, mucky waters host a
variety of wildlife, including several beaver lodges. Other wetlands that were
created by impoundments include Brown Hill and Black Spruce ponds. The
conservation education center adjoining Pine Acres Pond includes a native
wildflower garden and an interpretive stewardship demonstration trail. A
short distance north of the main entrance are more large fields on the west
side of Potter Road, where wildflowers such as milkweed, daisies, and black-
eyed Susans are interspersed with planted evergreens of various heights.

VIEWING

The wetland edges are the domain of northern water snakes, which are
often seen swimming in search of frogs, salamanders, fish, insects, and
even small birds and mammals and basking atop beaver lodges and dams,
tree branches, and wetland banks. Though their size can be rather intimi-
dating—some individuals grow as long as 55 inches—they pose no threats
to humans unless they are cornered or gathered. Motionlessly stalking the

The James L. Goodwin State Forest, which offers diverse habitats for wildlife, is one of several large preserves in eastern Connecticut.

same prey are great blue herons, while belted kingfishers and tree swallows make hunting dives over the water. Other familiar creatures include basking painted turtles and green frogs, whose banjolike *cluck* is a distinctive sound amid the chorus of amphibians.

At the north end of Pine Acres Pond, a short detour along the White Trail leads across a causeway to a small island; from the trail's end there is a view across the pond to a beaver lodge and wood-duck boxes. In midsummer, abundant dragonflies flittering about the wetland vegetation here include common whitetails, widow skimmers, and eastern pondhawks. The latter are especially colorful; males are bright blue with some pale green during immature stages, while females are electric green. Another beaver lodge is visible along the White Trail just north of the footbridges near the trailhead.

In the meadows and fields look carefully for white-tailed deer tunneling through patches of wildflowers and grassy areas; sometimes only the tips of their ears are visible. The dense, low vegetation provides cover for newborn fawns, whose survival strategy in early weeks is to remain motionless. By midsummer they grow large and strong enough to use their speed to escape potential threats. Butterflies such as monarchs, clouded and orange sulfurs, silver fritillaries, red-spotted purples, and red admirals feed on abundant milkweed and other wildflowers, while eastern towhees, common yellowthroats, eastern bluebirds, indigo buntings, and other edge-favoring species call from shrubs and treetops.

GETTING AROUND

The forest offers more than 10 miles of well-marked recreational trails, including several popular horseback and cross-country ski routes. Several of these paths, which traverse mostly easy terrain with a few rocky areas and minimal elevation gain, originate near the conservation center and explore the area east of Pine Acres Pond, including the White Trail, which leads along the shore, and the Yellow, which loops to nearby Brown Hill Marsh. The long-distance Natchaug Trail crosses the western portion of the preserve, passing by Black Spruce Pond. The fields adjacent to Potter Road are 0.2 mile north of the main entrance; parking is available along the road, and grassy paths offer easy walking. The southwest corner of Pine Acres Pond is easily accessed and viewed at the main entrance from the picnic area and boat launch, both of which are immediately below the parking area. The shortest route is the 0.7-mile interpretive Stewardship Trail, which begins at the gardens at the conservation center.

For those with three hours or so to spare, the Yellow, Red, and White trails can be combined as a 5.2-mile circuit with excellent diversity. From the main entrance follow the marked trails around the southeast corner of Pine Acres Pond, then bear right on the Yellow Trail, which leaves the water and leads though woods and along field edges to the causeway at Brown Hill Marsh. The trail then loops through the forests surrounding the impoundment, briefly following Cedar Swamp Road before reentering the woods opposite a residence.

After completing the loop, bear right and head north on the Red Trail, which leads through woods and past a network of stone walls as it curves west to meet the White Trail at a four-way junction at the northeast corner of Pine Acres Pond. Continue straight here across the causeway to a small island, where an observation area at the trail's end offers views across the pond. Backtrack to the junction, then turn right (south) and follow the periodically rocky White Trail along the east shores for 1.2 miles back to the junction with the Yellow Trail near the entrance.

A boat launch is available at the main entrance for those looking to explore Pine Hills Pond by canoe or kayak (electric motors are also allowed); the shallow water, exposed stumps and logs, and aquatic vegetation can make for a challenging paddle here.

Lighthouse Point Park

City of New Haven Parks, 203-946-8019, www.cityofnewhaven.com/parks

CLOSEST TOWN: New Haven

DIRECTIONS: From the west, take Interstate 95 north to exit 50 (Woodward Avenue). At the second traffic light turn right on Townsend Avenue and continue past a waterfront park to a right on Lighthouse Road. If coming from the east, take exit 51, then left at the traffic light on Townsend Avenue. A $10 fee is charged for non-New Haven residents from Memorial Day through Labor Day.

At first, Lighthouse Point Park, which is situated along the east side of New Haven Harbor amid the heavily developed greater New Haven area, might seem an unlikely place for wildlife watching and nature study, but this 84-acre urban park offers a surprising array of viewing opportunities in all seasons. Its namesake and main attraction is the historic Five Mile Point Lighthouse, which was erected in 1847 and named for its location five miles from the New Haven green. The city parks department acquired the property in 1924, and visitors to early baseball games held on the grounds included Babe Ruth and Ty Cobb. After most of the trees and buildings were destroyed by the 1938 hurricane, the park was rehabilitated in 1950. Though the light itself is no longer active, it remains as a popular attraction, along with a swimming beach, bathhouse, and historic carousel that make up half the preserve. The other half includes grassy fields and a small block of maritime oak forest, shrubs, and vines that provide cover for large groups of migrating birds and other wildlife. A public boat launch is available for leisure craft, and a car-top launch provides access to Morris Creek.

VIEWING

The point is one of New England's most productive hawk-watching sites, especially for species of the accipiter and falcon families. An overall average of more than 17,000 raptors are counted annually, with some of the best viewing occurring toward the end of September and early October, when American kestrels and merlins are on the move; the merlin count is exceeded only by a site across Long Island Sound on Fire Island. Because of their relatively small size and blue-gray coloration, merlins were once known as "pigeon hawks"; a few stay to overwinter along the coast annually. Watch for these sharp-eyed raptors diving to hunt migrating songbirds, which use the park's woodlands and shrubs as rest areas.

In winter, scan the sound for harbor seals and waterfowl such as American wigeons, canvasbacks, buffleheads, ring-necked ducks, greater and lesser scaups, black scoters, and common goldeneyes. Even familiar species such as blue jays, robins, and cedar waxwings often make for a spectacle here, as they travel about in giant flocks. Vagrants and rare species may show up at any time, as evidenced by the sighting of a tropical kingbird in 1990, the first time the species had been recorded in Connecticut.

The park is also home to a small butterfly garden at the edge of the parking area adjacent to the "Carousel Parking" signs; the garden includes plantings of lupine, butterfly weed, marigolds, coneflowers, and bee balm. Along with the shrubs and wildflowers across the road, it serves as a wayside that offers food and shelter for migrating monarch butterflies. Many other species, including red admiral and black and tiger swallowtail butterflies and twelve-spotted skimmer, blue dasher, and meadowhawk dragonflies, are evident from spring into fall.

Walk quietly along the short grassy paths through the thickets across the road from the parking area and you may glimpse a red fox making hunting rounds. The mixture of cover and open edges is ideal habitat for this familiar but often secretive canine, which excavates dens into dirt mounds and is relatively tolerant of developed areas.

 ## Pachaug State Forest

Connecticut Department of Forests and Parks, 860-376-4075,
www.ct.gov/dep
CLOSEST TOWN: Voluntown
DIRECTIONS: From Interstate 395 take exit 85 and follow CT 138 east for 9 miles to the junction with CT 49. Turn north on CT 49 and continue 1 mile to the entrance at Headquarters Road on the west side of the highway, opposite the Beachdale boat launch.

Connecticut's largest conservation area is the Pachaug State Forest, which protects nearly 25,000 acres in the state's southeast corner near the Rhode Island state line. The extensive forests visible today belie the region's past, when much of it was cleared for agriculture by English settlers, who also established mills along the waterways as early as 1711. Even after the farms were abandoned, the forests suffered significantly from the hurricane of 1938, but have recovered nicely and now provide food, cover, and travel corridors for creatures ranging from large mammals to songbirds.

The preserve is composed of two parcels, the Chapman and Green Falls areas. The former is the larger and more-visited, as it is home to several popular attractions, including Mount Misery, whose 441-foot summit ledges offer views across the countryside. The nearby rhododendron sanctuary is a favorite of naturalists, as it hosts colorful rosebay rhododendrons and a regionally uncommon Atlantic white cedar swamp. In the reservation's southeast corner near the main entrance is Beachdale Pond, one of several ponds and beaver wetlands along Mount Misery Brook. The woodlands include oak, hickory, hemlock, white pine, and dry scrub oak and pitch pine communities; the hemlocks have suffered infestation from hemlock woolly adelgids in recent years.

VIEWING

The ponds and wetlands offer the opportunity to view a variety of wildlife, including beavers and their sign, river otters, muskrat, raccoons, and mink. Amphibians present include Fowler's toads, spring peepers, and spotted salamanders. Common waterfowl include mallard, black, and wood ducks. In March and April and from September to December watch for migrating green-winged teal, which are distinguished by the male's chestnut-colored head and green eye-patch. They use the wetlands here as rest areas while migrating to and from summer breeding grounds, though some overwinter along the nearby south coast. Wading birds include great blue herons, green herons, and snowy egrets. Songbirds that favor wetlands and their edges include great-crested and olive-sided flycatchers, marsh wrens, eastern kingbirds, yellow and chestnut-sided warblers, and northern waterthrushes. Belted kingfishers nest in sandy burrows and hunt fish, insects, and small frogs in the brooks and ponds. A year-round resident that favors mixed woodlands and boggy habitats is the brown creeper, whose high-pitched call is difficult for some birders to hear. From Mount Misery's ledges, watch for migrating raptors in spring and fall, especially around the middle of September.

Mammals that frequent mixed forest-field habitats, including the fields near the campgrounds, include red and gray squirrels, striped skunks, eastern cottontails, eastern chipmunks, red foxes, eastern coyotes, and white-tailed deer.

GETTING AROUND

Maps and visitor information are available at the forest headquarters near the main entrance off Route 49 in the Chapman Area. Dirt roads provide seasonal vehicle access to much of the preserve, and a network of trails is available for a variety of recreational users. A viewing platform next to the picnic area at the main entrance overlooks Beachdale Pond and its surrounding shrubby vegetation. The long-distance Pachaug, Nehantic, and Quinebaug trails, 30, 15, and 7 miles long respectively, may be combined with side trails and the woods roads for a variety of loops.

Two short and interesting trails begin at the picnic area field near the junction of Headquarters and Cutoff roads. Here the universally accessible rhododendron sanctuary trail leads for 0.25 mile through the white cedar wetland to a viewing platform with views of Mount Misery Brook and the swamp; the rhododendrons bloom in early July. The nearby Pachaug Trail makes an easy 0.5-mile climb to Mount Misery's lookout.

For a short touring route that passes several wetland viewing areas and is open to vehicles, begin at the Beachdale Pond observation deck at the main entrance and follow the paved Headquarters Road to its end, then continue straight on Cutoff Road. Turn right on Trail 2 Road, which soon leads to Edwards Pond. After passing the Frog Hollow horse camps, turn left on Trail 1 Road, which winds to the Philips Pond area, 4.2 miles from the entrance. Trail 1 Road ends at a junction with Hell Huddle Road near the parcel's northern tip, a short distance west of Hell Huddle Pond.

The Beachdale Pond boat launch is situated on the east side of Route 49, opposite the main entrance. Paddlers here have the option of going north along Mount Misery Brook, or east to explore the wetlands along the Pachaug River.

Quaker Ridge, Audubon Greenwich

National Audubon (Greenwich), 203-869-5272, www.greenwich.audubon.org
CLOSEST TOWN: Greenwich
DIRECTIONS: From the Merritt Parkway (CT 15) in Greenwich take exit 28 and turn right (north) on Round Hill Road. Continue for 1.6 miles to a left on John Street, opposite a church. Follow John Street for 1.1 miles to a four-way intersection; the marked sanctuary entrance is on the right. The admission fee is $3 for adults and $1.50 for children and seniors.

Ideally situated where coastal breezes converge with warm thermal currents in Connecticut's southwest corner, Quaker Ridge is the site of some eye-popping single-day raptor migration spectacles. On September 15, 1995, 31,988 broad-winged hawks alone were counted, surpassing the previous high of 30,500 that was recorded on September 14, 1986. While one can't expect such numbers every year, this overlook is nevertheless one of New England's finest raptor viewing areas, with an average of more than 20,000 individuals recorded annually since official counts were started in 1972.

The ridge lies within the Audubon Center in Greenwich, whose 522 acres host a number of other features and habitats worth exploring in all seasons. Extensive hardwood forests of oak, beech, hickory, and maple cover most of the preserve, with a number of giant specimens along the various trails. Adjacent to the nature center are an old orchard and open field, and additional openings are maintained along the Pasture Trail. A short walk from the entrance leads to Mead Lake and its associated shrubby wetlands, formed by an impoundment of the Byram River; other wetlands include vernal pools and several wooded swamps in depressions near the northern boundary. The sanctuary is about as far south and west as one can go in New England and as such offers the opportunity to see early and late-season wildlife such as butterflies, dragonflies, and birds that may be absent from the colder interior regions.

The visitor center includes informative displays and a gift shop. During the peak of the migration period in mid-September, the sanctuary hosts a weekend festival that includes identification workshops and presentations of live birds, guided nature hikes, and children's programs.

VIEWING

The peak time for viewing broad-winged hawks, which are by far the most numerous species in overall number, as well as American kestrels and bald eagles, is generally September 15–20, while osprey are most common toward the end of September. Northern harriers and sharp-shinned hawks dominate the skies during first two weeks of October, while red-shouldered hawks, rare golden eagles (October 20–25), and red-tailed hawks (October 25–30) pass through toward the end of the month and into early November. The sight of a golden eagle, unmistakable thanks to its giant wingspan, is a true treat, as an average of only 7 are seen here annually, and the highest single-year total is 24 reports. Also keep an eye out for other migrants, including sandhill cranes, songbirds, and monarch butterflies.

Check the orchard near the visitor center and the clearings along the Old Pasture Trail for eastern bluebirds, indigo buntings, barn swallows, and purple martins. White-tailed deer are often seen in these clearings, as the preserve is home to a dense population characteristic of Connecticut and the south coast in general. These large herds can adversely impact other wildlife by consuming a high percentage of shrubs and tree saplings that provide cover, food, and nesting layers for other species. Other familiar mammals include red foxes, woodchucks, and eastern cottontails. The wildflowers nourish a variety of butterflies, including monarchs, silver fritillaries, red admirals, red-spotted purples, and red-banded hairstreaks, which are found in the southernmost regions of New England.

The wetlands and their edges are home to mink, snapping turtles, spring peepers, wood frogs, and American toads. The dam and boardwalk areas of Mead Lake are a good place to see dragonflies and damselflies such as eastern pondhawks, common whitetails, variable dancers, blue dashers, and eastern amberwings. Look for raccoon tracks in muddy areas bordering the Dogwood Lane Trail.

GETTING AROUND

The hawk-watch station is situated next to the sanctuary entrance and parking area. A full-time observer maintains a count from late August until November, and daily and seasonal totals are posted at the information kiosk. Landmarks such as individual trees and the visitor center are used as points of reference when tracking individuals.

Seven miles of well-marked trails explore the sanctuary's habitats, traversing mostly easy terrain with some gentle ups and downs. If you have limited time or want a short break from the lookout, the Lake Trail offers a half-mile walk from the parking area through the old orchard to the south corner of Mead Lake. Two viewing blinds are a short walk north from the dam, and the Lake and Boardwalk trails can be combined as a 0.8-mile circuit that circles the impoundment and its swampy wetlands.

For a longer 3-mile circuit that combines several of these paths, follow the Lake Trail past the dam and bird blinds, then continue north on the Riverbottom Trail. At the junction with the Pasture Trail make an optional short detour uphill (right) to the shrubby fields. Return to the Riverbottom Trail, which crosses the Byram River on a wood bridge and rises through a grove of beech trees. At a sharp left it becomes the Hemlock Trail, which winds along a knoll before meeting the Maple Swamp Loop at a three-way junction near the sanctuary's northwest boundary.

Turn right here on the Maple Swamp Loop, which follows a ridge above a wetland and passes rocky outcroppings, then bear right on the Dogwood Lane Trail, which skirts the edge of another swampy area before crossing its outlet on a short boardwalk. Continue straight at a marked junction, following signs for the Lake Trail and nature center. Bear south on the boardwalk portion of the Lake Trail, which leads across a shrubby wetland at the lake's northern tip, then complete the loop with an easy walk along the west shores and backtrack to the nature center.

Sharon Audubon Center

National Audubon (Sharon), 860-364-0520, www.sharon.audubon.org
CLOSEST TOWN: Sharon
DIRECTIONS: From the junction of US 7 and CT 4 at Cornwall Bridge, near the southern boundary of Housatonic Meadows State Park, follow CT 4 uphill for 5.1 miles to the sanctuary entrance on the south side of the highway. An admission fee of $3 is charged for adults, $1.50 for children and seniors.

In the rolling uplands above the Housatonic River lies the Sharon Audubon Center, which offers some of the most diverse habitats and wildlife viewing opportunities in Connecticut's scenic northwest hills region. This 1,147-acre property, which was once known as Bog Meadow Farm, was donated to Audubon by Clement and Kayo Ford in 1961. Within its eastern division are Ford and Bog Meadow ponds, which sit at elevations of 985 and 1,020 feet respectively, and their associated wetlands and woodland streams. In its southwest corner are large open fields spread along the gently rolling terrain at the old farm site. Much of the remainder of the preserve, or roughly two-thirds of its total area, is cloaked with moist and upland mixed woodlands that include a number of giant oak trees and groves of eastern hemlock and white pine.

The sanctuary visitor center includes natural history exhibits, aquariums with creatures such as spotted turtles, ball pythons, and walking sticks, and a gift shop. Adjacent Ford Pond is an aviary for rehabilitated birds of prey, including a bald eagle, American kestrel, great horned and eastern screech owls, raven, and broad-winged hawk.

VIEWING

On sunny days visitors may enjoy the unmistakable sight of a giant snapping turtle basking on an exposed rock at one of the ponds. Other turtles found throughout the preserve during the warm months include painted turtles and much rarer spotted, bog, box, and wood turtles. Another familiar reptile seen here is the northern water snake, which is often seen basking on tree climbs or hunting wetland edges. In early spring and mid to late autumn, check the ponds for flocks of ring-necked ducks, common and hooded mergansers, buffleheads, and other migratory waterfowl resting while heading to or coming from southern wintering grounds. Mallards and Canada geese are common breeders here, and wood ducks nest in tall trees and specially constructed boxes. American bitterns blend into marshy edges, staking out bullfrogs, green frogs, salamanders, and juvenile snakes. Beavers, river otters, mink, and muskrats may all be seen in these wetlands as well.

The sanctuary's diversity and its proximity to the Housatonic Valley corridor result in fine migratory songbird viewing as well; the calls of wood thrushes, eastern wood peewees, and ovenbirds are familiar sounds throughout the woodlands. The low vegetation along the edge of Bog Pond offers close views of edge-favoring species such as chestnut-sided and yellow warblers, northern orioles, eastern kingbirds, gray catbirds, and ruby-throated hummingbirds; listen for the low buzzing sound of the latter as they zip around while feeding on flowering shrubs and wildflowers. Watch for turkey vultures circling over the water, riding on columns of rising warm air known as thermals.

The open fields along the Woodchuck Trail offer the greatest chance to see eastern coyotes, red foxes, and bobcats, though these often-elusive predators are periodically glimpsed near the sanctuary buildings as well. The woodchucks themselves frequent field edges and the garden; when they are standing still their rust and gray fur allows them to blend in almost perfectly with rocks and stone walls. Nesting boxes provide homes for tree swallows and eastern bluebirds, while indigo buntings call from the top of trees and shrubs. In warm months a variety of butterflies may be observed, including clouded and orange sulfurs, pearl crescents, and tiny American coppers. White-tailed deer are common and may be encountered in both the woods and fields; watch for areas of disturbed leaves (or depressions in the snow in winter) near the edge of the woods where individuals or groups have bedded down. Look for eastern cottontails along the trail and field edges.

GETTING AROUND

The sanctuary trails and the raptor center are open from dawn to dusk, and the nature center and store are open Tuesday to Saturday from 9 to 5 and Sunday from 1 to 5. The trail network includes nine blazed footpaths that explore the various habitats. Ford Pond is easily reached in a short stroll east from the nature center; a large wooden observation blind is located along the Fern Trail on the south shore.

For a strongly recommended 2.5-mile loop with excellent habitat variety, from the nature center head east past the gardens to Ford Pond, then bear right and follow the Fern Trail along the south shore for another 10 minutes to the blind. From there continue along the Fern Trail to its end at the junction with the Hendrickson Bog Meadow Trail. Turn left on the latter and continue through a patch of moist woods and past a brook crossing to another junction 0.5 mile from the nature center. Bear left here on the Woodchuck Trail, which soon forks into a loop that winds across the open fields, passing an overlook with views across the countryside at the height-of-land and a series of nesting boxes.

At the close of the circuit, return to the Hendrickson Bog Meadow loop and follow it left to the edge of nearby Bog Pond. The trail, which includes a boardwalk, follows the north shore, passing a boggy area. A short side path leads to an overlook with fine views of the pond and surrounding hills. After leaving the pond edge, the Bog Meadow Trail passes through a small clearing and leads north back to the entrance.

Stewart B. McKinney National Wildlife Refuge: Salt Meadow Unit

U.S. Fish and Wildlife Service, 860-399-2513,
www.fws.gov/northeast/mckinney

CLOSEST TOWN: Westbrook

DIRECTIONS: From Interstate 95 in Westbrook take exit 64 and bear south at the end of the ramp. At the four-way intersection turn left on Old Clinton Road and continue for 1 mile to the refuge entrance on the right.

Spread along a 60-mile section of Connecticut's coast is a series of eight preserves collectively known as the Stewart McKinney National Wildlife Refuge that protect a total of 825 acres, including salt marshes, barrier beaches, tidal creeks, and maritime woodlands. Originally formed by a 150-acre donation in 1972, the refuge was expanded by the efforts of nonprofit groups and citizens who were concerned about the rapid loss of coastal habitats to development. The headquarters is located at the 247-acre Salt Meadow Unit in Westbrook, which is situated along tidal salt marshes at the confluence of Gatchen Creek and the Menunketesuck River near the latter's mouth at Long Island Sound. Its proximity to both the sound and the Connecticut River Valley makes the unit an important link in the Atlantic migratory corridor.

The bulk of this piece of the refuge is forested with mature maritime woodlands, including tall, spreading white oaks, hickory, and birch. From the edge of the woods bordering the salt marsh, a viewing platform with a mounted spotting scope offers a unique elevated perspective of the marshes and the meandering river, allowing visitors to pick out birds and other wildlife hidden amid the grassy vegetation. Adjacent to the entrance and headquarters building are old fields with dense shrubs and saplings that offer additional habitat diversity.

VIEWING

Thanks to their size and bright white plumage, great and snowy egrets are the most conspicuous wading birds of these marshes. To distinguish the two species, look for the yellow bill of the great egret; the slightly smaller snowy's is black. Great blue herons are common here as well (a few over-winter in the region), and other waders include glossy ibis, black and yellow-crowned night herons, green herons, and little blue herons, which are uncommon in New England. From the shore-level vantage across from the railroad tracks, look up the river for osprey and their nests. Other birds of prey include great horned owls, red-tailed hawks, and sharp-shinned hawks. Adaptable muskrats, which live in both salt and freshwater marshes, are a familiar mammal of these wetlands.

Winter visitors may be rewarded with views of birds that are largely absent from the colder interior regions during this time, including peregrine falcons, short-eared owls, hermit thrushes, eastern towhees, northern flickers, brown thrashers, gray catbirds, field and savannah sparrows, ruby-crowned kinglets, and common grackles. As spring sets in during April, large flocks of migrating northern parulas, magnolia warblers, American redstarts, bobolinks, and other songbirds pause to rest and feed in the trees and shrubby thickets. Watch for eastern bluebirds, indigo buntings, northern orioles, purple martins, veeries, American woodcock, and house and Carolina wrens in the fields near the entrance and the adjoining woods. The mature forest groves are ideal habitat for eastern wood peewees, aptly named for their drawn-out *pee-a-wee, pee-o* call. Northern cardinals and Carolina wrens, both southern species that have expanded their range into New England in recent decades, are regularly seen and heard here.

The old fields near the entrance are ideal habitat for one of New England's most familiar reptiles, the common garter snake, which thrives in overgrown areas, fields, gardens, and other habitats. Eastern cottontail rabbits are also easily observed feeding along the grassy paths in the early

Paddlers explore the Menunketesuck River at the Stewart B. McKinney National Wildlife Refuge Salt Meadow Unit.

morning and evening, when shadows offer a measure of cover from predators. Other small mammals such as meadow voles, eastern chipmunks, and gray squirrels serve as prey for red foxes and eastern coyotes, whose hunting grounds include clearings and the edges of the salt marshes.

Butterflies flitting on or over the vegetation include tiger swallowtails and much less flashy little wood satyrs, which are pale brown and distinguished by a series of black and yellow spots on their wings. White-tailed deer and wild turkeys are regularly seen in the woods and along field edges; look for their tracks in muddy areas along the forest trails.

GETTING AROUND

The refuge has 2.5 miles of walking trails, mostly in an easy circuit with just 110 feet of overall elevation gain, which explore the fields, forests, marshes, and riverbank. A short portion of this loop is a universally accessible trail that begins behind the information kiosk at the entrance and offers a 10-minute walk to the observation platform.

To make a clockwise circuit from the entrance, follow the grassy path across the shrubby fields (just beyond the trailhead is an interpretive sign detailing bluebird habitat). The trail then enters the forest and curves to the west, passing near railroad tracks as it approaches the river. At a rest bench, a short side path slopes down to the edge of the river and salt marsh near a railroad bridge. The main trail continues in the woods along the edge of the shore, passing another overlook before joining the universally accessible trail near the refuge's northwest boundary. Turn left here to reach the nearby viewing platform, then complete the loop by returning to the parking area via the accessible trail.

 ## White Memorial Foundation Conservation Center

White Memorial Foundation, 860-567-0857, www.whitememorialcc.org
CLOSEST TOWN: Litchfield
DIRECTIONS: From the junction of US 202, CT 118, and CT 63 in the center of Litchfield follow US 202 (Whitehall Road) west for 2 miles to the entrance. Access to the trails is free. Museum admission is $6 for adults, $3 for children 6–12; children under 6 and members are free.

In the rolling foothills between the Connecticut River Valley and the northwest Appalachian highlands, the White Memorial Conservation Center encompasses more than 4,000 acres of varied habitats within the watershed of the winding Bantam River, including the North Bay of popular Bantam Lake. In addition to the river, the wetlands here include beaver ponds, woodland streams, swamps, and extensive marshy areas ("Mallard Marsh" appropriately borders "Duck Pond" north of the entrance). Near the preserve's northern boundary is Little Pond, where a long boardwalk allows easy viewing of several wetland communities. The mixed forests here include extensive stands of upland hardwoods with colorful mountain laurel, as well as an area of old-growth eastern hemlocks and white pines known as the Caitlin Woods. Rising above the shores of Bantam Lake is 1,030-foot Windmill Hill.

The center was established in 1913 by Alain and Mary White, whose efforts included protecting many other lands throughout the state and the reintroduction of wood ducks to the region. Its extensive holdings include 35 miles of recreational trails, a museum, campgrounds, and facilities for outdoor education and meetings. The museum includes live animals, dioramas and murals, a rock cave, a honeybee hive, and interactive exhibits; workshops, viewing trips, and special programs are offered throughout the year.

Adjacent to the main entrance and museum are fields and plantings that have been landscaped to attract a variety of birds, including yellow-bellied sapsuckers, eastern bluebirds, scarlet tanagers, northern cardinals, red-breasted grosbeaks, and rusty blackbirds. A small observatory offers close-up views for birders and photographers. Nearby Ongley Pond is home to resident Canada geese, as well as painted and snapping turtles. Red foxes and eastern coyotes hunt mice, eastern cottontails, and gray squirrels in these open areas.

From the Little Pond boardwalk, scan the marshy areas carefully for American bitterns and Virginia rails. These elusive wading birds are more often seen than heard; listen for the unmistakable *unk-a-lunk* call of the bittern and the rail's raspy *kidd-ick*. Along the open west shores, tiny marsh wrens duck in and out of cattails and other aquatic plants. Though they also can be hard to spot in this tangle of vegetation, you'll know when they are active, as the male has a conspicuous call that is described in various guides as "abrasive," "gurgling," and "an old-fashioned treadle sowing machine," with more than 200 variations. Common nighthawks are also present here; their much simpler *beep*-like call is similar to the spring mating call of the American woodcock. Also watch for mallard and wood ducks, great blue herons, and uncommon pie-billed grebes.

The Little Pond Boardwalk Trail offers extended close-up views of marsh and river habitats.

Other familiar wetland residents include painted, snapping, and spotted turtles, as well as river otters and muskrats. Raccoons regularly visit the edges during their mostly nocturnal hunting rounds; narrow, five-toed tracks in mud and sand offer abundant evidence of their activities. One of the most distinctive of the preserve's amphibians is the blue-spotted salamander, which is easily identified by the many light blue dots flecked along its black body.

The forests provide cover for elusive black bears, which are making a strong comeback in Connecticut. Though actual sightings are rare, check for sign such as marks on trees and logs that have been torn apart in search of insects. Great horned and barred owls are regularly seen and heard here as well, as are songbirds such as blue-headed and warbling vireos; Laurel Hill is a productive area during the height of migrations.

From the observation platform that overlooks Bantam Lake, watch for waterfowl such as migrating white-winged scoters and common loons. Northbound shorebirds such as solitary and least sandpipers may be seen in muddy areas during April and May and from mid-July onward during their return south, while breeding killdeer remain on the grounds throughout the warm months.

GETTING AROUND

A 35-mile network of nature trails, old cart paths, and woods roads traverse the grounds and the various habitats. The museum is open from 9 to 5 from Monday through Saturday and 1 to 5 Sunday. Maps are posted at trailheads; paper copies are available at the museum for $3.

An especially good route for wildlife watchers is the Little Pond Boardwalk Trail, which loops around Little Pond and its associated marshy wetlands. This trail is accessed from a parking area where the path crosses White Woods Road (1.75-mile round-trip), at the end of South Lake Street (1.5-mile round-trip), or by walking to the trailhead from the main entrance (3.1-mile round-trip). If doing the latter, from the museum continue east for 0.2 mile to a junction at a pair of stone pillars. Turn left and follow the road past a wetland and the edge of the Bantam River, then cross Bissell Road. Shortly after entering the woods, turn right on the white-blazed Little Pond Trail, which soon crosses White Woods Road and continues for another quarter mile to the start of the loop.

For those making a counterclockwise circuit, the trail leads through swamp honeysuckle and other shrubs, then crosses a wood bridge over the Bantam River. After you continue amid more shrubs along the southeast shore, fine views of the pond and wetlands unfold as the trail curves west, then south along the 1.2-mile-long boardwalk.

Bantam Lake and its adjacent woods and wetlands are explored via the Lake Trail, which makes an easy 1-mile circuit from the fields at the main entrance to an observation platform with an overview of the north shore. This trail is easily combined with the 0.2-mile loop around Ongley Pond, which is just south of the museum.

Boaters may access the Bantam River from a launch on White Woods Road; downstream is a series of wetlands above Bantam Lake, while the outlet of Little Pond is 2 miles to the north.

MAINE

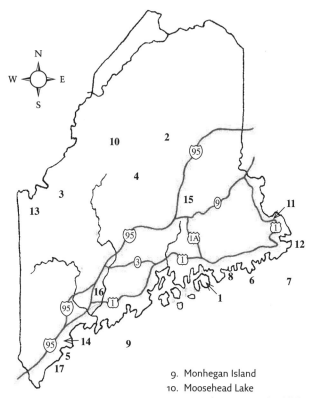

9. Monhegan Island
10. Moosehead Lake
11. Moosehorn National Wildlife
    Refuge
1. Acadia National Park
2. Baxter State Park
3. Bigelow Mountain Preserve
4. Borestone Mountain Audubon
   Sanctuary
5. East Point Sanctuary and
   Biddeford Pool
6. Great Wass Island
7. Machias Seal Island
8. Maine Coastal Islands National
   Wildlife Refuge: Petit Manan
   Division
12. Quoddy Head State Park
13. Rangeley Lake
14. Scarborough Marsh
15. Sunkhaze Meadows National
    Wildlife Refuge
16. Swan Island/Steve Powell Wildlife
    Management Area
17. Wells National Estuarine Reserve
    and Rachel Carson National
    Wildlife Refuge

Acadia National Park

U.S. National Park Service, 207-288-3338, www.nps.gov/acad

CLOSEST TOWN: Bar Harbor

DIRECTIONS: From the junction of US 1 and ME 3 in Ellsworth follow ME 3 south through Trenton and across the causeway to Mount Desert Island. To reach the Hull's Cove visitor center, continue to follow ME 3 south toward Bar Harbor, then bear right on the well-marked park road. To get to Ellsworth from Interstate 95, from Augusta take ME 3 east to US 1 north, from Bangor take US 1A east to US 1 north, or from the Brunswick/Portland area follow US 1 north via the more congested coastal route. A $5 (individual, one-day), $10 (seven-day), or $20 (seasonal) fee is charged at the Sand Beach entrance station.

At Acadia National Park, low granite mountains rise abruptly out of the ocean, forming one of New England's unique landscapes, rich in both scenery and natural diversity. Here visitors can explore tidal pools along rocky headlands and beaches, observe whales and sea ducks from ocean vistas, deer, foxes, and songbirds along upland forest trails, and snapping turtles in beaver ponds. The park and the adjacent ocean waters are home to more than 40 mammal species, 30 species of fish, and 300 varieties of birds.

Established as the first eastern national park in 1919, Acadia encompasses nearly 50,000 acres on Mount Desert Island, Schoondic Peninsula on the mainland, as well as several offshore islands. Mount Desert Island, which is the largest island along the Maine coast, is divided for most of its length by Somes Sound, the only fjord on the Atlantic coast. It is forested with spruce-fir woodlands interspersed with groves of deciduous birch and aspens that sprouted following the great fire of October 1947, which burned more than 20,000 acres and destroyed many homes.

Unquestionably Acadia's most popular feature, Cadillac Mountain's 1,530-foot granite summit is the highest point on the eastern seaboard, and the tallest of the island's numerous low mountains and hills. The harsh coastal climate and historical forest fires denuded much of the summit vegetation, opening up 360-degree views of Frenchman Bay, Bar Harbor, the Porcupine Islands, and the Atlantic Ocean.

VIEWING

The steep east face of Champlain Mountain is a well-known nesting site for peregrine falcons. During the late spring and summer, they are often visible at an observation area on the loop road north of the Sand Beach entrance booths. May and June generally offer the best viewing; by early summer the juveniles begin flying and may be observed in "training" flights along the cliffs, while the adults rest and recuperate from the incessant demands for food. The falcons are present during other months, but generally harder to observe. During the summer, rangers offer spotting scopes and other interpretive materials.

Though all the park's trails have birding potential, one of the best, and most easily accessible, woodland areas is that around the Sieur du Monts Spring, where wildflower gardens are maintained. Here colorful American redstarts, scarlet tanagers, warbling vireos, black-billed cuckoos, and other migratory songbirds are regularly observed; year-round northern residents include gray jays, boreal chickadees, black-backed woodpeckers, and spruce grouse. During spring and fall, watch for migrating raptors from the open summits, including Cadillac and Beech mountains. In winter, scan the rocks, coves, and offshore waters for purple sandpipers and winter ducks such as eiders, scoters, buffleheads, mergansers, and common loons, which head for the coast once the inland lakes freeze. Familiar seabirds include double-crested cormorants and black guillemots, which breed along most of the Maine coast.

Mammals present in the forests include red foxes, porcupines, raccoons, eastern coyotes, snowshoe hares, and the occasional black bear and moose, though the latter two are rarely seen on the island. White-tailed deer are common and may be encountered along any of the trails; they are often observed along the loop road from the Sieur du Monts area to Sand Beach in the early morning.

The island's beaver population has fluctuated considerably over the years. After they were nearly eliminated by trapping by 1900, a reintroduction program was successful enough that nuisance claims were prevalent within 30 years. Following a brief decline after the 1947 fires, the population rebounded to an estimated 300 by the 1970s, then declined to 100 by 1997. Two easily visible beaver ponds are located along the loop road south of the Sieur du Monts Spring and adjacent to the ocean bluffs at Seawall near Bass Harbor. Snapping and painted turtles are common throughout the freshwater ponds; other reptiles to watch for include milk, northern red-bellied, ringback, smooth green, and garter snakes.

The most common of the whales that inhabit the offshore waters from spring through fall is the finback, which at 70 feet is the world's second-largest mammal; humpback and minke whales are present as well. Harbor and gray seals are easiest to observe when basking on exposed ledges and sandbars at low to half tide. Though marine life can be viewed from shoreline lookouts, natural-history boat tours offer the best opportunities for good views.

The rocky shoreline offers abundant tide pool habitat; at low tide, check these pockets and basins for sea stars, lobsters, crabs, barnacles, and mussels. Some of the most accessible areas are along the Otter Cliffs and Sand Beach, and at Seawall.

GETTING AROUND

Many of the park's familiar features, including Cadillac Mountain, Otter Point and Sand Beach, the Sieur du Monts Spring, and Jordan Pond are reached via the park's 20-mile loop road. The road to the top of Cadillac Mountain begins near the Cadillac Mountain entrance just south of Bar Harbor. While the vast majority of visitors arrive by car, the summit can also be reached by hiking trails, including the spectacular 3.5-mile South Ridge Trail, which begins at the Blackwoods Campground and ascends along an open ridge to the top.

Outstanding views abound along the Ocean Path, which begins at the Sand Beach parking area on the island's southeast shore and follows the rocky headlands for 1.7 miles to its end at Otter Point. The 1.6-mile Great Head Trail also begins at Sand Beach and passes an overlook en route to rocky bluffs with more ocean views. Nearby 525-foot Gorham Mountain offers sweeping views from above the bluffs; its summit is reached via an easy-to-moderate 0.9-mile hike from the trailhead south of Thunder Hole.

Options for exploring the Jordan Pond area include a rocky 3.3-mile trail that encircles the pond, and a network of carriage roads that lead to nearby Eagle Lake and Day Mountain. Easy trails lead to the top of North and South Bubbles, where there are striking views of the pond and Bubble Rock, a glacial erratic that sits improbably balanced atop the edge of a high cliff, while longer outings explore 1,248-foot Pemetic Mountain, which features an open ridge with excellent views (3.3-mile round-trip via the West Cliff Trail). To the west lie Penobscot and Sargent mountains (1,194 and 1,373 feet respectively), connected by another open ridge.

One of the best hikes on the island's quieter, less-visited west side—and a fine alternative for those looking to avoid the crowds on Cadillac Mountain—is the easy 1.2-mile loop over 852-foot Beech Mountain, where the summit tower and other viewpoints offer fine vistas of the eastern mountains, Northeast Harbor and Southwest Harbor, and nearby Long Pond.

Beech and Canada cliffs, which are easily accessible by short paths from the parking area at the end of Beech Hill Road, offer striking views from ledges that rise high above Echo Lake.

For a complete perspective, be sure to include at least one boat tour. The variety of options includes whale watches, lobster and seal tours, general scenic and lighthouse cruises (some of which include stops on the offshore islands), and sea kayak excursions. Information is available at visitor centers and in the park's free *Acadia Weekly* publication.

Baxter State Park

Maine Bureau of Parks and Lands, 207-723-5140,
www.baxterstateparkauthority.com

CLOSEST TOWN: Millinocket

DIRECTIONS: From Interstate 95 in Medway take exit 244 and follow ME 157 west for 11 miles through Medway and East Millinocket to Millinocket (it's a good idea to fill up at one of the gas stations here). From Millinocket follow the well-marked road to the park for 17 miles to the Togue Pond gatehouse. A $12 daily fee ($37 for a season pass) is charged for non-Maine residents.

Encompassing more than 200,000 acres of magnificent wilderness where Mount Katahdin and 46 other peaks of the Longfellow Range preside over central Maine's forest plateau, Baxter State Park is a natural area unlike any other in New England. Here wilderness takes precedence over convenience: the entrances are roughly 20 miles from the nearest towns, and there are no paved roads, gas stations, or electricity. The park is the legacy of former Maine governor Percival Baxter, who spent more than 30 years working to acquire the land and also left a series of deeds arranging for the preserve to remain undeveloped. The isolation of the area is evidenced by the fact that the first known climb of Katahdin by settlers was documented in 1804, more than 130 years after Darby Field's 1672 ascent of Mount Washington.

Baxter's central and signature feature is Mount Katahdin, famed for its distinctive summit that includes a mile-long plateau above treeline known as the "tableland." The highest of Katahdin's peaks is Baxter (5,267 feet), and six other summits surpass 4,700 feet. This extensive zone is home to numerous alpine plants, as well as an endemic form of the Polixenes Arctic butterfly. Moving glaciers carved several distinctive cirques into Katahdin's slopes, including the famous Great Basin. The surrounding mountains

A subspecies of the red-spotted admiral, the beautiful white admiral butterfly is a familiar sight in northern and western New England.

include 18 summits that exceed 3,000 feet. More than 90 percent of the park is forested with northern hardwoods and spruce. There are numerous ponds, beaver wetlands, streams, and brooks. Open fields may be viewed at Nesowadnehunk Field and at the northern entrance.

VIEWING AND GETTING AROUND

From drive-up views and short hikes to ponds and fields, to multiday wilderness adventures in the backcountry, options for explorers run the gamut at this expansive area. There are 175 miles' worth of trails, all of which have viewing potential. Some of the most reliable and accessible areas are detailed here.

The historic Nesowadnehunk Tote Road provides access to most of the trailheads, ponds, and campgrounds. Unlike most park auto roads, it is a narrow, winding, and often dusty dirt road, with only a handful of open views scattered along its 46-mile length. Sandy Stream Pond and the Roaring Brook area are reached by an 8-mile road that begins at the Togue Pond gatehouse. While some viewing can be done by car, the best way to experience the park and see wildlife is to explore the ponds and trails. Though they may seem tolerant of humans, the moose and other wildlife should be observed from a respectful distance at all times.

Nestled at the base of Katahdin and South Turner Mountain in the park's southwest corner, Sandy Stream Pond offers an unmatched combination of scenery and wildlife, especially moose. In late spring and early summer, watch for mothers with newborn calves, whose coats are light brown in their early weeks. During the autumn mating season, known as the "rut," fortunate observers may glimpse a bull (or two) courting a cow. Other interesting behaviors may include a territorial dispute or even a mother searching for a lost calf. Common mergansers, belted kingfishers, and white-tailed deer also frequent the pond, while dragonflies and damselflies patrol the edges during warm months. The viewing areas along the east shore are easily reached by a 10-minute walk from the Roaring Brook campground parking area. Along Roaring Brook, watch for Philadelphia vireos and least flycatchers. This lot, which provides access to several popular hiking trails, fills up early on good-weather weekends and holidays, and late arrivals should be prepared to make alternate plans; short-term "moose watcher" passes may be issued on a first-come, first-served basis.

The Daicey Pond and Kidney Pond areas offer a network of trails that explore a cluster of scenic water bodies near the park's western boundary, including Rocky, Grassy, and Elbow ponds. Moose and loons are often easily viewed from the campground and pondside trails; one reliable lookout is a short walk north from the Kidney Pond campground. Canoes are available for rent for a minimal fee. A pleasant, easy section of the Appalachian Trail follows the edge of Daicey Pond and Nesowadnehunk Stream south to Little and Big Niagara Falls and the site of an old toll dam.

Nesowadnehunk Field, near the park's western boundary at the midpoint of the tote road, is home to large meadows that offer habitat diversity. White-tailed deer are common here; in summer watch for fawns with spotted coats feeding with their mothers. Red foxes are often seen hopping and following the scent of mouse trails as they hunt the fields and openings near the campgrounds; other familiar mammals include red squirrels, raccoons, and eastern chipmunks. Check the outlet to Nesowadnehunk Stream for moose, beavers, river otters, and muskrats. A common butterfly here is the beautiful white admiral, easily identified by its dark body with white and blue wing bands.

The portion of the park from Nesowadnehunk Field north offers the best boreal forest viewing; species found here include three-toed and black-backed woodpeckers, spruce grouse, boreal chickadees, and bold, curious gray jays, who often visit campgrounds and picnic areas. The melodious *Sam-Peabody-Peabody* whistling call of white-throated sparrows is a familiar sound throughout these woodlands. Catch a fisher by surprise along a trail or by a pond and you may witness it shooting up and down trees at a remarkable rate of speed. Snowshoe hares frequent road and trail edges, seeking cover from bobcat and Canada lynx. Black bears are often seen crossing the roads and trails, in blueberry and raspberry patches during summer and in beech ridges in autumn.

A short distance south of the northern entrance gate is another scenic campground at South Branch Pond, where common loons cruise the waters below Traveler and North Traveler mountains. Here the relatively easy North Traveler Mountain Trail explores a ridge where historic fires have created an open meadow, abundant blueberries, and continuous long open views. Look for moose and black bear sign here, particularly near the summit, which is 2.5 miles from the trailhead.

Bigelow Mountain Preserve

Maine Bureau of Parks and Lands, 207-778-4111, www.maine.gov/doc/parks
CLOSEST TOWN: Stratton
DIRECTIONS: For the Stratton Brook Pond trailheads, from the center of Stratton follow ME 16/27 east for 4.5 miles, then turn north on the dirt Stratton Brook Road. Continue 1.6 miles to the parking area, which includes an information sign with a trail map. For the boat launch near Stratton, at the junction of ME 27 and ME 16 in the village center, follow ME 27 north for a mile to the parking area.

Established in 1976 by a referendum of the citizens of Maine, the 36,000-acre Bigelow Mountain Preserve encompasses some of Maine's most scenic and rugged terrain. It includes the ridge of Bigelow and Little Bigelow Mountains, as well as 21 miles of frontage along the south shores of adjacent Flagstaff Lake, a large reservoir formed by an impoundment of the Dead River in 1949. Bigelow Mountain's highest points are, from west to east, Cranberry Peak (3,194 feet), the twin North and South Horn peaks, (3,792 and 3,805 respectively), West Peak (at 4,145 feet the highest point), and Avery Peak (4,088). From these open vistas there are expansive views across the mountains, hills, and wetlands of western Maine. The extensive forest transitions from northern hardwoods at the lower elevations to boreal spruce-fir above 2,000 feet; the ridge is largely wooded but open above 3,800 feet, with more than 170 acres of alpine terrain. High-elevation wetlands include Cranberry and Horns ponds along the ridge and a bog that is visible on the Horns Pond Trail.

Bigelow Mountain is separated from the neighboring Saddleback Mountain Range by the narrow Carrabassett Valley. Here Stratton Brook Pond and its associated wetlands, which are fed by the numerous streams and brooks that drain the mountain slopes, offer additional habitat diversity. The two ridges are home to 9 of Maine's 14 mountain summits above 4,000 feet.

Often quieter in the woods than squirrels and chipmunks, moose may be encountered along any of the trails, especially near wetlands such as Flagstaff Lake and Stratton Brook Pond. They are also often seen by boaters on Flagstaff Lake. Also present in the forests here are white-tailed deer, fishers, bobcats, pine martens, and red foxes. Porcupines, black bears, and eastern coyotes den in the abundant rocky outcroppings. Small mammals include red and gray squirrels, eastern chipmunks, little brown bats, and rock and meadow voles. The lake and other wetlands are frequented by beavers, river otters, mink, muskrats, and raccoons. Stratton Brook Pond is rich in brook trout.

The forests also provide habitat for numerous songbirds, including bay-breasted, Tennessee, and magnolia warblers, wood, Swainson's, and gray-cheeked thrushes, American redstarts, ovenbirds, and solitary vireos. Northern species include pine siskins, boreal chickadees, pine and evening grosbeaks, yellow-bellied sapsuckers, ruby and golden-crowned kinglets, winter wrens, spruce grouse, and gray jays. Watch for olive-sided and alder flycatchers along the edges of beaver ponds and bogs.

Among the birds of prey here are bald eagles and osprey, which are often seen at Flagstaff Lake. Another, less celebrated species that is also recovering from mid-twentieth-century declines caused by DDT and other pesticides is the Cooper's hawk, which thrives in dense woodlands.

GETTING AROUND

With an early start, fit day hikers have the option of a 12.4-mile circuit that begins on the Fire Warden's Trail at the Stratton Brook Road trailhead. This route passes Stratton Pond and its wetlands before climbing to a junction at 1.6 miles, where the loop begins. Here the Horns Pond Trail branches to the left and offers a much gentler climb to the ridge than the Fire Warden's Trail, which becomes very steep as it approaches the summit. After passing the bog at 3 miles, the Horns Pond Trail steepens as it rises to join the Appalachian Trail on the ridge at South Horn Pond. The Appalachian Trail passes the North and South Horn peaks, then follows rolling terrain along the forested ridge for 2 miles before emerging above the trees at West Peak (a detour to Avery Peak adds an extra mile). Begin the descent by following the Appalachian Trail for another 0.4 mile to a right on the Fire Warden's Trail, which descends steeply for 1.5 miles before moderating as it returns to the trailhead, 4.6 miles from the ridge.

For distance backpackers, the 16.7-mile (one way) traverse of the ridge, which includes a portion of the Appalachian Trail, generally takes two days to complete from trailheads located off Routes 16 and 27 just east of Stratton and East Flagstaff roads on the preserve's eastern boundary.

Flagstaff Lake is a highlight of the 740-mile Northern Forest Canoe Trail, which stretches from New York State to Maine. The state boat launch on Route 27 north of Stratton offers easy access to the western corner of the lake, which is considered a paddle of intermediate difficulty; be alert and prepared for changing winds throughout the day. A short segment of the Appalachian Trail follows the southeast shores near Round Top Mountain and Long Falls Dam Road.

Borestone Mountain Audubon Sanctuary

Maine Audubon Society, 207-781-2330, www.maineaudubon.org

CLOSEST TOWN: Monson

DIRECTIONS: From ME 15 in Monson turn north on Elliotsville Road, marked with a sign for Borestone Mountain, and continue 8 miles to the bridge over Big Wilson Falls. Bear left after the crossing and continue to the parking area on the left-hand side of the road, opposite the entrance gate. A $4 fee ($2 for students, seniors, and nonprofits) is collected at the nature center at Sunrise Pond.

Perhaps no other small New England mountain has a larger feel than 1,954-foot Borestone Mountain, whose rocky, windswept summit ridge is home to a pair of distinct, open peaks that offer 360-degree views across the surrounding ponds, lakes, and hills of central Maine. The mountain is the centerpiece of a 1,600-acre sanctuary that is an oasis of protected land amid the industrial timberlands north of Monson and the Piscatiquis River. Nestled roughly 700 feet below the summit is a series of picturesque, high-elevation alpine tarns known as the Moore Ponds, the lowest of which is Sunrise Pond, where the sanctuary's nature center is located. Here several exhibits detail the natural history of the mountain, and a staff naturalist is available from June to October. Nearby Sunset Pond is home to a historic Adirondack-style lodge that is a holdover from a fox ranch that operated on the mountain in the early twentieth century.

VIEWING

The mountain's hardwood forests offer good bird-watching opportunities year-round; diversity is greatest in late spring and early summer. Characteristic northern species include boreal chickadees, yellow-bellied sap-suckers, red-breasted nuthatches, and white-throated sparrows. Migratory songbirds include bay-breasted, blackburnian, and Cape May warblers and hermit thrushes, whose beautiful, flutelike call is evident from late spring through summer. Red squirrels provide food for pine martens, bobcats, fishers, and coyotes. You may see a red fox that is a descendant from individuals that were once bred at the fox ranch. Porcupines den in the rocky ledges, while raccoons make homes in tree cavities. Check for sign of black bear and white-tailed deer along the forest trails. The preserve is near the southern range limit for Canada lynx, which feed primarily on snowshoe hares. Look for webbed tracks of the lynx in snow.

The ponds below the summit are home to kingfishers as well as beavers, river otters, and mink. From the crest of the ridge at the West and East peaks, scan the wetlands below for a unique perspective of moose and other wildlife from above. Ravens and turkey vultures glide along the thermal currents and wind gusts along the exposed ridge, while osprey hunt fish in the ponds. Immature peregrine falcons were released on the mountain as part of a reintroduction effort, and they have successfully recolonized the cliffs. Listen for the call of common loons echoing from Lake Onawa and the other numerous lakes and ponds that surround the preserve. Amphibians present in these wetlands include gray tree, leopard, and bull frogs.

GETTING AROUND

From the parking area on Elliotsville Road, the Base Trail winds on an easy-to-moderate mile-long ascent through the woods to the nature center at the edge of Sunrise Pond below the summit ridge. Hikers also have the option of walking the sanctuary's dirt access road, which is slightly longer (1.3 miles) but offers easier footing. From the pond there are views across the water to the mountain's upper slopes. Here visitors have the option of returning to the parking area or continuing the steep but fairly short ascent to the ridge.

After crossing the outlet of Sunrise Pond behind the nature center, the Summit Trail follows a steeper, rockier grade for 0.7 mile as it rises to the open top of West Peak, with some minor scrambling over boulders just below the summit. Here there are fine views of the ponds and wetlands below and the surrounding mountains and hills of central Maine. From West Peak the trail continues for another 0.3 mile to the end of the ridge at East Peak. The one-way climb from the parking area to the ridge can be as short as 1.7 miles (via the Base Trail and ending atop the West Peak) or as long as 2.3 miles (via the access road and ending at the East Peak).

East Point Sanctuary and Biddeford Pool

Maine Audubon Society (East Point Sanctuary), 207-781-2330, www.maineaudubon.org

CLOSEST TOWN: Biddeford

DIRECTIONS: From the center of Biddeford follow combined ME 9 / ME 208 south for 5 miles, then bear left on ME 208 and continue for 0.5 mile to a T junction at the edge of the pool. Turn left at the stop sign and follow ME 208 along the pool, then continue to the road's end at the junction with Ocean Avenue, 1.7 miles from the stop sign. The East Point Sanctuary entrance is on the left, with limited parking on the right-hand side of the road.

From the tip of a small rocky peninsula that juts into the Gulf of Maine just east of Saco and north of Kennebunkport, the East Point Sanctuary offers sweeping vistas and varied habitats within its compact 30 acres. Here rocky headlands and an open wildflower meadow offer fine views along the southern Maine coast, including Wood Island and its lighthouse across the channel, Gooseberry and Beach Islands, and the distant hotels bordering Old Orchard Beach. Ringing the point are rocky beaches with numerous tide pools, and groves of pitch pine and birch woods and shrubs offer additional diversity.

A short distance to the west lies Biddeford Pool, a mile-long tidal cove where mudflats offer uncommonly good shorebird viewing during migration periods. The pool is part of the Rachel Carson National Wildlife Refuge, the headquarters for which are a short distance to the south in Wells.

VIEWING

From the ocean bluffs at East Point from late fall to spring, watch for wintering seabirds such as king eiders, ruddy turnstones, purple sandpipers, common murres, dovekies, razorbills, common and red-throated loons, and even Atlantic puffins. Snowy owls and rough-legged hawks may be seen across the channel on Wood Island during this time. The rocky shoreline offers fine tide pool habitat, where the variety of unique creatures includes starfish, blue mussels, and crabs.

In warmer months look for wading birds such as black-crowned night herons and glossy ibises, which also nest on Wood Island. During spring and fall migrations, watch for merlins navigating the breezes above the open fields and edges of East Point. These small members of the falcon family, which favor these openings, hunt songbirds and shorebirds, which are also on the move during these times. Other raptors on the hunt include peregrine falcons, which reach speeds nearing 200 miles per hour in hunting dives. Yellow-breasted chats and orange-crowned warblers are among the songbirds that use the shrubby thickets to rest during this time. Check the open meadow and the edge of the golf course near the entrance for red foxes and wild turkeys.

Shorebird viewing at Biddeford Pool is best during the height of the late-summer migrations, though May is also a good time to check for northbound travelers. Watch for Baird's and buff-breasted sandpipers, long-billed dowitchers, and marbled godwits, and common, least, arctic, and roseate terns. Also watch for long-legged wading birds such as glossy ibises, great blue and green herons, and snowy and great egrets, and Barrow's and common goldeneyes, buffleheads, black ducks, and other waterfowl. Winter visitors may see snow buntings, goldeneyes, and Lapland longspurs, which breed in far northern polar regions.

GETTING AROUND

The East Point Sanctuary's easy walking trail offers a round-trip of slightly less than a mile that is especially good for families. From the roadside gate this path briefly skirts the edge of the adjacent golf course before bearing right to follow an old road toward the ocean. Watch carefully for a narrow path on the right that explores the wildflower meadow and the edge of the bluffs. This trail soon rejoins the road, then continues above the rocky beach before ending at a junction with several overgrown paths; backtrack from here to the entrance for a round-trip of slightly less than a mile.

Though the pool is part of the Carson refuge, the surrounding lands are private, and viewing is done from Route 208 (also known as Mile Stretch Road).

 Great Wass Island

The Nature Conservancy, 207-729-5181, www.nature.org
CLOSEST TOWN: Jonesport
DIRECTIONS: From the junction of US 1 and ME 187 in Jonesport follow ME 187 south for 10.8 miles to the bridge to Beals Island. After crossing the bridge,

bear left and continue through the village. After crossing a causeway, turn right at a junction, following signs for the Nature Conservancy. The entrance and parking area is on the left-hand side of the road, 15.3 miles from US 1.

Lying just offshore from Jonesport is an archipelago of more than 40 often-fogbound islands of all sizes that host some of New England's most unusual natural communities. The largest of these rocky islands is 1,700-acre Great Wass, 1,576 acres of which have been protected since 1978 by the Nature Conservancy. Here the diverse habitats include a series of interconnected peatlands that form one of the finest examples of a coastal plateau bog along the Maine coast, granite ledges, a long rocky shoreline with numerous tidal pools and coves, and a small jack pine bog, the only known natural community of this type in the United States. The northernmost of the New World pine species, jack pines are at their southern limit in Maine and New Hampshire; though they generally require disturbances such as fire or logging to propagate, studies indicate that the Great Wass community has adapted to poor soils and may be self-sustaining. The bogs are home to northern pitcher plants and sundews, along with uncommon species such as dragon's mouth orchids and baked appleberry, and the edge habitat along the shore comes alive with prolific beachhead iris blooms in early summer.

The diverse habitats of Great Wass Island include rocky beaches and a unique jack-pine bog.

Along the interior forest trails watch for palm, Nashville, Canada, black-burnian, bay-breasted, and magnolia warblers, Swainson's thrushes, and other migrants during the warm months. Northern boreal species here include elusive spruce grouse, which enjoy abundant habitat in the extensive conifer woodlands, crossbills, boreal chickadees, and Lincoln's sparrows, which are characteristic of northern boreal bogs. Around the bogs these birds compete with carnivorous northern pitcher plants for ants, flies, and other insects; the unwary insects that enter the vaselike leaves will become trapped and digested.

The rocky shoreline offers an entirely different habitat and suite of species. Scan the offshore waters for "rafts," or large flocks, of common eiders; the feathers of these attractive sea ducks have long been prized for their insulating qualities. Other hardy denizens of these waters include double-crested cormorants, black guillemots, laughing gulls, razorbills, common and thick-billed murres, gray seals, and humpback whales. Harbor seals bask in large groups along the rocky ledges near Cape Cove and other spots along the east shores. Bald eagles, osprey, and peregrine falcons, all strongly recovering from severe population declines associated with DDT pesticide use during the mid-twentieth century, may be seen here as well; watch for the latter hunting unwary songbirds in high-speed dives. Migratory periods bring large flocks of shorebirds to the area in spring and from midsummer through autumn, including piping plovers.

While carefully watching the tides and your footing, check the numerous tide pools, coves, and pockets for a range of wonderfully unique creatures such as sea stars, sea urchins, rock and green crabs, sea cucumbers, and rock gunnels, which are small eel-like fish. Here seaweeds such as common rockweed provide a measure of cover for clamworms and mussels, which in turn sustain creatures higher on the food chain.

GETTING AROUND

The preserve has two trails that wind through the interior habitats to the shore. Though there is little elevation gain along these routes, they are quite narrow, with numerous rocks, tree roots, and wet areas that can make for slow going in places. Because the vegetation is often damp with fog, a waterproof jacket is recommended.

From the end of a short connecting path that begins at the back of the parking area, the Little Cape Point Trail branches right and leads east across the island's interior, winding through spruce, fir, and jack pine woodlands and across open granite ledges, passing an overlook and crossing a wood bridge that offers close-up views of a boggy area. After 2 miles it reaches the shore at Cape Cove, just south of Little Cape Point.

The 1.5-mile Mud Hole Trail heads left (north) from the junction and winds along more ledges before turning sharply east to follow the woods above a long cove to Mud Hole Point, where there are fine views of Eastern Bay and the nearby islands.

These routes may be connected as part of a strongly recommended 5.5-mile circuit by walking the 2 miles of shoreline between their endpoints. This route, which is marked with blue blazes and cairns, passes a fjord-like cove and tidal pools with continuous coastal views that are sweeping on clear days and artistic when foggy. The walking is mostly easy but requires negotiating rocky terrain in places; prominent signs are posted at both trailheads. Because of the moderately rugged character of the three trails and the numerous overlooks and diversions, a minimum of four to five hours should be allotted for the full circuit.

Machias Seal Island

Canadian Wildlife Service
CLOSEST TOWNS: Jonesport, Cutler Harbor
DIRECTIONS: See "Getting Around," below.

Renowned for its remarkable seabird viewing, Machias Seal Island has hosted a long list of prominent naturalists, writers, and filmmakers, including Roger Tory Peterson and Marlin Perkins. This rocky, treeless, 20-acre island is located where the Gulfs of Maine and Fundy meet, roughly 10 miles southwest of Cutler, Maine. Its countless crevices, pockets, and burrows offer extensive nesting habitat for Atlantic puffins, razorbills, terns, and other seabirds, which enjoy abundant stores of fish in the surrounding waters.

In addition to its wildlife, Machias Seal Island is well known as one of the disputed territories of the United States and Canada, thanks to an ambiguous clause in the treaty that followed the Revolutionary War. Both the United States and Great Britain claimed the island, which remained largely unknown and unsettled through the early nineteenth century; the British first established the lighthouse in 1832. Though Canada has subsequently continued to operate the lighthouse and administer the island, the United States does not recognize either as signifying ownership; in 1979 both countries agreed to allow the boundary to remain ambiguous.

VIEWING

Observation blinds offer fine close-up views of the seabirds as they meander around their nests and make hunting rounds. The viewing season generally runs from May through the middle of August, with the prime opportunities from mid-June to mid-July. Some 3,000 pairs of Atlantic puffins, which breed along the coast in warm months before moving far offshore during fall and winter, spend the summer here. They nest in the numerous pockets between the rocks and also excavate burrows in the ground.

While the puffins are the star attraction for most visitors, not to be overlooked are the other hardy seabirds that call the island home, including arctic terns, whose sleek bodies and long, thin bills offer a marked contrast to their more gaudy neighbors. During the course of their yearly migrations, arctic terns travel 20,000 miles or more, the greatest distance of any migratory bird. Lesser numbers of razorbills, which bear a resemblance to penguins with their body shape and black-and-white coloration, also nest amid the rocks here. Also watch for common murres, common terns, Leach's storm petrels, and flocks of common eider ducks.

During the boat ride from the mainland, watch for more seabirds such as Wilson's storm petrels, northern gannets, jaegers, sooty shearwaters, phalaropes, and double-crested cormorants, as well as harbor seals and a variety of whales and dolphins.

GETTING AROUND

Boat trips to Machias Seal Island are offered by Norton's of Jonesport, Maine (207-497-5933), Bold Coast Charters of Cutler Harbor, Maine (207-259-4484), and Sea Watch Tours of Grand Manan, New Brunswick, Canada (877-662-8552). Due to the short viewing season and restrictions on access and group size, advance reservations are strongly recommended; also ask the individual operators for specific information about departure times (which may be affected by weather and tides), group tours, and landing and access to the viewing blinds. Those that land on the island should use caution when getting out of the boat around slippery rocks and use care not to disturb any species encountered along the short paths to the blinds. Accommodations are available nearby in Machias, Jonesboro, and Lubec; Ellsworth and Acadia National Park are roughly an hour's drive south.

Maine Coastal Islands National Wildlife Refuge: Petit Manan Division

U.S. Fish and Wildlife Service, 207-546-2124,
www.fws.gov/northeast/mainecoastal

CLOSEST TOWN: Steuben

DIRECTIONS: From US 1 in Steuben turn south on Pigeon Hill Road and continue for 5.8 miles to the Birch Point Trail parking area near the refuge boundary, and an additional 0.4 mile to the Hollingsworth Trail.

For centuries Maine's seabirds, such as Atlantic puffins and terns, were decimated by unregulated hunting, habitat destruction, egg collecting, and expanding populations of predators such as gulls and introduced animals. During the 1970s the Maine Coastal Islands National Wildlife Complex, which encompasses more than 7,000 acres spread among numerous islands and divisions over 200 miles from Cutler to Portland, was established to provide habitat for recovering colonies. At Seal Island in the midcoast region, where puffins were eliminated during the late nineteenth century, a successful reintroduction program implemented by the National Audubon Society's Project Puffin during the 1980s has resulted in a thriving colony. Arctic, common, and roseate terns have also been restored to several of the islands. In 2009 a pair of Manx shearwaters nested at Matinicus Rock, becoming the first breeding pair noted along the Maine coast and only the second on record in New England.

Petit Manan Point, the refuge's largest and most easily accessible division, encompasses 2,166 acres of a narrow peninsula between Dyer Bay and Pigeon Hill Bay south of the town of Steuben. Here habitats include blueberry barrens characteristic of Washington County, grasslands and old pastures, forests of jack pine, balsam fir, tamarack, white cedar, birch, and aspen, salt marshes, swampy wetlands, and rocky shoreline ledges and beaches. Mid to late summer is an especially enjoyable time for a visit here, with abundant shorebirds and other southbound migrants to be seen and fruiting blueberries and other shrubs and wildflowers offering nourishment for a variety of wildlife.

VIEWING

Petit Manan Point's blueberry barrens and clearings provide habitat and food for white-tailed deer, black bear, wild turkey, ruffed grouse, savannah sparrows, bobolinks, and American woodcocks, whose unique courtship

Migrating shorebirds at rest along rocky shores at the Petit Manan National Wildlife Refuge in late summer.

flights can be observed on spring evenings. Forest-field edges are also frequented by eastern coyotes, which are fairly recent arrivals to the Maine coast, as well as red fox, striped skunks, porcupines, and snowshoe hares. Check the wetlands for beaver, mink, muskrat, and raccoons.

In the boreal woodlands watch for Nashville, blackburnian, and Canada warblers and other songbirds during spring and summer, and boreal chickadees, gray jays, and spruce grouse year-round. Autumn migrations bring waterfowl by the thousands, as large flocks use the refuge as a rest stop during the course of their journey south, particularly at the portion of Petit Manan Point known as Cranberry Flowage, where there is abundant wild rice. During the cold, windswept days of winter, hardy visitors include scoters, goldeneyes, oldsquaws, long-tailed ducks, common loons, and common eiders. A 2007 survey indicated nine pairs of breeding bald eagles at the refuge.

During the mid-1980s, common, arctic, and roseate terns were successfully restored to the point. Because roseates nest with large flocks of other terns, it was necessary to establish healthy populations of common and arctic terns as part of the process. From the rocky shoreline and cobble beaches scan the nearby ledges and islands for a variety of other shorebirds and seabirds, including black guillemots, laughing gulls, double-crested cormorants, and sandpipers. The refuge offers a unique opportunity to view Atlantic puffins from the mainland, particularly during the month of August. Harbor seals may also be observed feeding in these waters, especially at high tide.

GETTING AROUND

The refuge offers two trails that explore the habitats of Petit Manan Point. The longer of these is the 2-mile (one way) Birch Point Trail, which begins at a parking area on Pigeon Hill Road just south of the refuge boundary. This path, portions of which may be seasonally wet, explores a blueberry meadow, boreal forest groves, and salt marshes as it winds west, then north to overlooks at a narrow cove on Dyer Bay.

Roughly half a mile to the south is the trailhead for the more rugged, interpretive Hollingsworth Trail, which begins at a blueberry barren and makes a 1.5-mile circuit along the east side of the peninsula. It winds through woodlands of spruce, fir, and maple, over granite ledges, and follows a boardwalk through an Atlantic white cedar swamp before reaching the cobble beaches, ledges, and a brackish pond along the shores of Pigeon Hill Bay. Signs detail the various wildlife, habitats, and management practices.

Those looking to explore the islands by boat should contact the refuge prior to their visit. Four islands in the complex—Bois Bubert (which lies directly east of Petit Manan Point), Scotch, Cross, and Halifax—are open to the public year-round; the others are closed from April through August to protect nesting birds. Commercial operators offer views of seabirds on Petit Manan Island; contact the refuge for more details.

Monhegan Island

Monhegan Associates, www.monheganassociates.org

CLOSEST TOWN: Monhegan Village

DIRECTIONS: Boats serving Monhegan Island depart from New Harbor (Hardy Boat Cruises, 207-677-2026), Port Clyde (Monhegan Thomaston Boat Line, 207-372-8848), and Boothbay Harbor (Balmy Days Cruises, 800-298-2284).

A jewel of the Maine coast, Monhegan Island is often characterized as a miniature Mount Desert Island minus the national park. Situated in the

Gulf of Maine 11 miles east of the mainland, Monhegan is roughly a mile long by half a mile wide with rugged, rocky headlands and extensive interior woodlands of spruce and balsam fir. The gulf's productive fisheries drew Native Americans to the area in historical times, and early European explorers from 1497 on included John Cabot, George Weymouth, and John Smith.

The island's most dramatic attractions are the steep cliffs along the east shore, where Burnthead, Whitehead, and Blackhead points rise 140 to 160 feet above the ocean, offering sweeping views of the rocky coastline and coves from a variety of perspectives. The historic Monhegan Lighthouse presides over the island's interior height-of-land at an elevation of 168 feet, where there's another fine overview of the village and the mainland across the gulf. A short distance south of the village is Lobster Cove, where the rusted hull of a wrecked tugboat serves as a reminder of these treacherous waters.

The island owes its largely pristine character to the efforts of the Monhegan Associates, who maintain nearly 500 acres, or roughly two-thirds of its total area, in an undeveloped state. The association, which primarily functions as a land trust, was founded with a 300-acre acquisition during the 1950s and has subsequently added holdings through purchases and donations. For more than a century, the village, which has a year-round population of roughly 65 residents, has hosted a well-known seasonal colony for artists.

VIEWING

Monhegan is one of New England's premiere coastal "migrant traps," or areas in especially favorable locations to attract large resting groups of migrants and accidental visitors such as blue grosbeaks, dickcissels, summer tanagers, and red-headed woodpeckers. The village offers fine bird viewing at a small meadow and the Ice Pond, and at properties with planted apple trees and lilac bushes. During migrations look for blackburnian, orange-crowned, Tennessee, Cape May, and chestnut-sided warblers, as well as raptors such as bald eagles, peregrine falcons, American kestrels, and merlins. Butterflies such as mourning cloaks and monarchs may be seen along the edge of the forests; the latter are often observed moving south in large numbers during fall migrations.

Beneath the cliffs and along the rocks are large groups of shorebirds and seagulls, including double-crested and great cormorants, black guillemots, eider ducks, northern gannets, white-winged scoters, and Corey's,

Manx, and greater shearwaters. Lobster Cove at the island's southern end is a productive and easily accessible spot for shorebird viewing. When walking the trails along the west side, watch for harbor seals, which often congregate on exposed rocks and ledges along the shore.

Like other islands along the Maine coast, Monhegan once hosted a white-tailed deer population of more than 100 individuals per square mile. This overpopulation had several consequences for the herd and village residents, including widespread Lyme disease and food shortages that caused the deer to grow barely larger than dogs and does to bear only single offspring, and the deer were ultimately removed from the island in 1999. Other mammals that have been present here include muskrats and Norway rats; a population of feral rabbits briefly existed during the 1980s.

The boat trip from the mainland to the island takes about an hour and is a good time to sample the marine life of Muscongus Bay, which includes harbor seals, minke, pilot, and humpback whales, harbor porpoises, white-sided dolphins, and Atlantic puffins.

GETTING AROUND

The island's 17-mile trail network is divided into 18 numbered routes of various lengths that wind along the seaside cliffs and through the interior forest. The Monhegan Associates trail map, available in the village, details the trails, junctions, and other features. The best way to explore the island is to spend at least one night in the village, which allows time to sample the trail network and enjoy the often spectacular sunrises and sunsets. Automobiles are not allowed on the island.

The full circuit around the island via the Cliff Trails (Trails 1 and 1A) and the village roads is approximately 3.7 miles. The narrow paths traverse some moderately rolling and rugged terrain, but the views are well worth the effort. As you follow the perimeter of the island, the perspective changes as the views shift from the cliffs toward the coast, and the shorter interior trails offer numerous opportunities to detour into the spruce woodlands. Half a day is recommended for this loop, as there are numerous vistas and diversions in the village. You also have the option of making a shorter loop to the north or south by using either Trail 7 (via Whitehead Cliff) or Trail 10 (via Blackhead) as a cutoff route; two hours is sufficient time for either.

Shorter one-way options appropriate for day visitors with limited time include Trail 7, which makes a 0.4-mile beeline from the lighthouse to the Whitehead Cliffs, and Trail 4, which leads from the village to Burnthead Cliff. Both are roughly half an hour's walk from the village center, with minor elevation gain. Lobster and Christmas coves are easily reached by a 0.6-mile stroll south from the wharf.

 Moosehead Lake

Maine Bureau of Parks and Lands (Lily Bay State Park), 207-695-2700, www.maine.gov/doc/parks

CLOSEST TOWN: Greenville

DIRECTIONS: For Lily Bay State Park, from the center of Greenville follow Lily Bay Road north for 8 miles to the marked entrance road on the left. The admission fee for adults is $4.50 (out of state) and $3 (Maine residents), with reduced rates for children and seniors. For Lazy Tom Bog, from Greenville follow Lily Bay Road north for 18 miles to Kokadjo village, then continue 1 mile to a left turn that leads for 0.5 mile to the bog, which is easily viewed from the road.

Among the many visitors to Moosehead Lake during the mid-nineteenth century was Henry David Thoreau, who explored the region during visits in 1853 and 1857. Indeed, this largely undeveloped lake, so named for its vague resemblance to a heavy-antlered bull moose when viewed from the air or on a map, has long been a popular destination for tourists, sportsmen, and hikers. With 117 total square miles and more than 420 miles of shoreline, Moosehead is the largest lake that lies entirely within the boundaries of New England; Vermont's Champlain is larger but shares a border with New York and Canada. Fed by the Moose River from the north, Moosehead Lake serves as the headwaters for the Kennebec River, which winds southerly to Augusta and ultimately the Atlantic Ocean. The most distinctive of the surrounding mountains and hills is arguably wedge-shaped Mount Kineo, whose dramatic cliffs rise 800 feet above the northwest shores.

North of the lake's gateway town of Greenville lies Lily Bay State Park, which encompasses 925 acres at the lake's southeast corner centering on Rowell Cove. The habitats here include extensive northern hardwood-spruce/fir woodlands and lakeshore edge. Visitors enjoy a variety of facilities including boat launches, a sand beach, picnic areas, two campgrounds, and walking trails. Another prime location for viewing moose and other wildlife is Lazy Tom Bog, at the confluence of Lazy Tom Stream and the Roach River on the east shores near the village of Kokadjo, which is 18 miles north of Greenville.

A mother moose runs off a curious young bull that ventured too close to her calf.

VIEWING

The Moosehead region is renowned as sportsman's country, and familiar large mammals include black bears, white-tailed deer, and, of course, moose, which may be encountered anywhere along the lake edges, wetlands, and roads and trails. They are often seen at Lazy Tom Bog and from roads along the shores. Along the woodland trails keep an eye out for more elusive mink, pine martens, striped skunks, raccoons, coyotes, and red and gray foxes. Another midsize predator present here is the Canada lynx, the known populations of which in New England are restricted to a narrow band in northern Maine.

The lake's abundant fish, which include brook and lake trout, smelt fish, lake whitefish, and salmon, provide sustenance for a variety of birds, including common loons, waders such as great blue herons, and other waterfowl, and raptors including osprey and bald eagles. The laughing call of crow-size pileated woodpeckers is a familiar sound throughout the surrounding woodlands, which are also home to hardy year-round resident boreal forest birds such as gray jays and boreal chickadees. Warm months bring large groups of migrants such as mourning and blackburnian warblers, eastern wood peewees, and olive-sided flycatchers.

The state park boat ramps offer fine views across the water and allow for launching of watercraft of all sizes, including kayaks and canoes, which may be rented in Greenville. An easy, blazed 2-mile-long (one way) nature trail, with side paths to vistas, follows the woods along the horseshoe-shaped shore, connecting the Rowell and Dunn Point campgrounds. Walkers beginning at either of the campgrounds can make this a 4-mile out-and-back trip, or save roughly half a mile by making a loop with the park auto road. The park is open from 9 AM to sunset from mid-May to Columbus Day weekend; in the off-season visitors may park at the entrance gate.

From late June through October the Moosehead Marine Museum in Greenville offers tours aboard the historic SS *Katahdin*, a holdover from the days when more than 50 steamers regularly operated along the lake.

Moosehorn National Wildlife Refuge

U.S. Fish and Wildlife Service, 207-454-7161,
www.fws.gov/northeast/moosehorn
CLOSEST TOWN: Calais
DIRECTIONS: For the refuge headquarters at the Baring Unit, from the junction of US 1 and Charlotte Road south of Calais follow Charlotte Road south for 2.4 miles, then turn right on Headquarters Road and continue to the buildings and parking area at the road's end.

From bears to bald eagles, viewing opportunities abound throughout the many habitats of the 30,000-acre Moosehorn National Wildlife Refuge. Here a mosaic of controlled burns and small clear-cuts provides open and brushy habitats that benefit a wide variety of species, while other areas are designated wilderness zones where forests of maple, birch, aspen, spruce, and fir are maturing to old-growth characteristics. The refuge has four natural lakes and more than 50 water bodies created by impoundments where water levels are managed throughout the year, several of which are designed to facilitate the migration of anadromous alewife fish in spring. The 20,000-acre Baring Unit, where the refuge headquarters and visitor center are located, is bordered by the St. Croix River to the north and Meddybumps Lake to the west. The smaller, 8,800-acre Edmunds Unit lies to the south between the towns of Dennysville and Whiting, on the west shore of Dennys Bay.

The refuge is an active center for research on American woodcock, and large areas are cleared and burned to maintain the brushy fields and clearings that this teapot-shaped inland shorebird uses for its distinctive courtship flights at dusk and dawn from the onset of spring to the end of May. They are much less conspicuous during the daytime, as they remain mostly hidden among alder thickets and other shrubby vegetation. Nearly 2,000 woodcock breed throughout the refuge in spring and summer, while an additional estimated 3,000 use the grounds as a rest stop during migrations.

More than 220 species of birds have been recorded at the refuge, including the well-known pair of bald eagles that nest atop a platform along Route 1 in the Baring Unit, where an observation area includes a spotting scope. The ponds and marshes, including the Maguerrewock Impoundment, are frequented by common loons, black, wood, and ring-necked ducks, American bitterns, Virginia rails, soras, and great blue herons. Migratory songbirds arrive in force by mid-May, joining residents such as spruce grouse, gray jays, and boreal chickadees. Listen for whip-poor-wills and saw-whet owls along the roads and trails.

The refuge offers one of the best opportunities in New England for viewing black bears in the wild. Visitors are estimated to have a 30 percent chance of seeing a bear, and this may be greater at certain times of the year. The best places to check include grassy margins along the refuge roads, blueberry patches in July and August, and fields with apple trees in late summer and autumn. In spring watch for wandering yearlings that have been displaced by their mothers before the next cubs are born.

Check edges and thickets for snowshoe hares, which are easily distinguished from cottontails by their larger size and variable coats, which turn white in winter. This offers a level of protection from predators such as bobcats, which though rarely seen leave evidence such as tracks in mud or snow and covered scats in subtle scrapes dug into soft soil. Watch for other predators such as coyotes and foxes near field edges early and late in the day.

GETTING AROUND

The two divisions are home to a network of more than 50 miles of woods roads (closed to vehicles) and interpretive and wilderness trails. Maps and interpretive brochures are available at the refuge headquarters in the Baring Unit. There are two easy interpretive trails at the headquarters. The longer of the two, the 1.2-mile Raven Trail, explores a variety of habitats, including several forest types, a meadow, a timber harvest site, and Dudley Swamp. The universally accessible Woodcock Trail begins near the junction of Charlotte and Headquarters roads and makes a quick 0.3-mile circuit through the habitat for which it is named. Another short accessible trail is located on the east side of Charlotte Road 1.3 miles south of its junction with Route 1; this paved path leads past a field to an observation blind at Upper Maguerrewock Marsh.

A longer walking route with good potential for moose, waterfowl, and songbirds begins off of Charlotte Road opposite the turn for the refuge headquarters. Here Goodall Heath Road forks to the left and leads northeast to Vose Pond Road, where you can make a 1.7-mile circuit along a complex of wetlands, including Vose Pond and Popple and Boundary flowages. The out-and-back hike is approximately 3.7 miles; be prepared for bugs in late spring and summer. Several other Baring Unit wilderness trails are accessed via ME 191 south of its junction with US 1, including the Conic Lake Trail, which makes a 0.4-mile beeline to the lake's west shores.

Routes at the smaller Edmunds Unit include the North and South trails, which branch west off US 1 opposite Cobscook Bay State Park. These are connected by Crane Mill Road, where the Hallowell and Crane Mill flowages are easily viewed. To reach these routes, from the junction of ME 189 and US 1 follow the latter north for 4 miles to the South Road; the North Trail is a mile farther along.

A boat launch for nonmotorized watercraft is available at Bearce Lake off Route 191 in the western portion of the Baring Unit. Cobscook Bay State Park, home to a large campground, nature trails, and scenic vistas, adjoins the Edmunds Unit's southwest corner.

Quoddy Head State Park

Maine Bureau of Parks and Lands, 207-733-0911, www.maine.gov/doc/parks
CLOSEST TOWN: Lubec
DIRECTIONS: From the junction of US 1 and ME 189 in Whiting turn east on ME 189, following signs for Quoddy Head State Park and Lubec. Before reaching the center of Lubec, turn south on South Lubec Road and continue to the road's end at the park entrance.

Encompassing the easternmost point of land on the continental United States, Quoddy Head State Park is home to some of New England's most dramatic coastal scenery. Here seaside bluffs rise high above the Grand Manan Channel and the Bay of Fundy, offering views across the water to Canada's Grand Manan and Campobello islands (the latter is home to the 2,800-acre Roosevelt-Campobello International Park, which offers additional viewing opportunities and hiking trails). The most familiar attraction here is the distinctive, red-and-white-striped West Quoddy Head Lighthouse, erected in 1858 as a replacement for the original structure, which was built in 1808 not only to protect mariners but also to establish a territorial claim against the British.

Much of the park is forested with balsam fir and white spruce, both of which are well-adapted to the harsh climate and thin soils atop the bluffs. The grounds are also home to a pair of uncommon boreal peat bogs, including the seven-acre West Quoddy Bog near the park entrance; characteristic vegetation includes northern pitcher plants, sundews, leatherleaf, and black crowberry. Adjoining the park, and easily viewed from South Lubec Road near the entrance, are the South Lubec Sand Bar mudflats, which are frequented by large flocks of shorebirds during late-summer migrations.

VIEWING

From the lighthouse area and the overlooks along the Coastal Trail, scan the channel below for humpback, fin, and minke whales, as well as white-sided dolphins, gray and harbor seals, and harbor porpoises. In July and August, especially fortunate viewers may glimpse an endangered right whale feeding in the channel. Waterfowl and seabirds include eiders, scoters, and old squaw ducks, black-backed and Bonaparte's gulls, and seabirds such as northern gannets, purple sandpipers, dovekies, and kittiwakes. Birds of prey often observed hunting from overhead include bald eagles, ospreys, and merlins.

The park's spruce-fir woodlands are home to boreal chickadees, distinguished from their familiar black-capped relatives by their brown cap and more nasal call, spruce grouse, black-backed woodpeckers, winter wrens, pine siskins, red and white-winged crossbills, and red-breasted nuthatches. Migratory songbirds include nesting northern parulas and Wilson's warblers. Along the West Quoddy Bog boardwalk look for yellow and Nashville warblers and Lincoln's sparrows.

During spring, late summer, and early autumn check the mudflats at Carrying Place Cove and the South Lubec Sand Bar for migrating shorebirds, including whimbrels, ruddy turnstones, black-bellied plovers, American golden plovers, large flocks of semipalmated plovers, and short-billed dowitchers. The latter are among the first migrants to return south, as they may be seen as early as the first week of July. Uncommon species that have been seen here include marbled godwits and a common ringed plover, which was observed in 2003.

GETTING AROUND

The park's 4.5 miles of trails offer options ranging from walk-up views from the cliffs adjacent to the lighthouse to longer hikes along the bluffs and through the forests. The short Inland Trail leads away from the light-house past a series of vistas and a set of stairs that provides easy access to the cobble beach below. After a quarter mile it meets the Bog Trail, which offers a short walk to a 640-foot-long boardwalk loop that allows for safe close-up views of West Quoddy Bog.

For those with time for a longer outing, the Coastal Trail continues west along the bluffs and adjoining forests, passing a geological chasm known as Gulliver's Hole and scenic views of High Ledge and Green Point. At 2 miles from the entrance, it reaches its end at Carrying Place Cove, where it briefly descends to the beach. Here you have the option of backtracking to the entrance or making a circuit by returning via the Thompson Trail, which winds through the interior boreal forest for 1.3 miles to its end at the Bog Trail.

 Rangeley Lake

> Maine Bureau of Parks and Lands (Rangeley Lake State Park), 207-864-3858, www.maine.gov/doc/parks
>
> CLOSEST TOWN: Rangeley
>
> DIRECTIONS: For the state park, from the junction of ME 4 and ME 16 in Rangeley center follow ME 4 south for 3.5 miles, then turn right (west) on South Shore Drive and follow signs to the park entrance. South Shore Drive may also be accessed from the west via ME 17, the Rangeley Lakes Scenic Byway, which passes overlooks with outstanding views of Mooselookmeguntic and Rangeley lakes and the surrounding mountains. To reach the Hunter Cove Sanctuary, from Rangeley center follow ME 4 west for 5 miles and turn left (south) into the entrance and parking area.

In the heart of Maine's western mountains and hills lie the Rangeley Lakes, an especially scenic chain of interconnected water bodies that form the headwaters of the 120-mile-long Androscoggin River. With its proxim-

A well-antlered bull moose in its physical prime during the autumn mating season.

ity to the gateway town of Rangeley, 6,000-acre Rangeley Lake is the busiest and most visited of the group. Its southwest corner is home to a state park that encompasses 870 acres of forest and lakefront, including a large campground, beach, boat launch, and nature trails. Protecting an additional 100 acres along the north shore between Rangeley and Oquossoc village is the Hunter Cove Sanctuary, a quiet 100-acre preserve that was recently transferred from the Maine Audubon Society to the Rangeley Lakes Heritage Trust. The other lakes in the chain include Mooselookmeguntic (an Abenaki term meaning "moose feeding place"), Cupsuptic, Upper and Lower Richardson, and Umbagog, which straddles the New Hampshire border.

VIEWING

The lakes are renowned for their excellent fishing, as both wildlife and sportsmen enjoy fine stores of brook, brown, and lake trout, salmon, and bullhead. Watch for bald eagles, kingfishers, common loons, and osprey hunting the water, along with common and hooded mergansers, mallard and black ducks, and other waterfowl. Check the shrubby vegetation along the shoreline for a variety of dragonflies and damselflies, including several north woods bluets.

The northern hardwood and spruce-fir forests surrounding the lake provide food and cover for moose, fishers, eastern coyotes, raccoons, and mink. Black bear sightings were fairly common years ago but have decreased in recent years, though their sign is often evident at both the state park and Hunter Cove. Upland game birds with distinctive mating rituals include ruffed grouse, whose drumming call echoes through quiet woodlands, and American woodcock, which perform courtship flights in open areas during spring. These expansive woodlands also are home to songbirds such as gray jays and flycatchers; prime woodland warbler viewing is from May through August.

When driving any of the roads in the area, keep an eye out for moose, especially early and late in the day. While they may be encountered along any of the roads and trails, Route 16 from Rangeley to Stratton and Route 4 from Phillips to Rangeley are especially active "moose alleys," and caution should be used to avoid collisions.

GETTING AROUND

Rangeley Lake State Park is open seasonally from mid-May to early October. The beach, boat launch, and nature trails offer easily accessible views of the lake. An easy, mile-long nature trail connects the day-use area and boat launch near South Cove to the campground, following the woods along the shore. The launch serves canoes, kayaks, and other small watercraft; rentals are available in Rangeley. Winter use of the trails is allowed, though access can be difficult during periods of high snowfall.

At Hunter Cove the Red Trail begins at the picnic area at the entrance and leads for 0.5 mile through the forest to viewpoints along the shore. The walking is easy, though some areas may be wet in season.

Scarborough Marsh

Maine Inland Fisheries and Wildlife, Maine Audubon Society, 207-781-2330; www.scarboroughcrossroads.org/marsh (Friends of Scarborough Marsh)
CLOSEST TOWN: Scarborough
DIRECTIONS: From the junction of ME 9 and US 1 in Scarborough turn east on ME 9 (Pine Point Road) and continue for 0.8 mile to the Maine Audubon visitor center on the left. The Eastern Road recreation trail is a quarter mile east of the nature center.

Amid the development of the greater Portland area and popular Old Orchard Beach, the winding Dunstan and Nonesuch rivers meander through the 3,500-acre Scarborough Marsh, the largest salt marsh along Maine's coast. Situated at the terminus of a 60-square-mile coastal watershed, this ecologically rich area has long been used and altered by humans. In pre-colonial times it served as the hunting and fishing grounds for Sokokis Indians, then was cultivated for agriculture by European settlers, who harvested salt hay for livestock. During the nineteenth century the integrity of the marsh was further compromised by the construction of ditches, channels, and tidal gates, homes, and a railroad bed along the perimeter of this fragile area. Preservation efforts began in earnest in the late 1950s, after the town of Scarborough proposed filling the marsh and converting it to an industrial area.

Today, approximately 3,000 acres of the marsh are owned and protected by Maine Inland Fisheries and Wildlife. The primary habitat here is salt marsh of salt meadow and smooth cordgrass, with several rare plant species, while bordering woodlands and shrubby thickets offer diversity and cover. A 20-acre former pasture is maintained as a resting area for migratory ducks and Canada geese. The Maine Audubon Society operates a seasonal visitor center on Route 9 that offers boat rentals, canoe tours of the river, and a gift shop. Across the road from the center are a series of shallow pools known as "pannes," fed by high tides and rainwater, and a tidal creek.

VIEWING

The marsh offers outstanding bird-watching, with roughly 250 species on record. Shorebirds visible at the pannes opposite the nature center include willets, yellowlegs, Baird's, white-rumped, and stilt sandpipers, red knots, short-billed dowitchers, sanderlings, and uncommon long-billed dowitchers and eastern phalaropes. Great and snowy egrets, glossy ibises, and great blue herons are among the waders that hunt minnows in the wetlands here, along with belted kingfishers and uncommon tricolored and black-crowned night herons. Roughly 30 species of waterfowl use the marsh, including American wigeons, greater and lesser scaups, northern shovelers, long-tailed ducks, canvasbacks, and green-winged teal. The most conspicuous call heard here is the loud, territorial *conk-la-ree* of red-winged blackbirds. The mudflats at Pine Point at the town landing, where the Dunstan and Scarborough rivers meet at Saco Bay, are another good place to see gulls, shorebirds, and wading birds.

Birds of prey include six species of owls, including long and short-eared and northern saw-whet; in winter snowy owls and rough-legged hawks migrate to the area from northern breeding grounds. Peregrine falcons, gyrfalcons, merlins, and American kestrels also hunt the marsh. In spring and fall, migratory songbirds such as blackpoll, Nashville, Wilson's, bay-breasted, and Cape May warblers and northern waterthrushes pause to rest in the surrounding woodlands during their journey along the Atlantic Flyway.

Mammals present along the margins of the marsh include red foxes and eastern coyotes, which hunt smaller creatures such as deer mice and star-nosed moles along the edge of the grassy river and woody thickets early and late in the day. The latter are unmistakable thanks to their distinctive pink snout, which is ringed by more than 20 short tentacles. The area also serves as a wintering area for white-tailed deer and offers crucial shrubby habitat for endangered New England cottontails. River otters, muskrats, and mink may be seen in these wetlands at any time, along with an occasional harbor seal.

GETTING AROUND

The marsh has several public access and viewing points along and off of Pine Point Road (Route 9). An observation deck and car-top boat launch are available at the Maine Audubon Society visitor center, which offers canoe and kayak rentals and tours during seasonal operating hours. The short interpretive trail on the opposite side of the road offers views of the pannes, a tidal stream, a historic canal, and a grove of pine woods and shrubs. The center is open from 9:30 to 5:30 daily from June through August, during the Memorial Day weekend, and weekends in September.

A quarter mile east of the nature center is the trailhead for Eastern Road, a gravel recreational path for walkers, bikers, and cross-country skiers that connects Pine Point and Black Point roads. From the parking area this straight, level trail crosses a bridge over the Dunstan River and leads across the heart of the marsh, with fine open views of the tidal creeks, mudflats, and backwaters. It takes roughly 25 minutes to reach the woods opposite the parking area.

The edge of the marsh where the Dunstan River and several other waterways converge with the Scarborough River near its mouth at Saco Bay can be viewed at the town landing, which is located at the end of Pine Point Road.

Sunkhaze Meadows National Wildlife Refuge

U.S. Fish and Wildlife Service, Maine Coastal Islands National Wildlife Refuge, 207-236-6970, www.fws.gov/northeast/me/sunkhazemeadows; Friends of Sunkhaze Meadows National Wildlife Refuge, www.sunkhaze.org

CLOSEST TOWN: Milford

DIRECTIONS: From Interstate 95 in Orono take exit 191 and follow US 2 east for 4 miles to Old Town. Continue through a series of traffic lights and cross the bridge over the Penobscot River to Milford. At the sixth light turn right (east) on County Road and continue for 4.2 miles to the refuge boundary.

Though peat bogs may lack the majesty of Mount Katahdin or the grandeur of Acadia and the coast, they are nevertheless an integral element of Maine's landscape, as they comprise roughly 900,000 acres, or 3 to 5 percent of the state's total area. The high acidity and lack of oxygen in these wetlands prevents plants from fully decomposing, creating deposits of partially decayed matter, which are known as "peat." The distinctive, characteristic botanical communities include carnivorous northern pitcher plants, bladderworts, and sundews, as well as orchids such as rose pogonias and showy lady's slippers.

Located just east of the Penobscot River in the heart of a 40-mile complex of deposits that stretches from Bangor to Lincoln, Sunkhaze Meadows is the second-largest peat bog in Maine. Like many wetlands, it was threatened by development, which prompted the establishment of the 12,289-acre Sunkhaze Meadows National Wildlife Refuge in 1988. Throughout the wetlands, "domes," or raised clumps of vegetation, are divided by streamside meadows. Associated vegetation includes floodplain forests of silver and red maple, cedar swamps, and wet meadows, and upland northern hardwood forests. At the heart of these wetlands is Sunkhaze Stream, which meanders through the refuge from Studmill Road to the Penobscot River. The original headquarters building in Old Town was closed in 2007, and the refuge is now part of the Maine Coastal Islands National Wildlife Refuge and largely maintained by the Friends of the Sunkhaze National Wildlife Refuge.

VIEWING

These wetlands and their surrounding vegetation are ideal habitat for a variety of insects, including subarctic and shadow darners, frosted whitefaces, and pygmy snaketail dragonflies. The latter, which is one of New

England's smallest dragonfly, is identified by its tiny, chalk-blue-colored body. Damselflies include Hagen's and lateral bluets, river and ebony jewelwings, eastern forktails, and variable dancers. Much more conspicuous by day are Canadian tiger swallowtail and monarch butterflies, while Pennsylvania fireflies light up open areas in early to mid summer.

More than 180 birds have been recorded throughout the refuge, including wood, black, and ringed-necked ducks, hooded mergansers, blue-winged teal, and other waterfowl. Common snipe and American bitterns, identifiable by their unmistakable, throaty *unk-a-lunk* call, breed here as well. Black terns, which are found in only a handful of areas in northern New England and are listed as endangered in Maine, nest at Carleton Pond Waterfowl Production Area in Troy, and the Benton and Unity Units of the refuge. Look for both ruffed and shier spruce grouse along the refuge trails. Nesting birds of prey include northern goshawks, red-shouldered, broad-winged, and sharp-shinned hawks, northern harriers, and northern saw-whet, barred, and great horned owls.

Commonly observed mammals in the wetlands include river otters, muskrats, mink, and beavers; late winter and early spring can yield especially productive viewing where open water meets ice. Beavers are continually altering the refuge's waterways, often providing a challenge to boaters. Moose and white-tailed deer may be seen in the wetlands, forests, and along the roadways that surround the refuge, particularly in the early morning and evening hours.

GETTING AROUND

Perhaps the best way to explore these extensive wetlands is by canoe or kayak; boat launches are located on County Road along the refuge's southern boundary and off Stud Mill Road to the north. Distance paddlers may need to carry their boats around numerous beaver dams. The wetlands associated with Buzzy Brook can also be viewed by car from Stud Mill Road; watch for moose here and yield to all logging trucks.

There are also several foot trails, including the Carter Meadow Trail, which explores the southern portion of the refuge. From the gate on Carter Meadow Road it's a quick quarter-mile walk along the road to an old cabin, where a 1.6-mile loop begins. For those making a counterclockwise circuit by continuing straight (the right fork of the loop), the trail follows along the edge of Little Birch Stream for 0.7 mile to the observation area, which offers fine views of the meadows and Sunkhaze Stream in the distance. The loop then returns southward through upland forest for another 0.9

mile to the cabin; backtrack from here to the parking area for a 2.1-mile round-trip.

A short distance to the north, the Johnson Brook Trail, a favorite of birders, offers a 2.5-mile outing that includes boardwalks over wetlands, vernal pools, and an uncommon Atlantic white cedar swamp forest. The northwest corner of the refuge is home to a series of unmaintained logging roads collectively known as the Buzzy Brook Trails. These are accessed via McLaughlin Road, which is used by logging trucks and snowmobiles, south of its junction with Stud Mill Road. The North Buzzy Brook Trail reaches the brook in 2.3 miles.

Swan Island / Steve Powell Wildlife Management Area

Maine Inland Department of Fisheries and Wildlife, 207-737-4307, www.maine.gov/ifw/education/swanisland

CLOSEST TOWN: Richmond

DIRECTIONS: To reach the ferry landing at Richmond, from Interstate 295 north of Portland take exit 43 and follow ME 197 east for 3 miles to the town center. At the intersection of ME 197 and ME 24, turn left, then park in the marked lot on the right. There is an admission fee of $8; children three years old and under are free.

At Merrymeeting Bay, five rivers in the Kennebec River watershed converge to form a 10,000-acre estuarine complex that serves as a magnet for a variety of wildlife. At the head of the bay lies four-mile-long, finger-shaped Swan Island, which has a long history of human use: it was home to Native American tribes before being settled as Perkins Township during the eighteenth and nineteenth centuries; early industries included farming, fishing, ice cutting, and shipbuilding. During the 1940s the state began acquiring the lands that form the present 1,755-acre Steve Powell Wildlife Management Area, named for a wildlife biologist who worked and lived on the island. In 1995 Swan Island was added to the National Registry of Historic Places, thanks to the combined efforts of the Maine Historic Preservation Commission and the Department of Inland Fisheries and Wildlife.

The island's wetlands include eight artificial ponds, freshwater marshes, and several hundred acres of tidal flats. The open fields are mowed every one to three years and planted with crops to support Canada geese and other waterfowl. Roughly 850 acres, or half the preserve, is forested with white oak, birch, butternut, and other species. Historical forest clearing and the continued presence of a large deer herd have had ongoing effects on the vegetation. The island, which is seasonally accessible to visitors with reservations, is unique among wildlife management areas in that it includes facilities for general visitor use, including a campground and nature trails.

VIEWING

For the past century the island has supported a dense population of white-tailed deer, thanks to a ban on hunting that has been in effect since 1890 and ideal habitat provided by the managed clearings and rejuvenated forests. The herd reached its peak of 200 to 300 individuals during the 1960s and 1970s, and while it declined in subsequent years, it remains highly visible today. An old enclosure just south of the Lilly-Wade House offers ample evidence of the impact deer have on the vegetation.

Other familiar denizens of upland forest edges and clearings include wild turkey, ruffed grouse, and American woodcock, red foxes, skunks, porcupines, woodchucks, raccoons, and coyotes; the arrival of the latter in the late twentieth century helped stabilize the deer population to some degree. Another prey species for these adaptable canines are meadow voles, which are common throughout New England but quite elusive, as they spend much of their lives in extensive networks of tunnels. Their abundance is largely due to a prolific reproductive rate; females may bear as many as 17 litters in a single year alone. Other residents of the open fields include grassland birds such as eastern bluebirds, bobolinks, eastern meadowlarks, grasshopper, savannah, and vesper sparrows, and upland sandpipers.

While there are no swans to be found on the island (its name is likely derived from the Abenaki word *swango*, or "island of eagles"), large congregations of waterfowl, including mergansers, common goldeneyes, wood ducks, and Canada geese, make extensive use of this area. Bald eagles nested in an old oak tree behind the Maxwell-Tarr House for more than 20 years, and other pairs have nested along the east shores and at Little Swan Island. Watch for both eagles and osprey along the banks of the Kennebec; they may be perched in trees or making fishing passes over the water.

GETTING AROUND

Access to Swan Island is by reservation only during the visiting season from May to Labor Day, though limited excursions may be offered in the fall by arrangement. A short ferry ride from Richmond brings visitors to the landing on the island's northern tip; vehicles are not allowed, though a truck is available for group tours. From the landing the main gravel road leads south across the island for 4.5 miles, passing nearly 40 historic sites and old homes along the way. Several nature trails branch off the road and explore the various habitats, the longest of which is the West Side Trail, which winds for 3 miles through the forests along the west shore, rejoining the main road near the tidal flats known as the "Middle Ground" at the island's southern tip. The half-mile-long Beaver Pond Trail leads through an open field and offers views of an artificial pond.

Camping is available by arrangement at the island campground, where several Adirondack shelters are available. Contact the Department of Inland Fisheries and Wildlife at 207-737-4307 or 207-547-5322 for further information and a reservation form.

Wells National Estuarine Reserve and Rachel Carson National Wildlife Refuge, Upper Wells Division

Wells National Estuarine Research Reserve, 207-646-1555,
www.wellsreserve.org; U.S. Fish and Wildlife Service, 207-646-9226
CLOSEST TOWN: Wells
DIRECTIONS: From Interstate 95 in Wells take exit 19 and follow ME 109 east
for 2 miles to its junction with US 1 and ME 9. Turn left (north) on combined
US 1 / ME 9 and continue for 2 miles, then bear right on ME 9 where the roads
split. To reach the Wells reserve, continue for 0.6 mile on ME 9 to a sharp right
on Skinner Mill Road, then left at the reserve entrance to the parking area and
nature center. The Carson refuge entrance is just beyond the junction of ME 9
and Skinner Mill Road, also on the right-hand side of the road. An admission
fee of $3 ($1.50 for children and seniors) is charged at the Wells reserve from
Memorial Day through Columbus Day.

A short distance north of popular Wells Beach, Branch Brook and the Merriland River combine to form the rather diminutive Little River, which winds a short distance to its mouth at Laudholm Beach. Encompassing this estuary are a network of contiguous conservation lands that are part of the Rachel Carson National Wildlife Refuge and the Wells National Estuarine Research Reserve. The latter is a 1,600-acre mosaic of diverse habitats that includes a patchwork of upland forests and fields on the grounds of an old farm, tidal salt marshes along the Merriland and Little rivers and the Webhannet River to the south, and a section of barrier beach. The old farmhouse now serves as a visitor center and gift shop.

Bordering the Wells reserve on the north side of the Merriland River is the Upper Wells Division of the Rachel Carson National Wildlife Refuge, which protects more than 5,000 acres in a series of divisions spread among 50 miles of coastline from Kittery to Cape Elizabeth. Named for the influential marine biologist and author whose writings were an integral part of the late-twentieth-century American environmental movement, the refuge features expansive tidal salt marshes, as well as tidal rivers, pools, beaches, dunes, bogs, and upland forests; these mixed communities support an equally diverse coastal wildlife community that ranges from moose and seals to nearly 250 bird species.

VIEWING

Once grazed by cows and sheep, the open fields next to the Wells reserve entrance are now the domain of white-tailed deer, which are abundant here and often easily viewed in the early morning and evening hours. Look carefully for shy antlered bucks during the autumn mating season and fawns with spotted coats in late spring and early summer. Red foxes and eastern coyotes thrive in the mixed field-woodlot habitat; uncommon black-phase forms of the former have been seen here. Bobolinks, eastern meadowlarks, tree and barn swallows, brown thrashers, and eastern bluebirds also benefit from these open areas, along with ruffed grouse, American woodcock, and wild turkeys, which take cover in the surrounding woodlots. The brushy thickets are maintained as habitat for endangered New England cottontail rabbits, which unlike the much more widespread and adaptable eastern cottontail are almost solely dependent on this sort of habitat, which has rapidly declined due to forest regrowth and suburban development in recent decades.

The marshy areas and mudflats associated with the Merriland, Little, and Webhannet rivers are frequented by green and great blue herons, great and snowy egrets, an occasional glossy ibis, American bitterns, and little blue herons. Nesting waterfowl include green and blue-winged teal, mallard, and black ducks; the Carson refuge divisions host large flocks of the latter in spring. Watch for muskrats, mink, beavers, and river otters here as well. As spring progresses, keep an eye (and ear) out for painted and spotted turtles, leopard frogs, spring peepers, and American toads.

In winter, common eiders, surf and white-winged scoters, common goldeneyes, common loons, mergansers, and buffleheads cruise the ocean waters and river mouths of adjacent Laudholm Beach. Snow buntings also visit the beaches, and wintering bald eagles soar above the coast. Shore-

The crow-size green heron
is often hidden amid dense
marsh vegetation in shallow
wetlands.

birds are most visible during the spring and mid to late summer, when black-bellied, semipalmated, and piping plovers, willets, dunlins, and short-billed dowitchers, as well as rarer ruddy turnstones, least sandpipers, and sanderlings may all be seen. The Carson refuge beaches provide nesting habitat for more than half of Maine's piping plover population.

In late summer and autumn watch for large flocks of raptors migrating south along the coast, including broad-winged hawks, peregrine falcons, merlins, and northern harriers. The upland forests and thickets provide rest areas for a long list of warblers, vireos, flycatchers, and other migratory songbirds, while monarch butterflies feed on late-summer field wildflowers.

A number of uncommon or vagrant species have been documented here, including tricolored herons, black skimmers, and scissor-tailed flycatchers.

The waters of Branch Brook and the Merriland and Little rivers are home to striped bass, bluefish, flounder, blue mussels, and soft-shelled clams. Look for harbor seals basking on exposed rocks at low tide and hunting the ocean and river waters during high water.

GETTING AROUND
The Wells Reserve has seven miles of easy foot trails that are open daily from 7 AM to sunset. The Barrier Beach Trail offers the most direct route

to Laudholm Beach, as it slopes east from the fields at the visitor center for 0.6 mile past forests and a maple swamp en route to the shore, where you can turn left and walk an additional three-quarters of a mile to the mouth of the Little River.

There are several loop options that combine the various paths, all of which traverse mixed habitats. A good route for viewing the salt marsh is to follow the Knight and Barrier Beach trails away from the entrance, then turn left on the Laird-Norton Trail, which leads north to an overlook with fine views of the marsh and inlet of the Little River. At the junction with the Cart Path, a short detour on the Farley Trail leads to the Little River overlook. Return to the entrance via the Cart Path for a 1.5-mile round-trip.

The southern portion of the reserve is explored by the Muskie and Pilger trails, which form a 1.8-mile loop. The former winds along the edge of the fields and woods near the entrance, then meets the Pilger Trail a short distance from the Drake's Island overlook, where there is a fine view of the marshes bordering the Webhannet River. The Pilger Trail leads east along more edge habitat before ending at the Barrier Beach Trail, which leads back to the trailhead.

At the nearby Carson refuge, an interpretive, mile-long universally accessible nature trail loops around the narrow neck where Branch Brook and the Merriland River converge. Observation decks and short boardwalks provide good views of both waterways and their associated marshes and pools. The office is open weekdays, though hours are variable during summer months. Contact the headquarters for information about other public access and viewing areas, which include a 1.8-mile woodland trail on Cotts Island Road in York and an overlook of Furbish Marsh on Route 1 in Wells.

MASSACHUSETTS

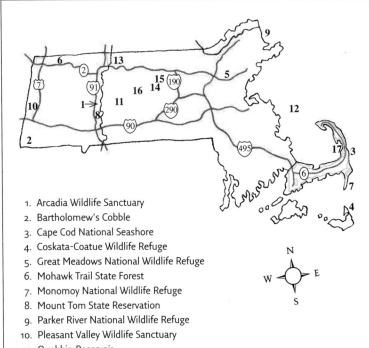

1. Arcadia Wildlife Sanctuary
2. Bartholomew's Cobble
3. Cape Cod National Seashore
4. Coskata-Coatue Wildlife Refuge
5. Great Meadows National Wildlife Refuge
6. Mohawk Trail State Forest
7. Monomoy National Wildlife Refuge
8. Mount Tom State Reservation
9. Parker River National Wildlife Refuge
10. Pleasant Valley Wildlife Sanctuary
11. Quabbin Reservoir
12. Stellwagen Bank National Marine Sanctuary
13. Upper Connecticut River: French King Gorge, Barton Cove, and Turners Falls Canal
14. Wachusett Meadows Wildlife Sanctuary
15. Wachusett Mountain State Reservation
16. Ware River Reservation
17. Wellfleet Bay Wildlife Sanctuary

MASSACHUSETTS

◎ Arcadia Wildlife Sanctuary

Massachusetts Audubon Society, 413-584-3009, www.massaudubon.org
CLOSEST TOWN: Easthampton
DIRECTIONS: From Interstate 91 in Northampton take exit 18 and follow US 5
south for 1.5 miles to a right on East Street. Follow East Street for 1 mile, then
turn right on Fort Hill Road, following signs for the sanctuary. Bear right at
the junction with Clapp Street, then turn left on the sanctuary entrance road.
Admission is $4 for adults, $3 for seniors and children 2–12, and free for
Massachusetts Audubon Society members.

Another wildlife area with similar habitats is the Fannie Stebbins Wildlife
Refuge, which encompasses 340 acres of wetlands, riparian forests, and
open fields along the floodplain of the Connecticut River in Longmeadow
near the Connecticut state line. To reach the entrance, from the Springfield-
Longmeadow town line drive south on US 5 for 2.4 miles, then turn right on
Bark Haul Road and continue for 0.4 mile to a parking area at the junction
with Pondside Road.

In 1836 the "Oxbow," a sharp bend in the Connecticut River at Easthampton, was immortalized as the subject of a famous landscape paint-
ing by artist Thomas Cole. Along its west banks is the mouth of the Mill
River, which originates in the hills west of the valley and flows east through
Northampton to its confluence with the Connecticut. Protecting 700 acres
worth of riverine and upland habitats where the two rivers meet is the Arcadia Wildlife Sanctuary, a property of the Massachusetts Audubon Society.

Among the many natural communities here is an uncommon floodplain
forest of silver maple, shagbark hickory, and black birch. Rising above a
complex of wetlands along the Mill River is an observation tower with fine
views of Arcadia Marsh; posted signs mark the remarkable extent of the
great floods of the late 1930s. Other habitats include an old orchard, vernal pools, a red maple swamp, and lowland and upland forest groves of
oak, pine, and hemlock. North of the oxbow are large, former agricultural
fields that were recently acquired by the sanctuary and are now maintained
as open grasslands. The nature center offers educational programs and a
popular summer day camp.

VIEWING

From the Fern and River trails and the observation tower, scan the Mill River
floodplain for river otters, mink, muskrats, and beavers; sign of the latter is

often evident along the trail. Wood, mallard, and black ducks are regularly seen here, along with green and great blue herons, Canada geese, kingfishers, and occasional great egrets and migrating snow geese. Dead standing trees along the floodplain provide food sources and nesting cavities for downy, hairy, pileated, and red-bellied woodpeckers. The latter, sometimes known as "zebrabacks," thanks to their checked feathers, have expanded their range from the south into New England during recent decades.

Coyotes and foxes hunt mice and meadow voles in the open fields adjacent to the entrance and north of the Mill River bridge; the fields are maintained for grassland and edge-favoring species such as eastern meadowlarks, bobolinks, eastern bluebirds, savannah sparrows, and American woodcock. Uncommon Cooper's hawks nest on the grounds, and other raptors such as sharp-shinned hawks and northern harriers are present during migrations. Ideally situated along the Connecticut Valley flyway, the adjoining woodlands and thickets provide waysides and homes for migratory songbirds such as melodious wood thrushes, veeries, brown creepers, red-eyed vireos, and black-throated green warblers. Check the old orchards for cedar waxwings, common yellowthroats, northern cardinals, and indigo buntings. All told, 215 bird species have been recorded throughout the sanctuary.

Frogs and painted turtles frequent the vernal pool and pond behind the nature center. Black bears are fairly common in this region of Massachusetts and, though often elusive, are periodically seen along the woodland trails and field edges.

GETTING AROUND

There are five miles of easy, well-marked foot trails that explore the various habitats. For a 1.3-mile circuit that explores the floodplain and adjacent woodlands, from the entrance follow the Old Coach Road through the upland forests for half a mile, then bear right at successive junctions on the River Trail, which offers good views of Wood Duck Pond and a silver maple swamp as it follows the edge of the floodplain. After crossing an old trolley line, this narrow footpath becomes the Fern Trail and leads to the observation tower. It then reaches a junction with several other trails near the nature center. Here the Horseshoe Trail winds through an old orchard and along the fields adjacent to the entrance before returning to the parking area via the Tulip Tree Trail. The trails are open daily from dawn to dusk; the visitor center is open weekdays from 8:30 to noon, Saturday from 8:30 to 3:30, and Sunday from noon to 3:30.

Though the grasslands are outside the foot trail network, they are easily viewed by vehicle or foot. From the junction of Combs Road (the sanctuary entrance road) and Old Springfield Road, follow the latter for 0.2 mile to the one-lane bridge over the mouth of the Mill River; the fields begin just beyond the bridge. Flooding may make the bridge impassable at times, especially in early spring. The dirt Pynchon Meadow Road bears off to the left and follows the fields for 0.8 mile.

Bartholomew's Cobble

The Trustees of Reservations, 413-229-8600, www.thetrustees.org
CLOSEST TOWN: Sheffield
DIRECTIONS: From the junction of US 7 and MA 7A in Sheffield follow MA 7A for 0.5 mile to a right on Rannapo Road. Follow Rannapo Road for 1.5 miles, then turn right on Wheatogue Road and continue to the parking area and visitor center. A $5 admission fee is charged for nonmembers of the Trustees of Reservations.

Renowned and recognized as a National Natural Landmark by the National Park Service for its exceptional biodiversity and rare plant species, the Bartholomew's Cobble Reservation is one of the most unusual and diverse natural areas of the Berkshire Hills. Here a pair of limestone and marble knolls along the banks of the Housatonic River provides nutrients for rich soils that support more than 800 plant species, including colorful woodland ephemerals in spring, more than 50 varieties of ferns, and regionally uncommon flora such as great blue lobelias.

In addition to its botanical treasures, the reservation hosts a wide diversity of wildlife, thanks to the variety of habitats within its compact 330 acres. Bordering the river are marshy edges, floodplain forests with giant silver maple and cottonwood trees, and rocky outcroppings. Rising out of the valley is 1,050-foot Hurlburt Hill, where a 20-acre sloping meadow at the summit offers long views across the southern Berkshires to Mount Greylock; at the hill's base are more open fields opposite the entrance. This variety, combined with the preserve's location along the Housatonic migratory corridor, is reflected by the nearly 250 species of birds that have been recorded on the grounds. The reservation is managed by the Massachusetts Trustees of Reservations, a private organization that protects approximately 100 natural areas statewide; a small visitor center offers natural history displays.

Along the banks of the Housatonic and its floodplain watch for beavers, river otters, mink, muskrats, bank swallows, waterfowl such as wood and black ducks, and bald eagles, which are most visible from January to March. Pileated woodpeckers, easily identifiable visually by their large size and audibly by their loud laughing calls, bore large cavities into dead standing trees here while searching for insects. The hairpin bend in the river known as Corbin's Neck is one of the region's best places to see migrating shorebirds, including semipalmated, solitary, and least sandpipers, and occasional black-bellied and lesser golden plovers. Other uncommon species such as little blue herons and dunlins have been recorded here as well. Reptiles include uncommon spotted and wood turtles; the latter are often well camouflaged along the river bottom.

Ashley Field and the open meadows atop Hurlburt Hill are home to field and edge-loving birds such as eastern bluebirds, tree swallows, wild turkeys, ruffed grouse, and mammals such as white-tailed deer, red foxes, and eastern coyotes. With its long views across the valley in three directions, the hill is an excellent hawk-watching site during spring and fall migrations, with peak viewing during the height of the broad-winged movement in mid-September.

Though they are much more elusive, black bears and bobcats are also present in the reservation's woodlands. Roughly 25 warbler species use these forests as a rest stop during migrations; breeders that remain to nest include American redstarts and magnolia, blackburnian, blue-winged, and chestnut-sided warblers.

GETTING AROUND

The reservation's four miles of foot trails are divided into a series of short paths that explore the various habitats. The easy half-mile Ledges Trail explores the cobbles near the visitor center, with views of Corbin's Neck to the east. The Bailey Trail branches off the Ledges and leads south along the west bank of the river to a junction at a giant cottonwood tree, where it meets the Spero Trail, which makes a loop along the floodplain, through a meadow, and past rocky outcroppings. The round-trip combining these three routes is 1.75 miles. The summit of Hurlburt Hill is reached from Ashley Field near the visitor center via the 0.9-mile (one way) Tractor Path Trail, which climbs at an easy-to-moderate grade to the open meadow.

For those with time for a longer outing, these routes are easily combined as a 3.3-mile circuit with excellent habitat variety. Begin by following the

Ledges Trail through the cobbles, then continue south along Bailey Trail to the Spero Trail junction. After making the circuit, backtrack on the Bailey to a left on the Tulip Tree Trail, which makes a moderate 0.5-mile climb up the east slopes of Hurlburt Hill. At the junction with the Tractor Path Trail, turn left and continue through the meadow to the trail's end at the summit. Complete the outing by following the Tractor Path Trail back to Ashley Field and the visitor center.

Cape Cod National Seashore

U.S. National Park Service, 508-255-3785, www.nps.gov/caco

CLOSEST TOWNS: Chatham, Eastham, Wellfleet, Truro, Provincetown

DIRECTIONS: All the access areas are reached via US 6. For the Salt Pond Visitor Center, from the rotary on the Eastham-Orleans town line continue east on US 6 for 2.9 miles, then turn right on Nauset Road. To reach the Province Lands area and visitor center, follow US 6 to Provincetown and turn right on Race Point Road. For Great Island, from US 6 in Wellfleet follow signs to Wellfleet center and harbor. Bear left toward the harbor on East Commercial Street, which becomes Chequesett Neck Road, and continue past the harbor for another 3.3 miles to the National Seashore parking area on the left, shortly after the bridge over the Herring River. Parking is free at the nature areas; fees at the beach lots are $15 a day for vehicles, $3 for pedestrians, bicyclists, and motorcycles; an annual pass is $45.

As improbable as it seems today, Cape Cod was once popularly regarded as a desolate, savage, and unfashionable place; it wasn't until the mid-twentieth century that this arm-shaped peninsula became a favored destination for millions of tourists annually. As recently as the early 1960s, property values remained low enough for Congress to authorize the purchase of the lands that form the Cape Cod National Seashore. As a result, 45,000 acres of the narrow Outer Cape from Chatham to the tip of Race Point in Provincetown are permanently protected, ensuring homes for a wide variety of wildlife in the midst of a very popular and increasingly developed region. The national seashore is home to 32 species that are listed as rare or endangered in Massachusetts, and 25 that are federally protected.

In addition to its beaches, which attract an estimated five to six million visitors annually, the seashore also includes a number of unique natural communities, including Nauset Marsh, an uncommon Atlantic white cedar swamp, the Great Island peninsula, and the tall dunes and beech groves of

A least tern dives near its nest on an ocean beach at the Cape Cod National Seashore.

the Province Lands, all of which are easily explored by interpretive nature trails. The majority of the seashore encompasses the ocean beaches and adjacent habitats, but there is some land on the bay side, including Great Island. Visitor centers are located at Nauset Marsh in Eastham and at the Province Lands in Provincetown.

VIEWING

The open fields at the Fort Hill area in Eastham are frequented by birds of prey such as bald eagles, northern harriers, and red-tailed hawks that feed on eastern cottontails, squirrels, and mice. Birds include colorful goldfinches, noisy red-winged blackbirds, and migratory songbirds. Woodcocks perform evening courtship displays from early to mid spring, while large flights of monarch butterflies mark the onset of autumn. Eastern coyotes and white-tailed deer are most active in the early morning and evening. From overlooks watch for peregrine falcons hunting the nearby Nauset Marsh. The Fort Hill Trail leads past the meadows and woodlands to an overlook and interpretive shelter at Skiff Hill. Here it joins the Red Maple Swamp Trail, which explores the heart of a swamp on a long boardwalk, then passes the historic Penniman House as it returns to the trailhead.

The 1.2-mile trail at the Salt Pond visitor center offers more views of Nauset Marsh and a kettle pond where osprey, bald eagles, great blue and green herons, Canada geese, mute swans, double-crested cormorants, loons, and an occasional river otter or muskrat may all be seen. During low tide, wading birds and shorebirds hunt crabs and fish on the exposed mudflats. After passing an overlook with sweeping views of the marsh, the trail winds through groves of oak, pine, and cedar as it loops back to the visitor center, joining the Buttonbush Trail (specially designed for the visually impaired) near the parking area.

With a unique and varied 7-mile circuit trail that is regarded as one of New England's classic hikes, the Great Island peninsula in Wellfleet offers explorers plenty of opportunities to observe a full suite of coastal wildlife. This narrow promontory, which actually once was an island until the ever-shifting sands connected it to the mainland during the 1830s, juts out of Chequesett Neck in Wellfleet into Cape Cod Bay. Along its east side are tidal marshes bordering a narrow neck known as the Gut, where you may observe colonies of fiddler crabs, great blue herons and other wading birds, and horseshoe crabs. The interior woodlands host migratory songbirds such as pine warblers and ovenbirds and also provide cover for white-tailed deer, eastern coyotes, and red foxes. The peninsula reaches its end at Jeremy Point, a narrow spit that is covered at high tides. Harbor seals are common here in winter. Along the three-mile section of bay beach, look for piping plovers, eider ducks, seagulls, and a variety of migrating shorebirds in late summer. In winter the bay hosts large flocks of waterfowl, including northern gannets, red-breasted mergansers, and common and red-throated loons.

During migratory periods in the spring and early autumn, the panoramic overlooks at the Pilgrim Spring Area in Truro offer close-up views of raptors, which pass a short distance above as they attempt to navigate this narrow, curving neck of the Cape. In fall the birds are joined by southbound monarch butterflies and, in some years, large swarms of migrating dragonflies such as common green darners. Two easy 0.75-mile interpretive loop trails lead through an old farm site in a kettle hole and a spring visited by the Pilgrims in 1620.

The Beech Forest Trail at the Province Lands, named for its mature woodlands that include an uncommon grove of coastal beech trees, is an excellent route for viewing songbirds during the spring and summer. Among the numerous species present are scarlet tanagers, northern orioles, and more than two dozen varieties of warblers. This 1.4-mile trail also encircles a shallow pond that is home to bull and green frogs, great blue herons, and painted turtles.

The nearby Herring Cove and Race Point beaches are good places to view whales and other marine mammals from early spring to early autumn; May is an especially active month. Humpback, fin, and minke whales are the most commonly observed species, while fortunate observers may glimpse one of the 300 right whales that are estimated to occur worldwide.

The seashore's beaches offer crucial habitat for threatened least terns and approximately 5 percent of the entire Atlantic Coast piping plover populations. Wire enclosures protect nest sites from predators such as raccoons and coyotes, as well as from human recreational users and dogs. Among the amphibians that use the freshwater wetlands are eastern spadefoot and Fowler's toads, green and pickerel frogs, and spotted, four-toed, and red-backed salamanders. An uncommon reptile that is especially well suited to sandy habitats is the eastern hog-nosed snake, which uses its upturned snout to burrow in search of toads and other prey. Winter brings greatly reduced human crowds and the opportunity to observe cold-weather visitors such as northern gannets, black guillemots, razorbills, and scoter ducks. Reliable places to view harbor and gray seals include the inlet to Nauset Marsh, the Head of the Meadow Beach in Truro, and the Province Lands beaches.

Coskata-Coatue Wildlife Refuge

The Trustees of Reservations, 508-228-0006, www.thetrustees.org
CLOSEST TOWN: Nantucket Town
DIRECTIONS: From the Nantucket town rotary follow Polpis Road east for 6 miles, then turn left on Wauwinet Road and follow it to its end at the refuge entrance.

Thanks to conservation efforts that have protected some 40 percent of its 35,000 acres, Nantucket Island, the easternmost of Massachusetts' offshore islands, retains a quiet, rural character. Perhaps nowhere is this more evident than along the long, narrow, fishhook-shaped sliver of beach capped by Great Point that extends north out of the island's northeast corner. Here nearly 1,400 acres are protected by several preserves, the largest of which is the Trustees of Reservation's Coskata-Coatue Wildlife Refuge.

Within its bounds are a host of diverse coastal natural communities, including the Coskata Woods, a 40-acre block of mature maritime oak that was never cut in colonial times due to the point's remote location, and the larger Cedars, 400 acres of red cedar savannah and woodlands. Wetlands include the Glades, a complex of salt marsh and maritime shrubland where elevation changes of just a few feet have significant effects on the ecosystem, Coskata Pond, and Great Point Lagoon. There are also approximately 200 acres of dunes, stabilized by vegetation such as bayberry, beach plum, and rugosa rose. The beaches have been constantly reshaped by storms such as the hurricane of 1896, which opened a breach that cut off the point. The lighthouse at the tip of Great Point, which is part of the adjacent Nantucket National Wildlife Refuge, was destroyed by another storm in 1984 but rebuilt in 1986.

VIEWING

The fertile fishing grounds off Great Point provide sustenance for harbor and gray seals, along with less common hooded and harp seals. Fully one-third of the entire Massachusetts least tern population also calls the point home, along with piping plovers, sanderlings, and other shorebirds. Check the tidal flats for distinctive, orange-beaked American oystercatchers, a familiar species of the mid-Atlantic coast that is near its northern range limit here, and large groups of common, arctic, and roseate terns. Wading birds hunting the flats and marsh edges include black-crowned night, tricolored, great blue, little blue, and green herons, as well as great and snowy egrets. Herring, Bonaparte's, black-backed and lesser black-backed, ring-billed, and laughing gulls frequent these areas as well, feeding off a multitude of oysters and clams.

The sand dunes and woodlands offer additional diversity; watch and listen for melodious song sparrows, horned larks, killdeer, and tree and barn swallows, as well as white-tailed deer. Look for six-spotted green tiger beetles, easily identifiable thanks to their bright green coloration, hopping along sandy openings along the trails. Overhead circle birds of prey such as northern harriers, kestrels, red-tailed hawks, and osprey, which take advantage of the refuge's nesting platforms. One of the resident osprey ("Mr. Hannah") is presently being monitored by a university research group that has tracked and mapped its travels throughout the year, including the winter migration to South America (www.bioweb.uncc.edu/Bierregaard/maps09/Hannah-2009.htm).

In winter, scan the offshore waters for seabirds, including black scoters, buffleheads, oldsquaws, mergansers, and common and red-throated loons, and check open areas for snowy owls, which periodically migrate to the area from the north.

Access to the refuge is via the Wauwinet gatehouse at the end of Wauwinet Road. There are 16 miles of hiking trails and over-sand vehicle routes that explore the various habitats and both shores. The trails and beaches are free for pedestrians; an annual pass ($140) is required for an over-sand vehicle permit. Portions of the beaches may be closed during the shorebird nesting season. Please respect the private residences north of the entrance. Visitors are advised to contact the gatehouse at 508-228-0006 for updated information about access prior to their visit.

From the gatehouse the main route leads north for 1.1 miles to the refuge boundary, then soon reaches a four-way junction at marker 1. Here the trail on the left leads west toward the outlet of Coskata Pond, while a right leads to the ocean shore. At junction 2 at 2.6 miles, another trail leads west across the Cedars to explore the shores of Nantucket Sound. The main trail continues to the outer beaches and the lighthouse at Great Point, which it reaches at 5.5 miles. The full-length hike is rated as strenuous, as it traverses extended sections with soft sand.

Great Meadows National Wildlife Refuge

U.S. Fish and Wildlife Service, 978-443-4661,
www.fws.gov/northeast/greatmeadows

CLOSEST TOWN: Concord

DIRECTIONS: For the Concord Unit, from the junction of MA 62 and MA 2A in the center of Concord follow MA 62 east for 1.4 miles to a left on Monsen Road. Continue 0.3 mile to a nearly hidden left turn at a sign for the refuge, and follow this road to the refuge entrance and parking area. For the Sudbury Unit, from MA 27 on the Sudbury-Wayland town line turn north on Old Water Row and continue for 1.9 miles to a right on Lincoln Road. Follow Lincoln Road for 0.4 mile, then turn left on Weir Hill Road and continue 0.3 mile to the refuge entrance road.

When exploring the 3,800 acres of wild, riverine habitats that lie within the Great Meadows National Wildlife Refuge, it is hard to imagine that the greater Boston area lies just a few miles to the east. The refuge exists in two divisions, the northernmost of which encompasses the watershed of the Concord River a short distance from Concord's historic town center. Here two impoundments of the river, known as the Upper Pool and Lower Pool, are divided by a dike and bordered by walking trails that offer excel-

Painted turtles basking on a muskrat lodge at the Great Meadows National Wildlife Refuge.

lent close-up views of the varied wildlife that inhabit these ponds and the floodplain. The impoundment is drained into the river during the summer, opening up extensive mudflats that are heavily used by southbound migratory waterfowl and songbirds.

To the south lies the nearby Sudbury Unit, which is part of a network of conservation areas along the Sudbury River. The refuge headquarters and visitor center are situated here at the base of Weir Hill, a 190-foot glacial hill that rises above a sharp bend in the river; other habitats include a red maple swamp, upland forests of red and white oak, white pine, and hemlock, marshes, and a glacial kettle hole atop the hill. Relics of Native American activity along both rivers have been dated to 5500 BCE. Great Meadows is part of the overall Eastern Massachusetts Wildlife Refuge Complex, which also includes the Assabet River and Oxbow refuges. These three preserves offer more than 7,000 acres of habitat for wildlife in the heart of New England's most populous region.

VIEWING

The marshy areas that border the trails at the Concord impoundment offer excellent views of muskrats and their houses, which are composed primarily of cattail reeds and are much smaller than beaver lodges. Other mammals present throughout the wetlands of both divisions include beavers, river otters, mink, and raccoons, while white-tailed deer, red and gray foxes, eastern coyotes, bobcats, and fishers roam the upland forests. The Concord Unit hosts one of New England's largest populations of threatened Blanding's turtles, which are distinguished from other turtles by their bright yellow throat and chin. Though they spend most of their lives in the shallow, vegetated impoundment, females venture on land to make nests in open areas such as agricultural fields and backyards. Other reptiles and amphibians include painted, spotted, and snapping turtles, bullfrogs and leopard frogs, and northern water and garter snakes. In late April watch for the striking sight of thousands of exotic carp attempting to enter the Concord impoundment from the river.

The refuge is one of the region's finest inland bird-watching destinations, with more than 220 recorded species. The Concord Unit is among a handful of sites in Massachusetts that hosts breeding marsh wrens, which may be observed along the Dike Trail. Other marsh birds include rarely seen soras, Virginia rails, and great blue, green, and black-crowned night herons. Familiar songbirds of wetland edges include northern waterthrushes, swamp sparrows, yellow warblers, and great-crested flycatchers, while northern orioles, red-breasted grosbeaks, scarlet tanagers, phoebes, and eastern wood pewees add splashes of color and sound to the surrounding oak-pine-maple woodlands.

Thanks to an active nest box program, the refuge hosts a healthy contingent of wood ducks, which have recovered from historical declines caused by hunting and loss of mature nesting trees. Other common breeders include blue-winged teal, mallards, grebes, black ducks, and Canada geese, while American wigeons, gadwalls, and other waterfowl pass through during migrations. In spring and from midsummer to early autumn, check exposed muddy areas for migrating shorebirds such as dunlins, killdeer, greater and lesser yellowlegs, and a variety of sandpipers. Year-round residents include great horned and eastern screech owls, red-bellied and pileated woodpeckers, and wild turkeys.

GETTING AROUND

The Concord Unit's main walking route is the popular 1.7-mile Dike Trail, which begins at the main entrance and follows a causeway between the Upper and Lower pools to a three-way junction. Here the main loop continues right (northeast), with continuous views of the pool and floodplain forest, while the path to the left offers an optional one-way detour to the refuge boundary, with more fine wetland views. As the circuit nears the southeast corner of the Lower Pool, it passes the Timber and Edge trails, both of which offer easy 0.4-mile loops that explore the forests and shoreline. An observation tower next to the parking area provides a fine overview of the refuge.

At the Sudbury Unit, two interpretive trails form an easy 1-mile circuit that is excellent for families. From the visitor center, where there are good views from an observation deck on the building's second level, the Weir Hill Trail follows the west bank of the river to the refuge boat launch. It rises easily to explore the kettle hole and a hemlock grove atop Weir Hill, then descends and crosses the entrance road, where it becomes the Red Maple Swamp Trail. This path winds through a wetland, passing a side trail that leads to the adjacent Round Hill conservation area, then ends with a quick circuit around a small pond near the edge of the floodplain. For those with additional time, there are trails that explore the nearby Round Hill, Lincoln Meadows, and other conservation areas.

Boat launches are available along the river roads near both divisions. A small launch for car-top boats is available at the Sudbury Unit; it requires a five-minute walk over easy terrain on the Weir Trail.

Mohawk Trail State Forest

Massachusetts Department of Conservation and Recreation, 413-339-5504, www.mass.gov/dcr/parks/western/mhwk

CLOSEST TOWN: Charlemont

DIRECTIONS: From the center of Charlemont follow MA 2 west for 4 miles to the main entrance road on the right-hand (north) side of the highway. Cross the bridge over the Cold River and turn left to reach the ranger station and campground parking area. Several pullouts and picnic areas are located along the highway and river west of the entrance. A $5 fee per vehicle is charged from May to mid-October at the ranger station.

In the heart of the region made famous by the opening of the Mohawk Trail highway are a series of dramatic hills and valleys where the Cold and Deerfield rivers wind across the east slopes of the Berkshire Hills. Protecting 6,500 acres of the steep, rugged terrain here is the Mohawk Trail State Forest, which is part of a network of state-owned conservation lands in this scenic area. These hills and ridges are cloaked with hardwood forests of maple, birch, beech, and oak, interspersed with softwood hemlocks, pines, spruce, and colorful stands of mountain laurel. The steep slopes made logging impractical throughout much of this area during historical times, sparing pockets of virgin forest during an era when much of the surrounding landscape was cleared for agriculture; as a result many of the state's oldest and tallest trees are found here. From headwaters in the nearby Hoosac Range, the Cold River traces an easterly course as it parallels the highway to its confluence with the Deerfield, which is one of New England's best-known recreational waterways.

VIEWING

The hills of western Massachusetts are prime black bear country, and the Mohawk Trail State Forest is one of the region's finest sites to look for these elusive mammals and their sign. While actual sightings in the wild are uncommon (though the campground is periodically visited by regular raiders), evidence of their activities includes claw marks on beech trees, shredded logs, digs in the ground, and plops of scat along the edge of trails and fields. Other mammals here include moose, bobcats, coyotes, fishers, red and gray foxes, red and gray squirrels, porcupines, striped skunks, and white-tailed deer; look for the latter in open areas bordering forest edges along and near the campground nature trail, particularly near oak groves.

These openings are also frequented by wild turkeys, ruffed grouse, American woodcock, and eastern bluebirds, while the mature woodlands host migratory songbirds such as hermit thrushes, veeries, black-throated green warblers, and scarlet tanagers. Listen for the beautiful warbling call of winter wrens, which lasts for as long as eight seconds, on the lower slopes and ravines. From the ridgetops watch for migrating raptors such as broad-winged and sharp-shinned hawks during spring and late summer. Both the Deerfield and Cold rivers offer fine stores of trout for river otters, mink, and human anglers.

GETTING AROUND

The state forest offers several hiking trails of varying difficulty and a popular 56-site campground. The valley's rugged character is most evident along the Indian Trail, which begins at the end of the campground road and makes a short but very steep climb to the saddle between Clark and Todd mountains, gaining 700 feet in half a mile. At the crest of the climb turn right (east) and follow the much gentler trail for another 0.5 mile to an open ledge on Todd Mountain that offers the best view along the ridge.

Backtrack to the trailhead for a 4-mile round-trip that takes roughly three hours to complete.

The south side of the valley is explored by the one-way Totem Trail, which begins at a trailhead on the south side of Route 2 one mile west of the state forest entrance road and climbs at a moderate grade through the forest for 1.1 miles to an overlook with a partially open view north to the slopes of the Deerfield River valley.

A much gentler option is the Nature Trail, a mile-long path that begins east of the right fork of the campground road and explores the area along the south bank of the Deerfield River. It leads to fields that are maintained for wildlife, a grove of some of the country's largest white pine trees, a small pond, old pine plantations, and several historical features, including the grave of a Revolutionary War soldier. Allow 35 minutes to an hour to complete this circuit.

Monomoy National Wildlife Refuge

U.S. Fish and Wildlife Service, 508-945-0594,
www.fws.gov/northeast/monomoy
CLOSEST TOWN: Chatham
DIRECTIONS: From the junction of US 6 and MA 137 in Chatham take MA 137 south for 3 miles to the junction with MA 28, then follow MA 28 east for another 3.5 miles to a rotary. Continue straight here and follow Main Street to a T intersection with Shore Road. Turn right and drive past the Chatham Lighthouse and Coast Guard Station, then bear left on Morris Island Road, then take the first right and follow the causeway to the refuge entrance and visitor center.

At the elbow of Cape Cod lies one of the richest wildlife areas along the New England coast, an ever-changing mosaic of barrier beaches, sandbars, and tidal flats known as Monomoy Point. A half century ago, the point was an eight-mile barrier beach that extended south from the mainland at Chatham, before winter storms in 1958 and 1978 eroded gaps that separated it from the mainland and created North and South Monomoy islands. In 2006 another storm created a sandy peninsula between Chatham's South Beach and North Monomoy, and by the time you read this the area may well have undergone another transformation.

Established in 1944, the Monomoy National Wildlife Refuge encompasses 7,600 acres, including the barrier chain and a 40-acre tract on

An American oystercatcher (largest bird in the image) joins a variety of other shorebirds feeding on tidal flats at the Monomoy National Wildlife Refuge.

nearby Morris Island, where the refuge headquarters and visitor center are located. Across the channel is North Monomoy, which is an especially productive shorebird viewing area with tidal flats, a salt marsh, and beaches and dunes. Five-mile-long South Monomoy is roughly twice as large and offers additional habitats, including shrublands and freshwater ponds.

VIEWING

After nearly a century's absence, gray seals returned to breed on South Monomoy in 1989, and today their colonies may be viewed on the ever-shifting sandbars from tour boats. Known as "horseheads" because of their large, drooping snouts, they weigh as much as 800 pounds and are much larger than harbor seals, which are more common along the New England coast and winter off Monomoy in great numbers. The refuge's overall seal count, including harbors, peaked at an estimated 6,000 during the 1990s. The 2006 storm effectively cut off the seals from an easy passage to Nantucket Sound, and the population has dwindled to roughly 1,500 in recent years. Numbers during this time have increased at certain places such as the nearby Chatham Fish Pier, where the seals enjoy easy access to sand lances, one of their preferred foods. A good place near the refuge to watch for both gray and harbor seals is from the overlook and beach adjacent to the Chatham Lighthouse.

Along the beach, look for the molted shells of horseshoe crabs, which venture up from the depths to lay eggs along the shoreline during spring and summer. The flats hold great food stores for migrating birds and other wildlife, including clams, mussels, and oysters.

More than 300 bird species have been recorded here throughout the various seasons. No fewer than 8,000 pairs of common terns, the second-largest concentration of the species along the Atlantic coast, breed throughout the refuge. Monomoy is also an important nesting site for uncommon roseate terns, distinguished from other terns by their black beaks; a mere 3,000 individuals inhabit a handful of islands along the Northeast coast. Among the most colorful and recognizable species are American oystercatchers and black skimmers, both of which are at their northern range limit here. Other shorebirds include American avocets, Hudsonian godwits, black-bellied plovers, and a variety of sandpipers.

Waterfowl include northern shovelers, American wigeons, gadwalls, pintails, mallards, and black ducks; in winter large groups of sea ducks, including as many as 100,000 common eiders, are present. Check marshy areas for black-crowned night herons, snowy egrets, and other wading birds. During spring and fall migrations large flocks of songbirds use South Monomoy's scrubby vegetation and thickets as rest areas.

The land mammals, whose presence on these sandbars and beaches testifies to their overall adaptability, include white-tailed deer, muskrats, long-tailed weasels, raccoons, and coyotes. The latter often are a threat to breeding birds by raiding nests and eggs. Look for Fowler's toads, which are distinguished from the familiar American toad by their bleatlike call and preference for sandy habitats, on the offshore islands, and red-backed and spotted salamanders on Morris Island.

GETTING AROUND

The refuge headquarters and visitor center are located at Morris Island, which is connected to the mainland by a causeway and easily reached by car. An interpretive foot trail begins at the visitor center entrance and leads to a pair of overlooks atop bluffs with long views east across the barrier chain. It then descends to the beach below and follows it for a short distance south, then bears right to explore a pitch pine grove and salt marsh. When the trail returns to the beach, you may turn left to return to the entrance (0.75 mile round-trip), or right to follow the beach as it arcs to the refuge boundary before backtracking (1.5 mile round-trip).

The best way for visitors to experience the refuge and see the greatest variety of wildlife is by boat. Several conservation groups and local operators, including the Cape Cod Museum of Natural History (508-896-3867), Massachusetts Audubon Society (508-349-2615), Monomoy Island Excursions (508-430-7772), Outermost Adventures (508-945-5858), and Rip Ryder Seal Cruises and Ferry (508-681-9769), offer natural history tours or shuttles to the islands, including excursions to view the seals, shorebirds, and the lighthouse at the tip of South Monomoy. Contact the individual operators for specific information about times of departure, departure location, and the areas and features each tour visits; advance reservations are recommended.

 ## Mount Tom State Reservation

Massachusetts Department of Conservation and Recreation, 413-534-1186, www.mass.gov/dcr/parks/central/mtom

CLOSEST TOWNS: Easthampton, Holyoke

DIRECTIONS: For the main entrance on Smith's Ferry Road: from US 5 two miles south of the Easthampton-Holyoke town line (accessible from Interstate 91 via exit 18 from the north and exit 17A from the south), turn west on Reservation Road and continue one-quarter mile to the reservation entrance gate. For the southern entrance: from I-91 in Holyoke take exit 17B and follow MA 141 west uphill for 2.1 miles, then turn right at the height-of-land and enter the reservation via Christopher Clark Road opposite the Hilltop Tavern. A $2 fee is charged per vehicle on weekends and holidays from Memorial Day to Columbus Day.

A prominent landmark of the Connecticut River Valley, Mount Tom rises dramatically above the west bank of the river opposite the Holyoke Range. Its 1,201-foot summit is the highest point of the Metacomet Range, a series of traprock hills formed by ancient volcanoes that stretches more than 100 miles from New Haven, Connecticut, to Greenfield, Massachusetts. Other peaks of the ridge, which includes many unique geologic features and formations and offers continuous views west to the Berkshire Hills, are 1,014-foot Whiting Peak and 1,110-foot Deadtop. The antenna-capped summit of Mount Tom itself lies just outside the state park boundary.

The 2,081-acre Mount Tom State Reservation encompasses the bulk of the mountain and its natural habitats, including woodlands, rocky talus slopes and basalt cliffs, open balds, ponds, vernal pools, and springs and brooks, which together host a number of regionally uncommon species. At the base of the east slopes, just above the main entrance, is a complex of wetlands including Lake Bray, Bray Brook Marsh, and Kennedy Swamp. The mountain, which is an oasis of protected land in a developed area, lies in the heart of the Connecticut Valley flyway and as such is an excellent place to observe migrating birds, especially raptors, in spring and fall.

VIEWING

Mount Tom was designated as New England's first official hawk-watch site in 1936, and it remains one of the region's finest places to view migrating raptors. In early to mid-September, the overall numbers peak during the broad-winged hawk movement; on days with good updrafts spotters may see 2,500 or more individuals in large groups known as "kettles." Accompanying the broad-wings are lesser numbers of sharp-shinned hawks, American kestrels, northern harriers, bald eagles, osprey, merlins, and turkey vultures. In 2007 a pair of peregrine falcons reclaimed a historic nesting location on the mountain.

The traprock ridge of Mount Tom offers excellent views of raptors and songbirds as they migrate along the Connecticut River Valley flyway.

The reservation's extensive forest provides habitat for migrating and breeding songbirds, including more than 20 warbler species. During the prime viewing season in late spring and early summer, look for black and white, cerulian, Canada, blackburnian, and worm-eating warblers, red-breasted grosbeaks, wood and hermit thrushes, eastern wood pewees, and whip-poor-wills. The woods and rocky outcroppings offer year-round cover and travel corridors for black bear, white-tailed deer, bobcat, porcupines, and fishers. In 1851 the last documented wild turkey in Massachusetts was killed on the mountain, but they are thriving today, thanks to successful reintroduction programs and conservation efforts.

Lake Bray and its associated wetlands are home to Louisiana water-thrushes, red-winged blackbirds, mallard ducks, kingfishers, and green herons, which feed on panfish and bass. Though beavers abandoned the wetland adjoining the lake in 2005, the dam, dead trees, and other sign are easily viewed from the Loop and Inner Loop trails. You may glimpse a mink or river otter stalking the edges in search of a meal here. Late-season darner dragonflies remain on the wing here through the end of October.

Three-quarters of the amphibians and reptiles native to Massachusetts are found throughout the reservation, including uncommon or threatened species such as Jefferson, marbled, spring, and four-toed salamanders and spotted, wood, and eastern box turtles.

GETTING AROUND

The reservation offers an extensive network of trails and two paved auto roads that provide access to the many overlooks and natural features. From the east entrance on Route 5, Smith's Ferry Road passes Lake Bray and climbs to its junction with Christopher Clark Road, which follows a contour below the summit from the southern entrance off Route 141. The Bray Lookout Tower is located at the junction of the two roads, and the tower atop 822-foot Goat Peak, which is a favored raptor viewing site, is half a mile north of the junction. Several roadside vistas with views to the west are located along Clark Road.

Though it requires a moderately rugged hike, the portion of the long-distance Metacomet-Monadnock Trail (which recently became part of the New England National Scenic Trail) that follows the crest of the traprock ridge is one of the region's most spectacular footpaths. Within the reservation this trail is accessed where it crosses the upper end of Smith Ferry Road or via the Quarry Trail on Clark Road; from the south it crosses Route 141 south of the park entrance. A one-way traverse between the Route 141 entrance and Smith's Ferry Road is 2.7 miles; there are several options for loops.

The shortest and easiest of the trails that explore the Lake Bray area is the Inner Loop, which combines several paths to form a 0.8-mile circuit. From the brown gate at the lake parking area above the main entrance bear left and follow the universally accessible trail past a viewing area above the shore. The Lake Edge Trail forks off this path and leads to a bridge that crosses between the tip of the lake and an adjacent beaver wetland. A left turn after the crossing leads back to Smith's Ferry Road near the parking area, with views of a swampy area below the dam. The yellow-blazed Bray Loop is a slightly longer and more rugged route that explores the ravine's forests before looping back to join the Inner Loop at the bridge. The lake is a short distance from the main entrance gate and easily reached on foot if the auto road is closed.

Parker River National Wildlife Refuge

U.S. Fish and Wildlife Service, 978-465-5753,
www.fws.gov/northeast/parkerriver
CLOSEST TOWN: Newburyport
DIRECTIONS: From Interstate 95 take exit 57 and follow MA 113 east for 3.5 miles to the traffic light near the Newbury town common. Turn left here on Rolfe's Lane and continue for 0.5 mile, then turn right on the Plum Island Turnpike for 2 miles. After crossing the bridge to the island, take the first right on Sunset Drive and continue 0.5 mile to the refuge entrance.

The refuge headquarters and visitor center are located at 6 Plum Avenue Turnpike in Newburyport, opposite the Massachusetts Audubon Society Joppa Flats Education Center. The visitor center is open from 11 to 4 daily; the administrative office is open weekdays from 8 to 4:30.

Known as one of the finest bird-watching destinations in the eastern United States, the Parker River National Wildlife Refuge encompasses the bulk of Plum Island, a narrow, eight-mile-long barrier beach island that separates the Atlantic Ocean from the estuary at the convergence of the Parker, Rowley, and Plum Island rivers. This area has long been prized for its natural resources, as Native Americans established fishing camps here before European settlement, which began in the early seventeenth century following the explorations of Samuel de Champlain and John Smith. Today, the 4,662-acre refuge includes a diverse suite of coastal habitats, including beaches and dunes, tidal salt marshes and mudflats, coastal forests, shrubby thickets, a red maple swamp, a series of freshwater marshes that were created during the 1950s for waterfowl and other wildlife, and a tract of land on the mainland at the mouth of the Parker and Plum Island rivers. Adjoining the refuge is the tiny Sandy Point State Reservation, which protects Plum Island's southern tip.

VIEWING

More than 350 bird species have been recorded here, including vagrants such as western tanagers, scissor-tailed flycatchers, Ross's and ivory gulls, and sandhill cranes. Each season brings new viewing opportunities. Among the first migrants to return each spring are piping plovers, which arrive in March to nest on the beaches. In April and early May watch for northbound raptors such as American kestrels, sharp-shinned hawks, peregrine falcons, and rough-legged hawks. May is the prime month for viewing songbirds, including American redstarts, scarlet tanagers, and warblers; uncommon species to watch for include yellow-throated vireos, golden-winged, prothonotary, and worm-eating warblers, and yellow-breasted chats; best viewing is in the shrubby vegetation along the trails at the Hellcat Observation Area and the refuge road. Check marshy areas for great blue and green herons, great and snowy egrets, glossy ibises, and clapper, king, and Virginia rails.

The arrival of southbound shorebirds in July marks the beginning of the winter migrations. Some 43 varieties of shorebirds, including American golden plovers, red knots, western and Baird's sandpipers, and red-necked phalaropes, have been seen at the refuge, with peak diversity in August and early September. They are best viewed at the Salt Pannes area near the entrance, and at the North, Bill Forward, and Stage Island pools when water levels are low. At the height of waterfowl migration in late fall, more than 25,000 individuals, including flocks of green-winged teal, northern pintails, and buffleheads, may be observed.

From mid-October through the winter months look from the beaches for eiders, oldsquaws, scoters, loons, grebes, and occasional purple sandpipers, particularly near Emerson Rocks near the reservation's southern tip (parking lot 7). Snowy owls may be seen in open areas bordering the park road, as well as at the dikes at the Hellcat area.

While birds are the main attraction here, there are plenty of other creatures to watch for. In winter, harbor and less common gray seals "haul out" along the beaches at low tide, particularly near the Emerson Rocks.

A bull moose feeding during an autumn morning at Baxter State Park beneath the backdrop of Mount Katahdin.

Portions of the Moosehorn National Wildlife Refuge near Calais, Maine, are managed for American woodcock, which make twilight courtship flights during spring.

Large colonies of Atlantic puffins (*top*) and razorbills (*bottom*) inhabit Machias Seal Island off the Maine coast during the warm months.

A newborn white-tailed deer fawn lies motionless in an oak forest days after its birth in late May. The spotted coat provides camouflage by breaking up its form.

Gulls circle the summit of Gorham Mountain in the southeast corner of Acadia National Park.

Habitats of Maine's Bigelow Mountain Preserve include high-elevation bogs, a partially open ridge, Flagstaff Lake, and Stratton Brook Pond and its associated wetlands (*above*).

Coyotes migrated into the Northeast during the twentieth century and, in the absence of mountain lions and wolves, are the region's top predator.

The Sunkhaze Meadows National Wildlife Refuge encompasses a large complex of wetlands, including one of the state's largest peat bogs.

Apart from humans, no other animal impacts its surrounding environment more than beavers, whose wetlands benefit many other species.

Also known as the "varying hare" thanks to its changeable winter coat, the snowshoe hare is an important prey species for predators such as Canada lynx, bobcat, and fishers.

Mount Washington and the Presidential Range rise above Cherry Pond at the Pondicherry Wildlife Refuge in New Hampshire's White Mountains.

The largest preserve on the New Hampshire coast, Odiorne Point State Park offers extensive tide pool habitat and coastal views.

A gray fox on the hunt. Gray foxes are somewhat more secretive than red foxes and can climb trees.

Areas where different habitats meet, such as this meadow and spruce forest at the Bill Sladyk Wildlife Management Area in northern Vermont, are especially important for wildlife.

The Moose River meanders through the Victory Basin Wildlife Management Area, part of a large wildlands network in Vermont's Northeast Kingdom region.

A monarch butterfly pauses to feed on asters during the course of its long migration south to the mountains of Mexico.

White-tailed deer and wild turkeys have recovered from historic declines and are once again common throughout most of New England.

Two gray seals duel for a favored basking site on a sandbar at the Monomoy National Wildlife Refuge at the elbow of Cape Cod.

Hawk watchers on the summit of Wachusett Mountain in central Massachusetts during a prime mid-September viewing day.

(*opposite*) The Quabbin Reservoir and its surrounding habitats form a 40-square-mile wilderness that is the largest conservation area in southern New England.

A humpback whale breaches the Atlantic Ocean at Stellwagen Bank off the Massachusetts coast. Courtesy of Brooks Mathewson.

The Parker River National Wildlife Refuge, which encompasses most of Plum Island in northeastern Massachusetts, is one of the finest bird-watching destinations along the Atlantic Flyway.

A pair of red fox kits await the return of their mother to their den in a woodlot adjacent to a farm field.

Scenic Bog Meadow Pond and its associated wetlands are among the many habitats at the Sharon Audubon Center in the hills of northwestern Connecticut.

Colorful migratory songbirds such as magnolia warblers are most visible from mid to late spring through midsummer. Courtesy of Brooks Mathewson.

Another familiar species that has made a strong recovery in recent years is the great blue heron, which benefits from the increase in beaver wetlands.

Tidal marshes and observation tower at the mouth of the Connecticut River near Lyme, Connecticut.

Nesting ospreys are among the most visible of the many inhabitants of the Great Swamp Wildlife Management Area in southern Rhode Island.

The Hanging Rock Trail at the Norman Bird Sanctuary in Rhode Island offers a unique ridge, along with views of ocean, ponds, coastal forests, and marshes.

Check edges and clearings for white-tailed deer, eastern coyotes, red foxes, striped skunks, and raccoons, which may also be seen resting in nooks of mature trees. Beavers arrived at the refuge during the 1970s; a lodge is visible at a bend in the North Pool below the tower at the Hellcat Observation Area. Also present in the wetlands are muskrats and painted and snapping turtles. The refuge is home to one of Massachusetts' largest populations of spadefoot toads, named for the oddly shaped feet that enable them to easily burrow into their favored underground habitats. American toads, spring peepers, and garter snakes are also common.

GETTING AROUND

The refuge's 6.5-mile auto road provides easy access to the various observation areas, trails, and beach lots. From April to mid-August the beaches are closed to public access to protect nesting shorebirds. Some areas are reopened in July; contact the refuge for updated information. The refuge may fill to capacity and be temporarily closed during warm-weather weekends; an early or late-day visit (when wildlife viewing is often best) is recommended during these times.

Productive viewing areas include the Salt Pannes Observation Area, a series of pools that may be seen from the road south of the entrance, and the North Pool Overlook. At parking area 5, the universally accessible Pines Trail offers an easy 0.3-mile walk with more good views. Another observation platform overlooks the Stage Island Pool area near the reservation's southern boundary.

The Hellcat Observation Area at parking area 4 offers an observation tower with an excellent overview of the refuge and a pair of easy interpretive trails. Here the 0.8-mile Marsh Trail forks into a short loop that follows a boardwalk along the edge of the large freshwater wetland that borders the North Pool. At a junction near station 5, a short one-way side trail leads to an observation blind. From the same trailhead the 0.6-mile Dunes Trail passes an oak grove and swamp before crossing the auto road and looping over a tall dune via wooden stairs.

 ## Pleasant Valley Wildlife Sanctuary

Massachusetts Audubon Society, 413-637-0320, www.massaudubon.org
CLOSEST TOWN: Lenox
DIRECTIONS: From the junction of US 7 and MA 20 follow US 7 north for 3 miles

to a left turn on Dugway Road, marked with a sign for the sanctuary. Follow Dugway Road for 0.75 mile, then bear left on West Mountain Road and continue 0.8 mile to the roadside parking area. The trails are open daily dawn to dusk, with the exception of Mondays from Columbus Day to late June; a $4 fee is charged for non-Massachusetts Audubon members ($3 for seniors and children).

The nearby Canoe Meadows Sanctuary, which is also managed by the Massachusetts Audubon Society and is easily combined with a visit to Pleasant Valley, encompasses 262 acres of wetlands, hay fields, and forests along the Housatonic River in Pittsfield. The easy footpaths at Canoe Meadows include the Sacred Way Trail, which winds along beaver wetlands, meadows, and the river itself; a wooden observation building in the middle of the preserve offers fine views of a large beaver wetland. To reach the entrance, from the junction of us 7 and Dugway Road near Pleasant Valley, follow us 7 north for 1.4 miles, then turn right (east) on Holmes Road and continue for 2.7 miles to the entrance on your right.

In the heart of the southern Berkshires, the Pleasant Valley Wildlife Sanctuary encompasses 1,300 acres of prime wildlife habitats along and below the east slopes of 2,126-foot Lenox Mountain, the summit of which is owned and managed by the state. Here visitors may explore a series of ponds and beaver wetlands along Yokun Brook, which is a tributary of the nearby Housatonic River, open grassy meadows, northern hardwood and hemlock forests, cascading streams, and rocky ledges. Like Bartholomew's Cobble, which lies along this same valley to the south, the sanctuary features outstanding diversity on several counts: the rich soils host more than 700 species of plants, many of which are rare or endangered statewide, and nearly 170 bird species have been recorded throughout the various habitats, including 80 breeding residents.

VIEWING

In 1932 the sanctuary became one of the first places in Massachusetts to host reintroduced beavers, and their progeny's continuing work remains highly visible here today.

Pike's Pond and the wetlands along the Yokun Brook and Beaver Lodge trails are reliable places for observing these active engineers, and there are also good wetland views from Dugway Road on the way to the entrance. The beavers are most active and visible early and late in the day, when they may be seen feeding on bark, taking trees down, and building and maintain-

Pikes Pond is part of a wildlife-rich complex of wetlands at the Pleasant Valley
Wildlife Sanctuary.

ing their lodges and dams. River otters, mink, and muskrats are all present
here as well.

Also benefiting from these wetlands are wood, black, and mallard ducks
and hooded mergansers, all of which return as the ponds thaw in early
spring. Green and blue-winged teal are also rare visitors during migrations.
Northern and Louisiana waterthrushes, alder flycatchers, and swamp sparrows breed along the wetland edges, where other familiar seasonal residents include belted kingfishers, red-winged blackbirds, and great blue
herons. Among the most visible of the reptiles and amphibians are painted
turtles, which can been seen basking on rocks and logs in the wetlands,
snapping turtles, which make forays to lay eggs near the gravel roadway
and field edges, garter and ribbon snakes, and bull, green, pickerel, and
tree frogs and spring peepers.

The colorful wildflowers and gardens next to the nature center are frequented by ruby-throated hummingbirds during the summer months; listen for the buzzing sound created by their wings, which beat more than 50
times per second in flight. Tree swallows and eastern bluebirds use nesting

boxes in the nearby grasslands. More than 50 butterfly species have been recorded here, including wood nymphs, great spangled fritillaries, pearl crescents, skippers, hairstreaks, and tiger swallowtails and monarchs. Watch for red and gray foxes and white-tailed deer near the field-forest edges.

Along the trails that ascend Lenox Mountain, including the Overbrook Trail, look for sign, and rare glimpses, of black bears, which periodically visit the fields to feed on fruiting berries. Woodland birds include winter wrens, red-tailed hawks, pileated woodpeckers, and yellow-bellied sapsuckers. Nesting around the summit are dark-eyed juncos and white-throated sparrows, both of which are northern species at home in this high elevation, while red-shouldered hawks and turkey vultures soar on thermal currents along the ridge.

GETTING AROUND

Seven miles of well-marked walking trails offer a variety of options ranging from easy strolls around the ponds and fields near the nature center to a more strenuous climb up Lenox Mountain. A fine option for families is the 0.6-mile circuit trail around Pike's Pond, which begins behind the center and follows boardwalks along the perimeter of the pond and its wetlands.

For a longer but easy field-forest-wetland loop, follow the Bluebird Trail through the fields behind the nature center, then turn right on the Yokun Trail, which follows the edge of wetland along Yokun Brook, where there is a good view of a large beaver lodge. Turn left at a nearby junction on Wood Road, then left again on the Beaver Lodge Trail, which crosses boardwalks as it winds along the opposite bank. This trail soon rejoins the Bluebird Trail; turn left here and continue to a right on the western portion of the Yokun Trail, which follows the brook through the woods before meeting the Pikes Pond Trail. Turn right and complete the loop by following the Pikes Pond Trail around the pond and back to the parking area. This route can be completed in an hour.

The 1.25-mile Trail of the Ledges and the 1.3-mile Overbrook Trail both offer moderately difficult routes to the summit of Lenox Mountain, gaining roughly 800 feet from the entrance to the summit. The latter is recommended as a descending route.

Quabbin Reservoir

Massachusetts Department of Conservation and Recreation, 413-323-7221, www.mass.gov/dcr/parks/central/quabbin

CLOSEST TOWNS: Belchertown, Ware (Quabbin Park)

DIRECTIONS: Quabbin Park is reached by three marked entrances along the north side of MA 9 between Ware and Belchertown. The west entrance road (one way), which leads to the visitor center and Winsor Dam, is 3 miles east of the junction of MA 9 and US 202 in Belchertown. The east entrance road, which makes a loop to the middle entrance, is 4.3 miles west of the junction of MA 9 and MA 32 in the center of Ware.

In an ironic twist, southern New England's largest conservation area—a wilderness of nearly 40 square miles in the hills of central Massachusetts with thriving wildlife and unspoiled views—is the product of centuries of growth and development in the greater Boston area. From the time of European settlement onward, water supply has been an issue in Massachusetts, as state planners reached west for sources capable of meeting the demands of the eastern region. These efforts climaxed during the 1920s and 1930s with the creation of the massive Quabbin Reservoir by the flooding of the Swift River Valley, a controversial project in which four towns and numerous villages were abandoned and inundated, obliging 3,500 residents to relocate. With a capacity of 412 billion gallons, the reservoir serves more than 2.5 million residents of eastern Massachusetts with drinking water.

The West, Middle, and East branches of the Swift River, along with a number of smaller tributaries, are the sources of the Quabbin, which appropriately is a Nipmuc term for "meeting of the waters." To ensure water quality, an extensive forest buffer is maintained around the perimeter of the reservoir, with woodlands of various ages and species and a patchwork of timber harvests. Other habitats include ponds and abundant beaver wetlands, open meadows, rolling hills with rocky outcroppings and ledges, and seasonal mudflats and beaches along the perimeter of the reservoir.

The main visiting area is Quabbin Park, which encompasses the southernmost portion of the reservation, including the Winsor Dam and Goodnough Dike, the Enfield and Quabbin Hill lookouts, and numerous clearings and orchards that are maintained for wildlife. Artifacts and photographs of the lost towns and the reservoir's construction are displayed at the visitor center at Quabbin Park, where trail maps and recent wildlife sightings are also available.

VIEWING

From the time of its construction, the reservoir, with its surrounding habitats, has been a magnet for a variety of wildlife. Common loons arrived while it was still filling during the 1940s, and a dozen pairs now nest throughout the reservation. Reliable viewing areas include the Goodnough Dike and the shoreline road at gate 35 in New Salem. Bald eagles are the best known of several species that have been successfully reintroduced here, and they now occupy several nesting sites. In winter they are often seen from the Enfield Lookout; watch for individuals feeding at deer carcasses on frozen ice. Another uncommon but unmistakable raptor periodically seen here is the golden eagle, easily identified by its seven-foot wingspan.

White-tailed deer are common throughout Quabbin Park, especially in and near open and shrubby fields at Hank's Picnic Area and an old orchard adjacent to the rotary at the base of Quabbin Hill, especially in the evening. Hunting was prohibited throughout the reservation for more than half a century, resulting in abnormally high deer densities, with adverse effects for both the herd and the vegetation. A limited yearly hunt in the zones outside the park was implemented during the 1990s to bring the population density to the state average. Moose have thrived here since returning to the region over the past quarter century; they are especially common in the northern portion of the reservation.

Eastern coyotes, which are also recent arrivals to central Massachusetts, are common here; watch for the tracks of these adaptable canines in all habitats. One of the most likely times to see them is when they cross open ice in winter. Other predators include fishers, foxes, and bobcats, which den in rugged remote outcroppings. Beavers were reintroduced here during the mid-twentieth century and have created an extensive network of wetlands throughout the reservation. River otters may be seen in any of the ponds and streams. As the water levels drop in late summer, check exposed mudflats for shorebirds, including killdeer, greater yellowlegs, and uncommon migrants such as Baird's sandpipers.

Open fields are maintained in Quabbin Park and along several of the old roads, including gates 29/30 in New Salem and 40, the old Dana Common Road in Petersham. These clearings and edges are frequented by wild turkeys, indigo buntings, common yellowthroats, American woodcock, ruffed grouse, eastern towhees, eastern bluebirds, and a variety of insects.

The reservation's main visiting area is Quabbin Park, where the visitor center and auto road are located. The 5.3-mile road, which is open year-round, connects the east and middle entrances, passing a number of viewpoints and features, including the Enfield Lookout, the fields at Hank's Picnic Area, the spillway, and the road to the viewing tower atop Quabbin Hill. For close-up views of the reservoir, visitors can walk the paved roads atop the Winsor Dam and Goodnough Dike. The visitor center and a viewing area adjacent to the Winsor Dam are reached by a separate one-way road at the west entrance.

There are a handful of hiking trails in the park, several of which combine to form a mostly easy 3.5-mile circuit with excellent diversity. From gate WR 15 at the Hank's Picnic Area fields, follow Webster Road on an easy climb for 0.6 mile, then turn right on a yellow-blazed footpath that rises for another 0.4 mile to the summit of Quabbin Hill. The trail then descends through a shrubby area and open woods. After crossing a small field, turn right off the yellow trail and descend to the left-hand side of the Enfield Lookout at gate WR 18. From the gate the trail curves beneath the lookout, then drops to the reservoir shore. Complete the walk by following the path, now blazed again with yellow, along the shore and through the picnic area fields to the trailhead.

For a forest-wetland walk off the beaten path, park at the Goodnough Dike gate and follow the paved road on the right downhill. When it levels at the fields beneath the dike, turn right on an old woods road, then bear left on a yellow-blazed footpath (marked on the park map as Trail 42) that leads through the woods along the edge of a large cattail marsh. This trail continues along the wetland for about 20 minutes (stay left at two forks), then reaches a beaver dam at the inlet to Pepper's Mill Pond. The path continues between the pond and a wetland, with a close-up view of a beaver lodge. After exploring the pond, backtrack to the paved road, then turn right to continue the loop across the top of the dike and back to the parking area. This 3-mile round-trip can be completed in 1.5 hours.

The access gates outside the park are spread among seven towns, with public access allowed at all but gates 17–21 in New Salem. Walking is the main activity permitted on the trails, with bicycles and fishing allowed in designated areas. Though all the routes have viewing potential, some of the most diverse routes for wildlife watchers include gates 29/30 at the junction of Routes 122 and 202 in New Salem, gate 33 in New Salem, and gate 40 in Petersham, where the historic road to Dana Common passes a series of old fields and Pottapaug Pond.

Stellwagen Bank National Marine Sanctuary

National Oceanic and Atmospheric Administration, 508-747-1691,
www.stellwagen.noaa.gov

CLOSEST TOWNS: Provincetown, Gloucester, Boston (tour boats)

A short distance off the Massachusetts coast, roughly 25 miles east of Boston and just 3 miles from Cape Cod to the south and Cape Ann to the north, is a 120-square-mile underwater plateau renowned for its abundant, diverse, and often highly visible marine life. Here, from the decks of tour boats, thousands of visitors enjoy striking views of diving humpback whales, leaping dolphins, and uncommon seabirds. The bank owes its productivity to its variable underwater topography of sand and gravel banks, mud basins, rocky ledges, and boulders, which provides fertile habitat for phytoplankton and zooplankton, plants that are the foundation of the marine food web. The average depth of the bank, which was once connected to the tip of Cape Cod at Provincetown, is 100 feet, but in its southwest corner it is as little as 65 feet.

VIEWING

The bank's copious stores of plankton sustain large populations of key prey fish such as sand lances and herring. In turn, these species are an important staple in the diets of a wide variety of larger animals, including humpback, minke, and fin whales, Atlantic white-sided dolphins, and ridley, loggerback, and leatherback sea turtles. The whales and dolphins migrate north from the equator in early spring to take advantage of this food source and are present through the warm months; endangered right whales are most common around the bank from September to November. The star attraction is often the humpbacks, which are regularly seen breaching the surface and displaying their tail flukes while diving.

In addition to the mammals and reptiles, the bank is frequented by more than 40 species of seabirds, including Wilson's and Leach's storm petrels, a variety of gulls, double-crested cormorants, razorbills, common murres, northern gannets, and Atlantic puffins that feed on abundant prey fish such as cod and haddock.

GETTING AROUND

This 850-square-mile sanctuary is explored via whale-watching tour boats that depart from a number of harbors along the Massachusetts coast, including Boston, Provincetown, and Gloucester. Onboard naturalists provide information about the various marine creatures, and research is often collected during the trips as part of ongoing studies of the whales and other wildlife. Cruises generally operate from May into October, with best viewing during the summer months. Information about cruises is available at information centers, in guidebooks and brochures, and on the Internet.

Upper Connecticut River: French King Gorge, Barton Cove, and Turners Falls Canal

First Light Power / Northfield Mountain Recreation and Environmental Center, 800-859-2960, www.firstlightpower.com/northfield

CLOSEST TOWNS: Montague, Gill

DIRECTIONS: From the junction of MA 2 and Interstate 91 in Greenfield follow MA 2 east for 3.2 miles to the entrance to the Barton Cove natural area and 5.5 miles to the French King Bridge. To reach the Turners Falls Canal, from the center of Turners Falls follow Avenue A south past two traffic lights and a shopping center, then turn left on 11th Street. After crossing the bridge over the canal, turn left on G Street and continue 0.2 mile to the parking area.

As the Connecticut River meanders across the upper valley of Massachusetts, it traverses a series of distinctive natural and historical features. The best known and most dramatic of these is the French King Gorge, where the French King Bridge offers long views from 135 feet above the river for thousands of tourists annually. This chasm lies on a fault line where the African and North American continents diverged more than 200 million years ago; the rock on the east bank is millions of years older than that on the west. The Millers River discharges into the Connecticut at the base of the bridge.

Below the gorge, the Connecticut River turns abruptly northwest as it approaches the Turners Falls Dam. Above this hefty impoundment is picturesque Barton Cove, bordered by a rocky peninsula where dinosaur footprints have been found. A short distance downstream is the historic Turners Falls Canal, which was part of an active shipping route from 1798 through the mid-nineteenth century, then supplied waterpower for mills in the village. All these areas offer easily accessible wildlife viewing, with uncommon species regularly reported.

Watch for bald eagles and ospreys soaring above the river or perched in the trees along the banks. River otters and mink inhabit the water's edge, while bobcats den in the outcroppings high above the river. Dragonflies that inhabit this stretch of the river include arrow, riverine, spine-crowned, and cobra clubtails, umber and stygian shadowdragons, and rusty snake-tails; several of these species are regionally uncommon (though one may well hitch a ride on your canoe or kayak).

Barton Cove hosts waterfowl such as Canada geese, common gold-eneyes, mergansers, mallards, mute swans, black ducks, green-winged teal, and pintails, particularly during migration periods. Belted kingfish-ers are often observed darting and diving across the water from the tree-tops. The woodlands along the campground nature trail are frequented by pileated woodpeckers and migratory songbirds; uncommon species such as red-headed woodpeckers and slaty-backed gulls have been seen here as well. A storm in 2007 brought down a well-known bald eagle nest on the east side of the cove, but the eagles have established a new, less visible home in the area. Watch for them in the tall trees bordering the cove and entrance road.

Migratory Way, the paved road that parallels the Turners Falls Canal, of-fers easy viewing of waterfowl, including mallard ducks, mute swans, and less common Barrow's and common goldeneyes and whistling swans. You might spot, amid the large flocks of Canada geese, the similar but smaller cackling goose, which was recently designated a separate species after research indicated significant genetic differences. The narrow strip of floodplain forest between the canal and the Connecticut River is home to white-tailed deer, gray squirrels, raccoons, and eastern chipmunks. From mid-May to mid-June, migrating shad, sea lampreys, and occasional Atlan-tic salmon can be viewed at the nearby Turners Falls fish ladder.

GETTING AROUND

From June to October, interpretive cruises that explore the gorge and Bar-ton Cove are held aboard the historic *Quinnetuket II* tour boat. These 1.5-hour tours are offered by the Northfield Mountain Recreation Center, which also manages an extensive recreational trail network on nearby Northfield Mountain. Boat launches are located just north of the gorge at the Riverview Picnic Area off Route 63 and at Barton Cove, where canoe and kayak rentals are available in season. The gorge itself is safely viewed from the French King Bridge's walkway; the parking area is on the west side of the bridge.

The nature trail at Barton Cove offers a short walk to an observation platform with fine views across the cove and also combines with the campground road to form a 1.5-mile circuit that explores the perimeter of the cove. From the parking area walk up the paved road for a few hundred feet and watch for the path, marked with silver diamonds, on the right. The trail soon reaches the platform and adjacent rocky outcroppings. It briefly follows the campground road, then bears right and continues along rolling terrain past more ledges. After passing a side trail to the water, turn right at an unmarked junction, then bear right at another junction with the campground road. The path ultimately passes close by a small beach before entering the campground at site 25. To complete the circuit, follow the campground road all the way to the brown gate next to site 1, then continue back to the trailhead.

At the Turners Falls Canal, Migratory Road follows the west side of the canal, paralleling the river's floodplain forest. It reaches a fishermen's parking area in 0.6 mile and the entrance for the USGS anadromous fish research station at 0.8 mile. The road is open year-round to walkers and during posted hours for vehicles.

Wachusett Meadows Wildlife Sanctuary

Massachusetts Audubon Society, 978-464-2712, www.massaudubon.org
CLOSEST TOWN: Princeton
DIRECTIONS: From the junction of MA 62 and Goodnow Road 0.5 mile west of the Princeton town common, follow Goodnow Road north for 1.1 miles to its end at the sanctuary entrance at the parking area. A $4 fee for adults and $3 for children 2–12 and seniors is charged for non–Massachusetts Audubon Society members.

At the base of Wachusett Mountain lies the Wachusett Meadows Wildlife Sanctuary, which, like many New England nature preserves, was once the site of a large farm. In managing the 1,025-acre property for the benefit of a variety of wildlife, the Massachusetts Audubon Society maintains the old fields and pastures as open areas, including the expansive North and South meadows bordering the entrance, and a series of smaller clearings, employing a herd of resident sheep as active "land managers."

The old fields are one of many habitats here that benefit a wide variety of wildlife. Bordering the South Meadow are a 90-acre wetland, which drained in late 2008 when the beaver dam that had created it abruptly gave

The diverse habitats of the Wachusett Meadows Wildlife Sanctuary include an old beaver pond, wildflower meadows, forests, and rolling hills.

out, and the aptly named Wildlife Pond, which offers easy viewing of a variety of pond life. Rising above the old fields is 1,312-foot Brown Hill, the top of which is maintained as open habitat, with low shrubs such as juniper and lowbush blueberry, affording fine 360-degree views of the surrounding countryside and nearby Wachusett Mountain. The forests here, which suffered extensive damage from the December 2008 ice storm, include groves of hemlock, oak, maple, birch, ash, and old-field white pine.

VIEWING
The recently drained pond adjacent to the South Meadow offers a fascinating opportunity to view a beaver wetland in transition. Great blue herons have abandoned their large rookery here, though the old nests may still be viewed from the end of the Heron Rookery Trail. The nearby Wildlife Pond, adjacent to the sheep barn near the entrance, is home to river otters, beavers, mink, and waterfowl such as hooded mergansers and migrating bufflehead ducks. Amphibians include bullfrogs, which are easily viewed at the North Meadow's Farm Pond, and much rarer four-toed salaman-

ders. In warm months these wetland-field edges host colorful blue dasher, painted and spangled skimmer, eastern pondhawk, and meadowhawk dragonflies.

Familiar residents of the North and South meadows and the other fields include grassland and edge species such as bobolinks, bluebirds, barn and tree swallows, wild turkeys, meadow jumping mice, and eastern cottontails. These clearings are especially colorful during the summer months, when daisies, milkweed, goldenrod, and other wildflowers provide nourishment for more than 70 butterfly species, including tiger, black, and spicebush swallowtails, red-spotted purples, monarchs, and American ladies. Check the treetops bordering the meadows for red-tailed hawks staking out a meal.

The sanctuary's forests are home to nearly 20 species of breeding warblers, as well as other songbirds such as ovenbirds, veeries, and red-eyed vireos. On late summer and autumn days when the wind is blowing from the north, hike to the top of Brown Hill for views of raptors migrating along the corridor that includes nearby Wachusett Mountain. Winter tracking opportunities abound here, as moose, white-tailed deer, fishers, coyotes, bobcats, and red and gray foxes all inhabit the grounds; chances for viewing these elusive mammals are greatest early and late in the day along field and pond edges.

GETTING AROUND

The sanctuary trails are open daily from dawn until dusk year-round; the visitor center hours are 10 to 2 Tuesday to Friday, 10 to 4 Saturday, and 12:30 to 4 Sunday. Twelve miles of well-marked foot trails offer a choice of outings ranging from easy strolls through the meadows to half-day circuits. The summit of Brown Hill is easily reached via a 20-minute walk on the North Pasture and Summit trails, with a brief steep section below the summit. The 1.2-mile Brown Hill Loop makes a circuit along the base of the hill and leads to a viewing area at Otter Pond.

One especially good route for wildlife viewers is a 2.2-mile circuit that combines the Beaver Bend, Hemlock Seep, and Pasture trails. From the entrance follow the paved road to a metal gate, where the Beaver Bend Trail begins. Follow this trail straight, then left to a large field, then bear right on the Hemlock Seep Trail, which crosses a pasture and continues through a grove of hemlocks in moist woods. Bear left at the next junction on the Pasture Trail and follow it through an old pine plantation, past two junctions with the Fern Forest Trail, and across two fields. At the edge of the second clearing, the one-way Heron Rookery Trail offers a quick detour to a viewing area at the edge of the wetland. Continue on the Pasture Trail to the edge of the Second Pasture, then turn right on the Beaver Bend Trail, which winds along and near the large wetland for 0.5 mile, passing several viewing areas as it returns to the South Meadow. Complete the loop with a short walk around the perimeter of the meadow and the edge of Wildlife Pond.

Wachusett Mountain State Reservation

Massachusetts Department of Conservation and Recreation, 978-464-2987, www.mass.gov/dcr/parks/central/wach

CLOSEST TOWN: Princeton

DIRECTIONS: From MA 2 in Westminster take exit 25 and follow MA 140 south for 2 miles. Turn right on Mile Hill Road, then bear left at a split on Mountain Road, following signs for the state reservation. Follow Mountain Road past the ski area to the visitor center and auto road entrance on the right-hand side of the road. A $2 fee is charged for driving the road on weekends.

A nearby low mountain that also offers excellent raptor viewing is 1,830-foot Mount Watatic, at the southern terminus of the Wapack Range; both its upper and lower summits offer long views across Massachusetts and southern New Hampshire. From the parking area on MA 119 on the Ashburnham-Ashby town line, the Midstate Trail and State Line Trail form an easy-to-moderate 3.8-mile circuit that also crosses the partially open top of Nutting Hill; the summit may also be reached by a direct, 0.9-mile climb on the Midstate Trail.

The highest point in Massachusetts east of the Berkshires, 2,006-foot Wachusett Mountain is a familiar landmark visible from hundreds of viewpoints throughout western and central New England. The long views from this isolated, open summit include the city of Boston, Mount Greylock and the Berkshires, Vermont's Green Mountains, and Mount Monadnock and the hills of southern New Hampshire. Like many of New England's famous peaks, Wachusett Mountain has a long history of development; elaborate hotels were built on the summit during the nineteenth century, and communication towers are present today. A popular ski area operates on the north slopes.

Massachusetts established Wachusett Mountain State Reservation as its second state park in 1900, during a time when much of the mountain's slopes were barren and grazed by sheep. Today, stone walls are the only evidence of this activity, as mature forests of oak, hickory, maple, and birch are predominant. Interspersed are several pockets of old growth that include towering ancient hemlocks and unique, stunted yellow birches and red oaks below the summit, some of which are nearly 400 years old. Wetlands include Bolton Pond at the reservation's northern boundary, Echo Lake, and numerous streams, brooks, and vernal pools.

VIEWING

Thanks to the long views and easy access by the auto road, Wachusett Mountain is one of New England's finest hawk-watching sites. The mountain and the surrounding low hills offer an ideal corridor for migrants, as rising thermal currents provide lift. Exceptional single-day totals recorded here include 20,106 (September 13, 1983), 17,517 (September 17, 1984), and 16,062 (September 13, 1989), and an average of more than 12,000 are tallied annually. Broad-winged hawks dominate the species counts in mid-September, along with lesser numbers of sharp-shinned hawks. Other species visible throughout the fall include peregrine falcons, bald eagles, Cooper's hawks, osprey, and rare golden eagles.

The mountain's woodlands and rocky ledges provide cover and food for fishers, bobcat, coyotes, red and gray foxes, porcupines, an occasional black bear, white-tailed deer, and wild turkeys; the less-traveled trails and reservation roads offer fine tracking opportunities during winter. Scan the treetops for yellow-bellied sapsuckers, cedar waxwings, and a variety of migrating songbirds such as chestnut-sided and black-throated green warblers.

Inhabitants of the rocky streambeds include spotted, dusky, northern two-lined, and red-backed salamanders. Other reptiles and amphibians that may be seen at Echo Lake, Bolton Pond, and other wetlands include wood, green, and pickerel frogs and painted, snapping, and spotted turtles. Yellow-legged meadowhawks are among the most conspicuous of the dragonflies and damselflies that frequent wetland edges and openings along the roads and trails.

GETTING AROUND

The reservation's main entrance on Mountain Road in Princeton provides access to the auto road, several popular hiking trails, and the visitor center. The auto road, which is open from Memorial Day weekend through the end of October, passes several vistas and picnic areas as it winds from the visitor center to the summit. Hikers can take their choice of 17 miles' worth of trails, from easy to moderately rugged, that begin at the visitor center and trailheads on the roads surrounding the mountain. The shortest and most direct route is via the Pine Hill Trail, which makes a half-mile beeline to the summit, gaining 600 feet along the way. To avoid crowds and increase chances of viewing wildlife, the less-traveled trailheads such as Bolton Pond, West Side, and Echo Lake are recommended.

For a 3.4-mile circuit that explores a pond, brooks, old forests, and the summit, begin at the Westminster Road gate and follow the Echo Lake Trail for 0.4 mile to the shore of Echo Lake. Continue on the High Meadow Trail, which soon leads to the junction with the Jack Frost Trail. Turn right here and follow the Jack Frost Trail through a grove of old hemlocks to the Mountain House Trail, which makes a quick, steep rocky climb to the top. From the summit, follow the Old Indian Trail on a steep, rocky, 0.3-mile descent through stunted birch and maple old growth, then make successive lefts on the West Side and Semuhenna trails. Follow the latter for 0.5 mile to the Harrington Trail. Complete the hike by following the Harrington Trail to Administration Road, then turn left and make the easy walk downhill to the parking area.

Ware River Reservation

Massachusetts Department of Conservation and Recreation, 413-323-7221; U.S. Army Corps of Engineers, 508-928-4712; www.mass.gov/dcr/parks/central/ware

CLOSEST TOWNS: Hubbardston, Barre, Rutland

DIRECTIONS: For the entrance at Barre Falls Dam, where maps and information are available at the recreation area, from the junction of MA 62 and MA 68 in Hubbardston follow MA 62 west for 2.2 miles to the entrance road.

In the rolling uplands of the Ware River valley of central Massachusetts is one of the state's largest conservation areas, a 22,000-acre preserve that offers plenty of space for large mammals such as moose and black bear to roam. Here the contiguous Barre Falls Dam Recreational Area, Ware River Wildlife Management Area, and Rutland State Park encompass a variety of natural habitats, including large open wildflower meadows and brushy fields, beaver wetlands, marshy areas, swamps, and backwaters along the Ware River and its tributaries, and forest groves of oak, hickory, maple, pine, and hemlock. The Barre Falls flood control dam, which was built in 1958, has saved downstream communities millions of dollars by mitigating floodwaters during storms such as the rains of 1987.

VIEWING

In 1933 a local newspaper reported the sighting of a vagrant bull moose here "for the first time in 50 years." More than three-quarters of a century later, the reservation now hosts one of the state's largest moose populations; watch for sign (and the animals themselves) in the wetlands and forest openings along Stevens Brook and Blood Swamp and along timber harvest edges. Red foxes are frequently seen in open fields, along with white-tailed deer. In winter look for tracks of elusive bobcats along shrubby thickets, field edges, and stone walls. Black bears, which are less common in central Massachusetts than they are west of the Connecticut River, are periodically glimpsed scampering across fields and the dirt roads. Beavers, river otters, and muskrats are often seen throughout the numerous wetlands; lodges are easily viewed along Prison Camp Road and Blood Swamp along the Midstate Trail.

During the warm months the fields come alive with a variety of insects that feed on abundant wildflowers. Butterflies to watch for in mid to late spring include tiny silvery blues, which feed on vetches, and pearl crescents, skippers, and duskywings; dragonflies include dot-tailed whitefaces, lancet clubtails, and springtime darners.

The mix of forests, fields, and wetlands attracts a wide variety of bird species, including wild turkeys, ruffed grouse, introduced ring-necked pheasants, American woodcock, eastern bluebirds, indigo buntings, cedar waxwings, tree swallows, blue-winged and prairie warblers, and northern orioles. Check for wood, mallard, and black ducks, yellow warblers, waterthrushes, great blue herons, and eastern kingbirds around Blood Swamp and the other wetlands.

Though the overall totals aren't as high as nearby Wachusett Mountain and Mount Watatic, the parking area and overlook just north of the dam near the Route 62 entrance is a good area for viewing migrating raptors and monarch butterflies, as the hawks ride thermal currents above the valley.

GETTING AROUND

The main entrance, a recommended starting point for first-time visitors, is reached via the Barre Falls Dam recreation area off Route 62 in Hubbardston, where maps and information are available. The reservation may also be reached by Route 122 on the Barre-Oakham town line, and from Rutland State Park off Route 122A in Rutland. A network of dirt roads provides seasonal access, and Coldbrook Road from the dam to Route 122 is maintained in winter (it may be closed after severe storms or during spring high-water periods). This area is heavily hunted in late autumn, and visits during this time are recommended on Sundays, when shooting is prohibited.

A one-way route with good variety for vehicles, walkers, skiers, or bikers begins at the end of the paved road at the Barre Falls Dam recreation area next to a small cemetery. From here, follow the dirt Coldbrook Road south past a yellow gate for 1.1 miles to a left on Ruben Walker Road, which slopes downhill past the Midstate Trail crossing at a small pond to wetlands along Stevens Brook. At 2.6 miles turn right on Prison Camp Road, which passes a series of large fields. At 3.3 miles a quick detour left leads to a causeway with fine wetland views. Prison Camp Road continues past a large beaver wetland and ultimately reaches Whitehall Pond in Rutland State Park near Route 122 at 5.3 miles.

For those looking to escape into the woods on a hiker's path, the 92-mile-long Midstate Trail crosses the heart of the reservation, with one especially interesting segment that follows the edge of Blood Swamp. You can access the trail at the recreation area or at junctions where it crosses the interior woods roads. The most direct access to the swamp walk is at a small pullout where the trail crosses Ruben Walker Road, 0.2 mile from its junction with Coldbrook Road.

Boat launches are located on Route 122 near the Barre-Oakham town line, and also at the Barre Falls Dam recreation area.

Wellfleet Bay Wildlife Sanctuary

Massachusetts Audubon Society, 508-349-2615, www.massaudubon.org
CLOSEST TOWN: Wellfleet
DIRECTIONS: From the Eastham-Wellfleet town line follow US 6 north for
0.3 mile, then turn left (west) on the marked sanctuary road and continue
0.4 mile to the visitor center parking area. A $5 admission fee is charged for
non-Massachusetts Audubon Society members.

With its diverse habitats, abundant and visible wildlife, fine scenery, well-marked trails, and state-of-the art visitor center, the Wellfleet Bay Wildlife Sanctuary is an ideal destination for explorers of all ages looking to sample a wide range of Cape Cod's nature. This former asparagus farm and bird-banding research station, which was acquired by the Massachusetts Audubon Society in 1958, encompasses 1,100 acres of the east shores of Wellfleet Bay opposite the Great Island peninsula.

A painted turtle basks on water lilies in Silver Spring Brook at the Wellfleet Bay Wildlife Sanctuary.

Bordering the bay are tidal mudflats and creeks, salt marshes, an uncommon oak-hickory hummock, and a barrier beach. Inland are mature pitch pine and oak forests, shrubby heathlands, a sand-plain grassland, and Silver Spring and Goose ponds. The latter is drained during the summer and dammed in autumn to enhance its value for a variety of birdlife, including migrating shorebirds. The sanctuary visitor center offers natural history exhibits, including two large aquariums and a large butterfly garden.

VIEWING
The popular Try Island Trail, which traverses a long boardwalk as it winds to the bay, offers close-up views of colonies of fiddler crabs, which scramble in and around countless small den holes in the flats. The subspecies found here and along the coast south to Florida include mud fiddlers, which favor muddy marsh environments where they construct burrows that may be nearly two feet deep, and sand fiddlers, which are common to abundant in sandy and intertidal areas along marshes and tidal creeks. Both intermingle in areas where their preferred habitats overlap.

Along these exposed mudflats and marshes during the warm months are black and yellow-crowned night herons, snowy egrets, clapper rails, sandpipers, and great blue and green herons. The tidal flats at the end of the

Try Island Trail offer fine shorebird viewing, especially during the height of the mid- to late-summer migration when a number of species are present, including willets, whimbrels, ruddy turnstones, semipalmated plovers, greater and lesser yellowlegs, and large flocks of common terns.

The most visible of the sanctuary's five turtle species are painted turtles, which are easily viewed basking in groups in Silver Spring Pond near the nature center. From the bridge across Silver Spring Creek watch for much larger snapping turtles swimming below the surface, as well as river otters and muskrats. Fowler's toads are common in sandy habitats. From the low vegetation, dragonflies and damselflies such as slaty skimmers, blue dashers, and halloween pennants patrol the wetland edges, snapping up insects in hunting passes over the water. The short boardwalk and viewing blind at nearby Goose Pond allow easy observation of green herons and other wading birds and shorebirds.

Among the many songbirds present in the forests are pine warblers, named for their preference for tall pine trees such as those found along the Bay View and Silver Spring trails. Though visually similar to several other warblers, they are distinguished by their trilling call; some individuals overwinter in eastern Massachusetts. Nesting birds of prey include great horned and screech owls, red-tailed hawks, and northern harriers. Eastern cottontails and bobwhite quails, named for their unmistakable whistling call, take cover in shrubby vegetation along the sandy margins of the trails and clearings.

Offering additional diversity are the open fields near the entrance, where tree swallows and eastern bluebirds nest in the posted boxes; watch for white-tailed deer, eastern coyotes, and red foxes in the early morning and evening. The large butterfly garden nourishes ruby-throated humming-birds, tiger swallowtail and monarch butterflies, and a variety of bees and other insects.

GETTING AROUND

The sanctuary's five miles of trails are open from 8 AM to dusk daily (8 PM during the summer months). The visitor center is open daily from 8:30 to 5; it is closed Monday from Columbus Day through Memorial Day.

One recommended viewing route begins on the Goose Pond Trail, which branches to the left (south) from the main trailhead next to the visitor center. This path soon reaches Silver Spring Pond, where a 0.6-mile side trail loops along both banks of the brook and its wetlands, then continues to an observation blind and short boardwalk at Goose Pond. After passing an observation platform with views across the salt marsh, it reaches a junction at post 33. Here the Try Island Trail branches to the right and leads to a boardwalk that winds through the mudflats, salt marsh, and fiddler crab colonies to the mudflats where Hatches Creek meets the bay (keep an eye on the tides when exploring this area). This one-way walk is approximately 0.8 mile, or 1.4 miles if the Silver Spring loop is included.

The northern portion of the sanctuary is explored by the Bay View and Fresh Brook Pathway trails, which form a 1.6-mile circuit. The former begins at the entrance and follows the edge of the salt marsh, passing a junction with a cutoff that offers a shorter, mile-long loop through an open heathland. The main trail continues along the perimeter of the marsh, then meets the Fresh Brook Pathway, which winds over a knoll at the sanctuary boundary. From their second junction, the Bay View Trail continues through grassy pitch pine forests as it leads south past the campground to the fields at the entrance.

 NEW HAMPSHIRE

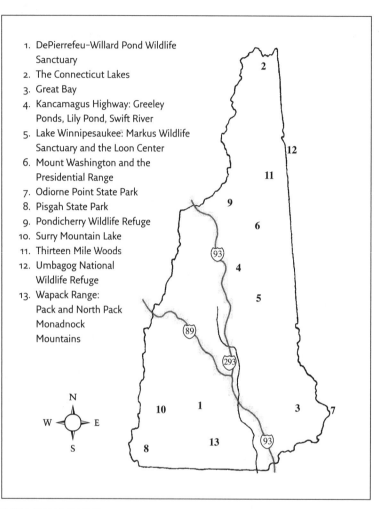

N

W ✦ E

S

NEW HAMPSHIRE

DePierrefeu–Willard Pond Wildlife Sanctuary

Audubon Society of New Hampshire, 603-224-9909, www.nhaudubon.org
CLOSEST TOWNS: Hancock, Antrim
DIRECTIONS: From the junction of NH 9 and NH 123 in Antrim follow NH 123
    south for 3.3 miles to a left on Willard Pond Road. Follow Willard Pond Road
    for 1.6 miles, bearing left at forks, to the large sanctuary parking lot and
    information sign on the left. The road ends at the boat launch just beyond
    the sanctuary entrance.

In the heart of an 18-mile-long corridor of protected lands in southern
New Hampshire's uplands is the 1,056-acre dePierrefeu–Willard Pond
Wildlife Sanctuary, which is the largest property of the New Hampshire
Audubon Society. Its namesake is pristine, 100-acre Willard Pond, which
is managed by the New Hampshire Fish and Game Department. Along its
shores are numerous glacial boulders, shrubs such as maple-leaved viburnum, hobblebush, and highbush blueberry, and a grove of white pines at
Pine Point, a small peninsula near the sanctuary's eastern boundary. The
pond's outflow feeds the adjacent Hatches Mill Pond, a much smaller,
shallow pond at the site of an old sawmill.

Rising some 900 feet above Willard Pond is Bald Mountain, so named
in the aftermath of a historical forest fire that destroyed much of its vegetation. Today, its steep, rocky slopes are again forested with oak, pine,
and maple, and a high-elevation red spruce grove at its 2,083-foot summit.
Open ledges below the summit offer fine panoramic views to nearby Mount
Monadnock and the Wapack Mountain ridge, and a lower overlook offers
a bird's-eye view of Willard Pond. The sanctuary encompasses the bulk of
the mountain, a portion of which is privately owned.

VIEWING

The clear waters of Willard Pond host a resident pair of common loons,
which may be observed from viewpoints along the Tudor Trail. Other
waterfowl often seen here include wood ducks and hooded mergansers.
"Hoodies," named for their distinctive hoodlike crests, breed throughout
much of New England; a few live year-round in southern regions, while others overwinter along the coast north to Maine. Watch for bald eagles and
osprey over the pond.

The nearby Mill Pond offers the opportunity to see mink, river otters,
and beaver; look for trees cut by the latter in the woods along the water's

edge. Pine warblers, appropriately enough, nest in the tall trees at Pine Point.

Along Bald Mountain's forest trails look for songbirds such as hermit thrushes, black-throated blue warblers, and veeries in spring and summer; winter wrens and white-throated sparrows frequent the area year-round. Abundant eastern chipmunks dart in and out of stone walls, the legacy of when the mountain's slopes were cleared pastures, while snowshoe hares and their sign may be seen along brushy edges. Along with red and gray squirrels and a variety of small rodents, these small mammals are prey species for predators such as fishers, bobcats, and eastern coyotes, which actively stalk the old walls during the course of their hunting rounds. White-tailed deer, black bears, and moose also reside in these woods and often use the mountain trails; the sign of the latter is often evident, even at the summit.

In the summit red spruce groves watch and listen for dark-eyed juncos, yellow-rumped warblers, golden-crowned kinglets, and beautifully colored blackburnian warblers, which are distinguished by their bright orange heads and breasts. All these species favor coniferous or mixed woodlands. Take note of subtle gaps in the forest, as even the smallest sunlit clearings attract insects such as swarming darner dragonflies and skipper and mourning cloak butterflies. From the open ledges watch for ravens and turkey vultures gliding on updrafts; migrating hawks are most visible during the late summer and autumn weeks.

GETTING AROUND

There are good views of, and access to, the south shores of Willard Pond from the boat launch, which is located at the end of Willard Pond Road north of the main parking area and the caretaker's cabin. The Tudor Trail begins near the cabin and follows periodically rocky ground along the west shore for 1 mile to its end at a small peninsula at Pine Point. The shortest path is the Mill Pond Trail, which begins opposite the Tudor Trail and makes a quick 0.4-mile loop past the old dam. Bald Mountain's summit is directly reached from the parking area by the Tamposi Trail, or from the shores of Willard Pond via the Bald Mountain Trail, which begins at a junction along the Willard Pond Trail (0.7 mile from the entrance) and rises for 1 mile to join the Tamposi Trail below the summit.

These routes may be walked individually or combined as a nicely varied 4.4-mile circuit that takes roughly three hours to complete. From the parking area follow the yellow-blazed Tamposi Trail as it ascends Bald Mountain at a moderate grade to a fork where a loop trail begins. Bear left here and continue the moderate-to-steep ascent to the forested summit. From the top follow the combined Bald Mountain and Tamposi trails to the open vista below the summit, then continue to another ledge with an overview of Willard Pond. Follow the Bald Mountain Trail as it descends to its junction with the Tudor Trail at the shore of Willard Pond. Turn left (north) here and make the short walk to the Tudor Trail's end at Pine Point, then backtrack and follow the trail south along the shore for 1 mile to Willard Pond Road. Complete the outing with the quick loop along the Mill Pond Trail, which emerges just south of the parking area.

A boat launch for nonmotorized watercraft is available at the end of Willard Pond Road; paddlers should respect all marked areas that are closed to protect nesting waterfowl.

The Connecticut Lakes

Various (private)

CLOSEST TOWN: Pittsburg

DIRECTIONS: From the town of Pittsburg, US 3 leads north for 22 miles to its end at the Canadian border. The access points to the lakes are all well marked along the highway. For the Forth Connecticut Lake Trail, follow US 3 all the way to the customs office at the border and park at the trailhead on the west side of the highway. For the Magalloway Mountain Trail, follow US 3 for 3 miles beyond the First Lake, then turn right on Magalloway Mountain Road and follow signs for the next 8.3 miles.

At an outlet along the south shore of the Forth Connecticut Lake, a small pond nestled amid the mountains along New Hampshire's border with Quebec, you can literally step across the headwaters of the Connecticut River as they begin their 410-mile journey south to Long Island Sound. As the river (more of a narrow, quiet stream at this point) meanders southward through the Great North Woods region, it serves as the source for a chain of scenic lakes nestled among dense spruce woodlands and rugged low mountains a world removed from the tidal marshes at its mouth.

South of the Forth Lake's outlet is the 278-acre Third Lake, which is a natural water body with a maximum depth of 100 feet. A short distance downstream are three much larger, artificial impoundments that are used for hydroelectric power, including the heart-shaped, 1,290-acre Second Lake, which lies in a scenic setting beneath the backdrop of Quebec's

Located in a remote valley along the Canadian border, the Forth Connecticut Lake is the source of the 410-mile Connecticut River.

Salmon Mountains, and the First Lake, which at 2,800 acres is the largest of the group. Just east of the region's gateway town of Pittsburg is 2,050-acre Lake Francis, which was formed by the construction of the Murphy Dam in 1940 and is home to a state park campground. Throughout the area are extensive beaver wetlands that provide an ever-changing mosaic of habitat diversity.

Thanks to a collaboration in 2003 between the state of New Hampshire, the Nature Conservancy, and the Trust for Public Land, more than 170,000 acres of the river's headwaters are now managed as a preserve for wildlife and recreational users; a timber company accommodates these uses with sustainable forestry practices. The Fourth Lake and its bordering woodlands are part of a 78-acre preserve that was donated to the Nature Conservancy on Earth Day 1990. Paralleling Route 3 from the Second Connecticut Lake to the Canadian border is the narrow Connecticut Lakes State Forest.

VIEWING

Route 3 from Pittsburg to the Canadian border is known as "Moose Alley," as sightings are almost guaranteed during late spring and summer mornings and evenings, particularly in wallows, or muddy areas along wetlands and the edge of the road. Adult females, or "cows," are most easily observed along the main highway; watch back roads and forest openings carefully for glimpses of shier bulls. Black bears and white-tailed deer are also common here, though less easily seen; check for their droppings in open areas. Midsize predators such as pine martens and bobcats patrol the forests in search of snowshoe hares, red squirrels, and other prey species.

This is also one of New Hampshire's most diverse birding destinations, as a number of both boreal and southern species are present. The forests surrounding the lakes and wetlands and bordering the highway are prime habitat for black-backed woodpeckers, spruce grouse, boreal chickadees, red-breasted nuthatches, pine siskins, white and red-winged crossbills, and tiny ruby-crowned kinglets. Late May and June are the best times for viewing Philadelphia vireos, olive-sided flycatchers, mourning warblers, and other migratory songbirds. Common loons are easily observed and heard along the lakes during the warm months, along with mergansers, goldeneyes, ring-necked ducks, and other waterfowl.

GETTING AROUND

Most visitors moose-watch from their cars along Route 3, which leads north past the lakes to the Canadian border. Drive-up views of portions of the lakes can be found along Route 3 and at the boat launches. Improved ramps for all types of watercraft are available at Lake Francis and the First and Second Connecticut lakes, and an unimproved ramp for car-top boats is located at the smaller Third Lake. Boaters should be alert and prepared for potentially choppy and windy conditions on the large lakes.

Though this region isn't as known for hiking as the nearby White Mountains, a handful of options are available for walkers. The quiet Forth Lake and its surrounding buffer are explored by a 1.7-mile (round-trip) trail that begins at a parking area next to the customs office on Route 3 at the border. This rocky, mildly rugged footpath follows the international border for 0.6 mile to the edge of the pond, where it forks into a half-mile loop that circles the source of the Connecticut River, crossing the outlet on the south shore.

The region's most popular hike is the moderately steep, 0.8-mile trail to the 3,360-foot summit of Magalloway Mountain, where a fire tower offers sweeping views of the lakes and the surrounding mountains and woodlands, half of which are across the border in Quebec. Another vista can be found atop Deer Mountain, located in the state park of the same name north of the Second Lake.

Great Bay

Great Bay National Estuarine Research Reserve, 603-778-0015, www.greatbay.org; U.S. Fish and Wildlife Service / Parker River National Wildlife Refuge, 978-465-5753, www.fws.gov/northeast/greatbay
CLOSEST TOWNS: Greenfield, Stratham, Portsmouth

DIRECTIONS: For the Great Bay Estuarine Reserve Discovery Center: from Interstate 95 take exit 3 and follow NH 33 west past the Greenland-Stratham town line, then turn right (north) on Depot Road. Bear left at the junction with Tidewater Farm Road and continue over railroad tracks to the entrance.

For the national wildlife refuge: from I-95 in Portsmouth take exit 4 and follow US 4 / NH 16 north to exit 1. At the traffic light at the end of the ramp bear left and continue for 0.5 mile toward the Pease Tradeport, then turn right on Arboretum Drive at a sign for the refuge and continue for 3 miles to the entrance and parking area at the road's end.

To reach Adams Point: from the junction of NH 108 and Durham Point Road 0.4 mile south of the center of Durham, turn east on Durham Point Road and continue for 3.6 miles, then turn left (east) on Adams Point Road / Jackson Estuarine Laboratory Road and continue 0.9 mile to the parking area at the road's end.

Fed by five major tributaries of the Piscataqua River 10 miles upstream from its mouth at the ocean, Great Bay is the largest inland saltwater bay along the eastern seaboard. Situated a short distance west of the greater Portsmouth area, this 4,500-acre tidal estuary is home to a wide range of habitats, including salt marshes, eelgrass beds, tidal creeks, mudflats, upland forests, beaver wetlands, and meadows. The bay and its surrounding environs are protected by a network of conservation lands managed by multiple agencies, ensuring a safe home for two dozen state-listed endangered and threatened animal and plant species.

The Discovery Center at the Great Bay National Estuarine Research Reserve, which protects more than 10,000 acres of the bay and its surrounding watersheds in a series of divisions, is a fine starting point for exploring the bay. Here an easy, well-marked interpretive boardwalk trail offers fine views of the southwest shores and information about the various habitats. The center includes natural history displays, a touch tank, and a boat launch.

Encompassing an additional 1,054 acres of the northeast shores is the Great Bay National Wildlife Refuge. Originally farmed by early settlers, the grounds were home to Portsmouth's municipal airport during the 1930s before becoming part of Pease Air Force Base from 1950 to 1991, and the old buildings and runway clearings are still visible from the refuge entrance.

The diverse habitats include beaver ponds, wildflower meadows, woods and thickets, vernal pools, an old orchard, marshes, Upper Peverly Pond, and a six-mile-long segment of the shoreline of the bay where it narrows

The south shores of New Hampshire's Great Bay as seen from the boat launch of the Great Bay National Estuarine Research Reserve.

into Furber Strait. The refuge is now under the management of the nearby Parker River National Wildlife Refuge in Newburyport, Massachusetts.

Directly across the bay from the wildlife refuge is Adams Point, an 82-acre peninsula that divides Great Bay and Little Bay. Once an island that was separated from the mainland, the peninsula encompasses marshes, rocky beaches, upland oak-pine forests, and bluffs with fine scenic views across the water.

VIEWING

In winter the bay hosts one of the region's largest concentrations of wintering bald eagles; as many as 19 individuals have been reported in recent years. Watch for them in the tall trees bordering Furber Strait, which are visible from both Adams Point and the platform on the Ferry Way Trail at the national wildlife refuge. Osprey have also been increasingly visible here from the 1990s onward. Some 1,000 to 2,000 black ducks also congregate in the area during the winter, a total considerably higher than at the state's other natural areas combined. Other waterfowl present include common loons, common goldeneyes, grebes, greater scaups, American wigeons, mallards, and Canada geese. In spring they are joined by flocks of migrating green-winged teal, horned and red-necked grebes, and hooded mergansers. Check rocky shoreline areas for double-crested cormorants and harbor seals. The bay is renowned among anglers for its bluefish, which migrate to the area during the summer months.

The salt marshes are home to Nelson's sharp-tailed and saltmarsh sparrows, which were once considered the same species; the bay lies within a narrow belt where the species overlap. Thirteen varieties of wading birds, including great blue and black-crowned night herons, great and snowy egrets, and glossy ibises, hunt the marshes and flats in search of fish, mussels, and amphibians. Eelgrass beds, which were nearly decimated throughout the Atlantic coast by a natural blight during the 1930s, provide habitat for lobsters, striped bass, and lined seahorses. In late spring, horseshoe crabs make brief onshore forays to lay eggs on the mudflats.

The surrounding upland habitats are frequented by wild turkeys, ruffed grouse, and American woodcock, while open fields support bluebirds, bobolinks, meadowlarks, field and Henslow's sparrows, sedge wrens, and upland sandpipers. Red foxes and eastern coyotes make hunting rounds seeking mice, voles, woodchucks, and eastern cottontails. Insects such as spangled and widow skimmers, meadowhawk, and darner dragonflies and monarch, buckeye, and cabbage white butterflies are common in open fields and along wetland edges during the summer months.

Familiar creatures of freshwater wetlands such as Upper Peverly Pond at the national wildlife refuge include beavers, river otters, wood ducks, green and blue-winged teal, and belted kingfishers; listen for the chattering call of the latter as it dives out of vegetation along the shore to hunt the water. Uncommon reptiles and amphibians include four-toed salamanders and hognose snakes.

GETTING AROUND

At the Discovery Center the family-friendly 0.5-mile Sandy Point Interpretive Trail leads past a small wildflower garden and lobster boat exhibit, then continues through woods of oak, shagbark hickory, ironwood, and birch to a boardwalk loop that offers fine views of the bay and its marshy edges. A forest path at the loop junction leads to another viewing area at the edge of the marsh. The boat launch, which is a short stroll from the entrance, offers more shoreline views. The nature center is open from 10 to 4, Wednesday through Sunday, from May 1 to October 1 and on weekends in October.

At the national wildlife refuge, the Ferry Way Trail begins across the road from the entrance and leads west along the edge of a clearing next to the old air force base buildings. It then follows a grassy road through shrubby thickets to a beaver pond and its associated wetland, where a loop begins. For those continuing straight (clockwise), the trail follows the edge of a large meadow and an old orchard, then narrows into a dirt path that leads through dense forest with vernal pools. It soon reaches the shores of the bay, where an observation platform with a mounted spotting scope offers views across the water. The path continues in the woods along the shore, then curves back toward the meadow and closes the loop at a short board-walk near the beaver pond. Backtrack from here to the parking area; allow an hour and 15 minutes for the 2-mile round-trip.

The universally accessible Peverly Pond Trail also begins at the refuge entrance and makes an easy half-mile loop through the woods to an obser-vation blind at Upper Peverly Pond. A portion of this trail was temporarily closed for renovations in 2009, but the route to the blind remains open.

At Adams Point a 1.5-mile trail begins at the parking area near the Uni-versity of New Hampshire research building and follows the perimeter of the peninsula. It skirts the edge of meadows above a narrow section of beach for half a mile before entering the woods, then continues to bluffs with fine views of the bay. After crossing a marshy area, the trail crosses Adams Point Road and loops back to the parking area. Other short paths allow exploration of the interior.

 ## Kancamagus Highway: Greeley Ponds, Lily Pond, Swift River

White Mountain National Forest, 603-447-5448,
www.fs.fed.us/r9/forests/white_mountain
CLOSEST TOWNS: Lincoln, Conway
DIRECTIONS: From the west: from the junction of Interstate 93 and NH 112 in Lincoln follow NH 112 east through the center of Lincoln to the national forest boundary, where the byway begins. From the east: from the junction of NH 16 and NH 112 in Conway drive west on NH 112. Parking passes are required at national forest fee areas ($3 a day, $5 for up to seven days, $20 annual pass).

Named for the last leader of the Penacook Confederacy of New Hamp-shire native tribes, the fabled Kancamagus Highway, a designated National Scenic Byway, offers a safe, picturesque passage across the southern White Mountains through the heart of the White Mountain National Forest, which protects more than 800,000 acres. This 35-mile route, which opened

Beaver lodge and dam at Lower Greeley Pond in a high-elevation valley between Mounts Osceola and Kancamagus.

in 1959, offers many attractions, including a series of overlooks near 2,855-foot Kancamagus Pass, the road's high point, views of and access to the Swift River and the historic Albany covered bridge, several campgrounds, and national forest trails that explore features such as Sabbaday Falls.

While best known for its scenic characteristics, the "Kanc" is also a fine place to sample the wildlife of the White Mountains, as more than 180 birds and 50 mammals have been recorded throughout the various seasons. Two of the most reliable roadside viewing areas are Lily Pond, a once-isolated high-elevation (at 2,060 feet) pond that became a popular attraction following the construction of the highway, and a series of wetlands associated with the Swift River near Oliverian Brook. West of the road's height-of-land is the Greeley Ponds Trail, which offers an easy route to a pair of scenic ponds nestled in the valley between the steep cliffs of Mounts Osceola and Kancamagus. The two-acre Upper Pond sits at an elevation of 2,245 feet, some 40 feet higher than the nearby Lower Pond, which is slightly larger and shallower.

VIEWING

Along the trail to the Greeley Ponds, keep an eye (and ear) out for black bears, especially early and late in the day. Though often elusive, they may be heard shuffling through leaves and shrubby vegetation (long-legged deer and moose tend to make more drawn-out bounding noises). In winter, this easy route offers the opportunity to view tracks of elusive midsize predators such as bobcats, fishers, eastern coyotes, pine martens, and long-tailed weasels. The latter, which are closely related to the similar, slightly smaller ermine, change their coat from brown to white in October, then molt back to brown in the spring. At the south end of the Lower Pond, the trail passes close by a view of a beaver dam and lodge near the outlet. Both ponds are rich in trout.

Some of the common forest birds found here include black-throated blue, black-throated green, and chestnut-sided warblers, common ravens, song sparrows, dark-eyed juncos, and winter wrens. Tree swallows snap up insects on hunting rounds over the water before departing the region in early autumn. Northern species include boreal chickadees, shy spruce grouse, and much bolder gray jays. Ruffed grouse may be seen feeding along the edges of the trail, though they are most often heard exploding out of cover as unwary hikers pass close by.

Moose are the main attraction at Lily Pond and the wetlands along the Swift River; they are often visible during the spring and summer months in the early morning and evening. Even if they are not present, heart-shaped tracks in the mud along the edges of both wetlands offer evidence of recent visits. In addition to spectacular foliage, an autumn visit offers the opportunity to observe mating-season behavior, when bulls seek potential female partners, who are often accompanied by confused calves.

GETTING AROUND

The highway, which is open year-round, winds for 35 miles between the towns of Lincoln and Conway. Numerous lookouts, pullouts, and trailheads offer places where you can stop and search for wildlife. Lily Pond is on the north side of the road, 2.5 miles east of its high point at Kancamagus Pass; a short path provides easy access to the shore. The wetlands along the Swift River are 5.5 miles east of Lily Pond and 1.6 miles west of the highway's junction with Bear Notch Road, which offers additional scenic views from a series of overlooks. Viewing can be done here from the roadside, or by walking the paths at the nearby Sawyer Pond and Oliverian Brook Trail parking areas. The road is often very congested during the height of autumn foliage season, but less so in the early morning and evening, when wildlife viewing is best.

The trailhead for the Greeley Ponds Trail is on the south side of the road,

9 miles east of the national forest boundary sign near Lincoln. This path climbs at a gentle grade for 1.8 miles to the Upper Pond and 2.2 miles to the Lower. Though there are a handful of stream and brook crossings, log bridges, and rocks and roots to navigate, this is one of the easier hikes in the White Mountains and an excellent trail for families. In late May this route comes alive with the blooms of hundreds of painted trilliums, along with red trilliums and violets. For winter visitors, a popular cross-country ski trail begins at a trailhead 0.2 mile west of the hiking trail and roughly parallels the foot trail to the ponds; the routes cross several times. Allow two hours for the out-and-back walk, plus time exploring the ponds.

Lake Winnipesaukee: Markus Wildlife Sanctuary and the Loon Center

Loon Preservation Committee, 603-476-5666, www.loon.org

CLOSEST TOWN: Moultonborough

DIRECTIONS: From NH 25 in Moultonborough turn south at the Moultonborough Central School on Blake Road, marked with a sign for the Loon Center. Follow Blake Road for 1 mile to its end, then turn right on Lees Mills Road and continue to entrance on the left.

A nearby destination of interest for wildlife enthusiasts is the Science Center at Squam Lake in Holderness, which offers views of native wildlife in enclosures, a trail to an overlook on Mount Fayal, and boat tours. The center is located on NH 113 in Holderness, just north of the junction of NH 113 and US 3.

At 72 square miles, Lake Winnipesaukee is as large as the 270 other water bodies combined that are spread across the rolling landscape of central New Hampshire's aptly named "Lakes Region." Fed by 60 source streams, Winnipesaukee, which sits at 500 feet above sea level, has nearly 300 miles of shoreline and more than 250 islands. The Winnipesaukee River flows out of the lake and joins the nearby Pemigewasset River to form the headwaters of the Merrimack River, one of New England's most historically significant industrial waterways. Adding to the lake's scenic characteristics are the surrounding ridges of the southern White Mountains, including the Belknap, Squam, and Ossipee ranges.

Protecting nearly a mile's worth of shoreline along Lake Winnipesaukee's northernmost arm is the Frederick and Paula Markus Wildlife Sanctuary. This 200-acre preserve is owned and managed by the Loon Preservation Committee, which operates a visitor center that offers exhibits,

A common loon pair near the Markus Sanctuary on the north shores of Lake Winnipesaukee in central New Hampshire.

educational videos and programs, and a gift shop. In addition to the waterfront, the habitats here include mixed upland woodlands, streams, and a large marshy area.

VIEWING

The common loon's loud, laughing call is a familiar and iconic sound throughout the lakes region, and while there aren't any guarantees of seeing a pair at the sanctuary (some visitors arrive expecting to find large flocks here), the nest platform visible from the Loon Nest Trail offers reliable viewing, especially during June and July. An unusual and unfortunate discovery was made during a recent winter, when a flock of 20 loons was found dead on the lake. Though the reason remains a mystery, it is believed that the birds may have mistaken a lightly frozen area for open water, landed, then were unable to take off. Indeed, one of the distinctive characteristics of loons is that they require at least a quarter mile of open water to take off.

Other waterfowl present include nesting hooded mergansers, black and mallard ducks, and migrating blue-winged teals, common mergansers, and buffleheads. The lake's fish include rainbow, brook, and lake trout, smallmouth bass, pickerel, salmon, yellow and white perch, hornpout (brown bullhead), and whitefish.

Though moose are often less visible in the lakes region than they are in the White Mountains and Connecticut Lakes to the north, they may be encountered along the woodland trails at any time, along with white-tailed deer, black bears, eastern coyotes, and red and gray foxes. Yellow warblers are among the most conspicuous of the migratory songbirds that frequent the low vegetation along the marshy edges. Reptiles and amphibians include painted, snapping, and wood turtles and tree frogs. Raptors to watch for overhead include turkey vultures, Cooper's hawks, northern goshawks, and red-tailed hawks.

GETTING AROUND

The Loon Center is open Monday through Saturday from 9 to 5 year-round and on Sunday as well from July to Columbus Day; the sanctuary trails are open dawn to dusk year-round. From the center the 1.5-mile Loon Nest Trail passes two junctions with the Forest Trail, a short side path that loops through the woods near the entrance, then continues south and east through the woods along the lakeshore, crossing several streams. After the last crossing it splits into a loop; bearing right here soon leads to an overlook with a view of the nesting site near two glacial boulders. The trail skirts the edge of an open marshy area along a narrow finger of the cove, then loops back to the junction. Backtrack from here to the center; the round-trip walk takes roughly one hour.

Boat access to this corner of the lake is available at the public landing at the end of Lees Mills Road, which is 0.2 mile from the center. From May to October, tour cruises of Lake Winnipesaukee are offered aboard the *SS Mount Washington II* from harbors at Weirs Beach, Wolfeboro, Center Harbor, and Meredith.

 ## Mount Washington and the Presidential Range

White Mountain National Forest, New Hampshire Division of Parks and Recreation, 603-528-8721, www.fs.fed.us/r9/forests/white_mountain
CLOSEST TOWNS: North Conway, Gorham
DIRECTIONS: To reach the Pinkham Notch Visitor Center, from the center of North Conway follow NH 16 north for 18 miles to the entrance on the west

(left) side of the highway. From the north, from the junction of NH 16 and US 2 in Gorham follow NH 16 south for 10 miles.

The Presidential Range is a landscape of extremes, an area unlike any other in the East. This 15-mile-long ridge, which rises a mile above the Mount Washington Valley and forms the west wall of Pinkham Notch, is home to New England's five highest summits, capped by 6,288-foot Mount Washington, the Northeast's highest peak. Thanks to the weather observatory that was established atop Mount Washington in 1932, there has been a daily record of the extraordinary weather at these heights. The summit averages nearly 100 inches of total precipitation and 21 feet of snow annually, and the highest temperature on record is only 72 degrees. Hurricane-force winds are a matter of course here, capped by a 231-mile-per-hour gust in 1934 that is the second-highest gust recorded on the planet, topped only by a recent cyclone measured near Australia. In effect, the range creates its own weather, as prevailing winds in the valley guide air into the cooler high elevations, often producing dense fog and intense storms that may form in a matter of minutes. A less welcome distinction the range holds is that of America's deadliest natural area, with more than 140 recorded fatalities over the past 160 years, though some of these have resulted from non-natural accidents involving the cog railway, aircraft, and the auto road.

A journey up the peaks of the Presidential Range is the equivalent of traveling to the boreal regions of Labrador. For every 1,000 feet of elevation, the temperature drops three to five degrees and precipitation increases by eight inches, resulting in a fascinating progression of natural communities. The lower slopes are forested with northern hardwood maples, birches, and beeches, mixed with some red oak, hemlock, and white pine. At around 2,000 feet a transition zone begins, and spruce and fir, which are best adapted to harsh environments, are predominant above 2,700 feet. At just below the timberline at 5,400 feet, the spruce-fir groves taper to clumps of stunted, nearly impenetrable thickets known as krummholz forest. The alpine zone is home to a variety of hardy, well-adapted plants including diapensia, moss campion, and alpine azalea. All told, the White Mountain region is home to 48 of the 67 mountain summits in New England that exceed 4,000 feet.

VIEWING

In spite of this harsh environment, the Presidential Range hosts a variety of wildlife, including a handful of unique species that favor the alpine zone and treeline communities. In the early 1990s American pipits were recorded nesting in an open meadow on Mount Washington at an elevation of 5,400 feet. Named for their distinctive *pip-it* flight call, these gray and white songbirds breed exclusively in alpine terrain throughout their range, which includes a handful of New England mountain peaks. Two butterflies, the White Mountain arctic and White Mountain fritillary, are endemic to Mount Washington's alpine zone. The former has a short flight season in late June and early July, while the latter is active from mid-July to as late as September. Rock voles have been recorded at elevations as high as 5,300 feet here.

Other birds present in the high-elevation spruce-fir groves include common ravens, white-throated sparrows, and boreal species such as spruce grouse, olive and yellow-sided flycatchers, gray jays, boreal chickadees, red and white-winged crossbills, and pine grosbeaks. At lower elevations watch for Canada, blackburnian, and black-and-white warblers; the latter are easily identified by their call, which sounds like a squeaky wheel. Red squirrels are half the size of gray squirrels, though this isn't reflected by their behavior; their drawn-out, chattering call boldly scolds hikers and other creatures that venture into their territories. The range offers ideal habitat for pine martens, which favor evergreen forests on mountain slopes, and porcupines, which den in rocky areas and even periodically visit the huts and shelters. Watch for black bears in the woods and along the edges of the Mount Washington auto road.

Though the unpredictability of moose has been amply demonstrated by individuals that have periodically been observed ambling along the open ridge, a much more likely place to see the world's largest deer is at the beaver wetland on the east side of Route 16 opposite the Appalachian Mountain Club's Pinkham Notch Visitor Center. Nearby Lost Pond offers a good view of Mount Washington and a chance to see river otters, mink, and waterfowl. Check the fields near the auto road entrance for red foxes, which are often seen hunting and loping along the grassy margins of the road.

GETTING AROUND

A recommended first stop for visitors is the AMC Pinkham Notch Visitor Center, where trail information, maps and guides, and equipment are all available. Presidential Range hikers should be in good physical condition, be prepared for the possibility of adverse weather at any time, allow plenty of time for the round-trip, and carry a detailed map and guidebook. Several popular trails ascend Mount Washington from the visitor center, including the Tuckerman Ravine Trail, which reaches the summit in 4.2 miles, gaining 4,250 feet from the trailhead. A much easier option for wildlife viewers is the Lost Pond Trail, which begins at the beaver pond opposite the visitor center and offers an easy, 1-mile round-trip to the pond.

A longer but less strenuous option for Presidential Range climbers is the Crawford Path, which begins at a trailhead in Crawford Notch State Park and makes a relatively gentle ascent over the southern peaks of the range, reaching Mount Washington's summit in 8.2 miles. The northern peaks are more rugged; one interesting route up Mount Adams is the Air Line Trail, which climbs steadily from the "Appalachia" trailhead on Route 2 to the long, open Durand Ridge and reaches the summit in 4.3 miles after gaining 4,500 feet. Many other options exist for hikers; consult a guidebook such as the AMC *White Mountain Guide* for full details.

For those not inclined to make the ascent on foot, the privately operated auto road ($20 toll), the entrance for which is on Route 16 north of the Pinkham Notch Visitor Center, winds steeply for 8 miles to Mount Washington's summit. There are parking areas and trail access points along the road, including the Alpine Garden Trail near the 6-mile marker, where viewers can stop and check for different species at the various elevations. In winter, Great Glen Tours offers snow coach rides up the auto road to the treeline.

Odiorne Point State Park

New Hampshire Division of Parks and Recreation, 603-436-7406, www.nhstateparks.com/odiorne

CLOSEST TOWNS: Rye, Portsmouth

DIRECTIONS: The main entrance and the Seacoast Science Center are located on the east side of NH 1A, north of Rye Beach and 3 miles south of the center of Portsmouth. The boat launch parking area is 0.6 mile north of the main entrance. A $4 fee for adults ($2 for children 6–11) is charged in season; a car/trailer fee of $10 is collected for those using the boat launch. The Seacoast Science Center is open daily 10 to 5 from April to October, and Saturday to Monday from November to March. A $5 admission fee is charged for adults, $2 for children 3–12.

At a mere 18 miles, New Hampshire has the smallest shoreline of any of the country's seacoast states, though one mired in the congestion of summer weekend beach traffic might well infer otherwise. Lying between

Portsmouth's city limits and popular Rye Beach is Odiorne Point, a landscape with a long and varied history. Originally the domain of Abenaki and Pennacook tribes, it was the first place in New Hampshire to be settled by Europeans, who arrived in 1623. Several generations of the Odiorne family operated farms on the point that served markets in Portsmouth. In more recent times it hosted resort homes and hotels before the government established the Fort Dearborn military reservation during World War II; the fort's bunkers and concrete casemates are still visible.

Sold to the state in 1961, the point now is the centerpiece of a 330-acre preserve that is the largest piece of protected land along this largely developed coast. Habitats include rocky shoreline with some of the region's finest tide pool habitat, sand and pebble beaches, mudflats, dunes, coastal woodlands and shrubby thickets, a freshwater impoundment, and salt marshes where Seavey Creek discharges into Little Harbor. From the beach there are fine views of Little Harbor, the Gulf of Maine, and the Whaleback Lighthouse. The grounds are also home to the Seacoast Science Center, which is operated by the Audubon Society of New Hampshire as part of a partnership with several groups. The center offers exhibits of the region's natural and cultural history, including aquariums with representative marine creatures.

VIEWING

Rejuvenated daily by ocean tides, the numerous pools within the rocky pockets are home to distinctive creatures such as sea urchins, mussels, moon snails, periwinkles, sea stars, spiral worms, and rock gunnels. Green crabs, whose northern range limit was once Cape Cod, have expanded north as ocean waters have warmed and are now found throughout the New England coast. Careful observers may also glimpse a hermit crab searching for an empty shell to cover its body.

The point's location along the Atlantic Flyway makes it a fine birding destination in all seasons. A winter visit may reveal sea ducks such as common eiders, surf scoters, grebes, and common loons. Check all of the region's beaches carefully for snowy owls and horned larks. Shorebirds include breeding willets in the salt marshes, overwintering sanderlings and dunlins, and a host of migrants, including greater and lesser yellowlegs, whimbrels, and solitary and pectoral sandpipers.

Familiar perching birds that favor the shrubby thickets include blue jays, gray catbirds, and northern mockingbirds, which mimic other bird calls and occasionally even noises such as car alarms, ringing telephones, and barking dogs. Though these imitations are often remarkably adept, mockingbirds are easily identified by their pattern of repeating individual calls three times in rapid succession before moving on to the next item in their repertoire. Migratory songbirds also benefit from the woodlands and shrubs in the midst of a largely developed area.

Eastern cottontail rabbits are common along the margins of the woods and shrubby areas; they can often be seen feeding along the trails during the late afternoon and evening. Woodchucks, chipmunks, and squirrels may greet visitors at the picnic area fields.

Whether reached via the park trails or by automobile, the boat launch area is worth a visit for its views of the salt marshes where Seavey Creek meets the bay. Here great and snowy egrets, great blue herons, and other wading birds feed on crabs, shrimp, clams, and mussels.

GETTING AROUND

A network of old roads and footpaths winds along the shore and through the woodlands, allowing visitors to explore the various habitats by foot, bicycle, or even skis when there is enough snow along the coast. These trails, which are posted on a large sign at the main entrance, are unmarked but fairly easy to navigate, as you are never far from either the shoreline or Route 1A.

The path that begins next to the Seacoast Science Center (at the edge of a parking area on the left-hand side of the building when facing the water) leads north to the edge of the rocky shore, where there are fine views across the beach and bay to the lighthouse. At the Colonial Dames Monument you have the option of leaving this trail to explore the tide pools and walk the rocky shoreline north to the breakwater and sandy beach at Frost Point, turning left to explore the interior woodlands, or continuing straight toward a small freshwater marsh and an old artillery casemate. Also connecting the main entrance to the boat launch is a paved bike path, though this mostly parallels Route 1A with no shore views.

 Pisgah State Park

New Hampshire Division of Parks and Recreation, 603-271-3254,
www.nhstateparks.org
CLOSEST TOWNS: Hinsdale, Winchester
DIRECTIONS: The various trailheads are well marked along NH 63 and NH 119.

For the Kilburn Road / Pisgah Ridge trailhead, from the junction of NH 63 and NH 119 in Hinsdale follow NH 63 north for 3.9 miles to the Kilburn Road parking area on the right. To reach the Horseshoe Road fields, from the Kilburn Road trailhead continue north on NH 63 for 3.4 miles to the center of Chesterfield. Turn right at a marked sign for the trailhead, then bear right on Horseshoe Road and continue to the parking area at the road's end.

In the quiet southwest corner of New Hampshire lies Pisgah State Park, a 13,500-acre expanse of low ridges, forests, and wetlands within the watershed of the Ashuelot River. It is named for Pisgah Mountain, which rises above the park's western boundary and offers long views across this wild, undeveloped countryside to the distinctive, oft-climbed profile of Mount Monadnock. Mixed second-growth woodlands of oak, maple, birch, beech, pine, and hemlock are the predominant component of this preserve, which like much of New England was logged and cleared for agriculture in historic times. Old homestead and mill sites along Old Chesterfield Road testify to past land uses.

Numerous wetlands, including seven ponds and the Pisgah Reservoir, are distributed throughout this expansive area, including Kilburn Pond near the base of the ridge, and Fullam Pond, which is accessible by car in season, along with beaver wetlands and their associated swampy areas and woodland streams and brooks. Adding more diversity, and a glimpse of the park's agricultural past, are large meadows of wildflowers and shrubs at the end of Horseshoe Road in the reservation's northeast corner.

VIEWING

The ponds and their associated wetlands offer excellent odenate viewing throughout the warm months. Watch for a variety of species, including shadow and Canada darners, band-winged and yellow-legged meadowhawks, and twelve-spotted and widow skimmers, all of which may be seen perched in vegetation bordering the ponds and in sunlit forest openings, or snapping up smaller insects on hunting passes over the water. Common damselflies include ebony and river jewelwings, aurora damsels, familiar bluets, and swamp and spotted spreadwings. More subtle but no less active and entertaining aquatic species include whirligig beetles and water striders.

These wetlands are also frequented by river otters, muskrats, mink, and beavers; a number of beaver ponds and swamps can be found throughout the preserve. Moose visit these water bodies during the warm months to feed on aquatic vegetation and seek relief from heat and biting insects. Black, mallard, and wood ducks all nest here and are joined by migrating ringed-neck ducks, common and hooded mergansers, and buffleheads just before and after winter thaws. "Woodies" find abundant mature trees for nesting here; listen for their high-pitched *o-eek* calls.

A winter visit will often produce a wealth of tracking opportunities, such as a fisher hunting along a stone wall, a bobcat navigating dense shrubs and logs beside a wetland, or a pair of eastern coyotes traveling and hunting together. White-tailed deer and black bear benefit from abundant beech trees and nuts; check large trees for claw marks of the latter. In spring and fall, tall trees and shrubs provide rest areas for migrating songbirds; a number of species, including vireos, ovenbirds, and black-throated green warblers, remain here to breed. From the overlooks along the ridge watch for ravens and turkey vultures, as well as raptors during spring and fall migrations.

At the Horseshoe Road fields, butterflies such as tiger swallowtails, silver fritillaries, buckeyes, viceroys, and monarchs feed on abundant daisies, milkweed, goldenrod, and other nourishing wildflowers throughout the spring and summer months. Red foxes, white-tailed deer, and porcupines are among many species that favor open and mixed habitats, along with birds such as indigo buntings, eastern towhees, common yellowthroats, wild turkeys, and American woodcock.

GETTING AROUND

A 20-mile network of well-marked recreational and backcountry trails traverses this large reservation; maps and information are available at the various trailheads. Be prepared for biting flies throughout the warm months, especially in the vicinity of the wetlands. Fullam Pond may be directly reached by vehicle when Old Chesterfield Road is open in season. From the orange gate at the park boundary, this dirt road leads north for 3 miles to a beaver wetland and cattail swamp at the pond's outlet; bear right at a nearby junction to the parking area. The fields at Horseshoe Road are easily accessible via a short drive from Chesterfield center.

The partially interconnected Pisgah Ridge and Kilburn Pond Loop trails are both accessed from Kilburn Road, which begins at a trailhead on Route 63 and leads east for 0.7 mile to a three-way junction. Here the blue-blazed pond loop bears to the right and leads south to several vantage points along the west shore. For those walking the entire 5-mile circuit, the trail continues through the woods along the ravine of a cascading stream, then descends along another stream at the outlet of a wetland. After crossing two wood bridges, it curves sharply to begin the return leg and rises along the opposite bank. It levels along a wetland, where a side path leads to a shore vista, then makes a long gradual climb through the woods, ultimately reaching a junction with the Ridge Trail at 4.3 miles. The pond trail bears west here and completes the circuit near the wetlands at its inlet.

The most direct route to the Pisgah Mountain views is to bear left at the Kilburn Road junction and follow the northern portion of the pond loop to a marked junction where the Ridge Trail branches east. From here it's a quick climb to the ridge, where there are several open views. The out-and-back hike to the ridge, not including a detour to Kilburn Pond, is 3.6 miles.

 ## Pondicherry Wildlife Refuge

U.S. Fish and Wildlife Service, 603-271-2214, www.fws.gov/r5soc
CLOSEST TOWNS: Whitefield, Jefferson
DIRECTIONS: From the junction of US 3 and NH 115 north of Twin Mountain follow NH 115 north for 4.4 miles. After passing a scenic overlook, turn left (west) on Airport Road (also known locally as Hazen Road) and continue 1.4 miles to a parking area on the right, where an information board is located. From the junction of US 2 and NH 115 in Jefferson take NH 115 southwest for 5.4 miles, then turn right on Airport Road.

Outstanding White Mountain views, abundant and varied wildlife and flora, and easy recreational trails characterize the Pondicherry Wildlife Refuge, which is centered on a complex of ponds and wetlands in the lowlands northwest of the Presidential Range. The largest of these is 100-acre Cherry Pond, whose open shores offer striking views of the west slopes of Mount Washington and the Presidential Range, the Pliny Range to the north, and nearby Cherry Mountain. A short distance to the west is the smaller Little Cherry Pond. Both water bodies, which are connected by the Johns River, are bordered by narrow rings of bog flora such as leatherleaf, Labrador tea, and rhodora; in a matter of a few thousand years the ponds will likely transition entirely into bogs. The remainder of the refuge is dominated by boreal forest consisting of black and white spruce, balsam fir, larch, paper birch, and aspen.

The 5,625-acre refuge, which was designated a National Natural Landmark in 1972, is part of the overall Silvio Conte National Fish and Wildlife Refuge, a series of preserves along the Connecticut River Valley and its environs, and is managed cooperatively by the U.S. Fish and Wildlife Service, New Hampshire Audubon, and the New Hampshire Department of Fish and Game.

VIEWING

The wooden observation platform at Cherry Pond offers close-up views of a large beaver lodge. In winter and early spring look for beavers, river otters, and muskrats feeding at small openings in ice near the pond edges and outlet. Moose, which benefit from wetlands that are created by beavers, are frequently observed here as well; their tracks are often conspicuous in mud, sand, or snow along the refuge roads and trails. Also watch for snow-shoe hares, white-tailed deer, bobcat, eastern coyotes, and wild turkeys, especially near shrubby areas, forest openings, and wetlands.

More than 235 species of birds have been recorded throughout the refuge. Waterfowl and wading birds that frequent the ponds and their boggy edges include common loons, green-winged teal, ring-necked ducks (which are at the southern limit of their breeding range here), American bittern, Virginia rails, and great blue herons, which nest in the wetland adjacent to Waumbek Junction and in the tall pines bordering Little Cherry Pond. The peak viewing for waterbirds is during September and October migrations, when more than 40 species may be present. May and June are the prime months for migratory songbirds such as warbling and blue-headed vireos, eastern wood peewees, northern waterthrushes, and Canada warblers. Marsh wrens nest amid the cattails at Moorhen Marsh east of Waumbek Junction. Boreal residents include black-backed woodpeckers, rusty blackbirds, spruce grouse, gray jays, and boreal chickadees. Birds of prey include osprey, northern harriers, and great horned, northern saw-whet, and barred owls.

The wetlands also provide habitat for amphibians such as northern dusky, northern two-lined, and spotted salamanders, and green, mink, and pickerel frogs. Reptiles include snapping and painted turtles and northern red-bellied and smooth green snakes.

Insects abound here as well, with more than 60 butterfly species, including black swallowtails, American painted ladies, Compton and Milbert's tortoiseshells, and numerous skipper, hairstreak, and commas. Two uncommon residents that specifically favor the refuge habitats are bog coppers and Nova Scotian arctics. The pond and road edges offer excellent dragonfly viewing; watch for fawn and Canada darners, beaverpond clubtails, and Hudsonian and frosted whitefaces.

The main access to the ponds is from the parking area on Airport Road near the biomass power plant. From the trailhead a portion of the Presidential Range Rail Trail makes a straight, level beeline for 1.5 miles along an old railroad bed to Waumbek Junction at the outlet of Cherry Pond, where it meets a lightly used rail line. Here the recreational trail forks to the right and leads to the nearby observation platform on the pond's south shore, then continues east for roughly half a mile to the Moorhen Marsh wetlands.

Bearing left (straight) at the junction leads to views of the Presidential Range from the pond's outlet and west shores; the Shore Path branches off the railroad bed and explores this scenic area. Visitors should be alert for occasional passing trains, as the tracks here are used a few times per week at low speeds. At 0.3 miles from Waumbek Junction, the Little Cherry Pond Trail, which was designated a National Recreation Trail in 2005, begins on the west side of the tracks. This narrow footpath, which forks into a short loop, winds through dense black spruce groves before emerging at a short boardwalk and viewing deck at the pond, 0.6 mile (25 minutes) from the trailhead. Wildflower enthusiasts will enjoy this trail in late May, when there are abundant blooms of painted trillium and bog rhodora.

The round-trip distances are 3.2 miles for Cherry Pond alone and 4.7 miles for both Cherry and Little Cherry ponds; a detour to Moorhen Marsh adds a mile to either outing. The level terrain, wide roads, and winter use by snowmobiles make for easy walking in all seasons.

Surry Mountain Lake

U.S. Army Corps of Engineers, 802-886-8111, www.nae.usace.army.mil
CLOSEST TOWNS: Keene, Surry
DIRECTIONS: From the junction of NH 12, NH 9, and NH 10 at the rotary in Keene, follow NH 12 / NH 9 north to the NH 12A exit. Turn right and follow NH 12A north for 3 miles to a fork. Here the road to the dam bears to the right, while NH 12A continues left for another mile to the recreation area entrance. To reach the fields, from the recreation area follow NH 12A north for 2.5 miles, then turn right on Dort Road and continue to the parking area at the road's end. A $1 fee ($4 maximum per car) is charged at the recreation area swimming beach, and a $2 fee is charged at the recreation area boat launch.

From headwaters near Mount Sunapee, the scenic Ashuelot River traces a southerly, then westerly course through the hills of southern New Hamp-

Scenic Surry Mountain Lake is formed by an impoundment of the Ashuelot River near Keene, New Hampshire.

shire to its confluence with the Connecticut River at Hinsdale, a little way downriver from Brattleboro, Vermont. As the Ashuelot winds through the hills north of Keene, it serves as the source of 265-acre Surry Mountain Lake, formed by an 1,800-foot-long dam that was built in 1942. The lake is the centerpiece of a diverse, 1,688-acre conservation area managed by the Army Corps of Engineers that includes a recreation area with a swimming beach, picnic tables, and a boat launch. A short distance upriver from its inlet are large fields and grasslands that were once the cornfields of a valley farm and are now maintained as open areas that benefit a variety of wildlife. Bordering the lake and fields are extensive mixed forests of hemlock, oak, and maple.

VIEWING

Among the early migrants that visit the lakeshores and swimming beach in spring are shorebirds such as least and semipalmated plovers and killdeer. The latter, named for its loud and distinctive *kill-dee* call, will often try to protect and divert attention from its young by feigning a broken wing to draw predators (and curious humans) away. Watch for bald eagles and osprey soaring against the backdrop of the ridge and diving to hunt the water. With binoculars or a spotting scope, scan the marshy areas along the far edge of the lake for waterfowl such as migrating common mergansers and ring-necked ducks and resident mallards and wood ducks, and mammals such as mink, river otters, and muskrats.

Next to the recreation area entrance is a small wetland associated with an old beaver pond, where great blue herons hunt green frogs and bullfrogs. White-tailed deer frequent the narrow strip of woods between the lake and the highway, as well as the fields north of the lake. Check the forest trails for sign of moose, bobcat, eastern coyotes, and fishers.

The fields and grasslands are home to grassland birds such as bobolinks, eastern bluebirds, meadowlarks, and tree swallows; indigo buntings, common yellowthroats, chestnut-sided warblers, American woodcock, ruffed grouse, and flocks of wild turkeys are all common here as well. Spring and summer days offer the spectacle of hundreds of butterflies, including mourning cloaks, checkerspots, clouded and orange sulfurs, tiger swallowtails, viceroys, and red-spotted purples feeding on abundant colorful field wildflowers. Eastern coyotes and red and gray foxes hunt these clearings in early morning and evening; watch for their sign along the adjacent gravel roads.

GETTING AROUND

The dam, lake, and fields are easily reached and viewed via separate entrances off Route 12A. From the parking area below the dam you can walk the paved road that crosses the impoundment, which offers views across the southern end of the lake and the forested valley. From the edge of the dam, dirt roads branch out to explore the woods and shoreline. At the recreation area there are good views across the water from the beach and picnic area. Several short, unmarked trails explore the surrounding woods, including a partially overgrown path that begins left of the entrance gate and winds above the old beaver pond, and a more prominent trail that leads from the paved road to the right of the gate to the lakeshore. The boat launch provides easy access to a pleasant, undeveloped four-mile stretch of the river.

The open fields are easily viewed from the parking area at the Dort Road entrance. A gravel road continues beyond the yellow gate, soon arriving at a fork. Here a side path on the left leads across a field to a wood bridge that crosses the Ashuelot River; other trails explore the forests on the opposite bank. The main road curves to the right and continues south for half a mile along the edge of the fields before ending at a picnic table and shelter in a large clearing.

 Thirteen Mile Woods

Various (private)

CLOSEST TOWNS: Errol, Berlin

DIRECTIONS: From the junction of US 2 and NH 16 in Gorham follow NH 16 north for 15 miles through Berlin to Dummer. The Thirteen Mile Woods begins 1.5 miles south of the Dummer-Cambridge town line and ends at Errol. Mollidgewock State Park is 3 miles south of Errol and 28 miles north of Berlin.

As the mighty Androscoggin River tumbles south from its headwaters at Lake Umbagog, it passes through a long corridor of prime wildlife habitat and protected land known as the Thirteen Mile Woods. During the region's historic lumbering era, great numbers of logs were driven downstream through this scenic valley to markets in the nearby towns of Berlin and Gorham; at times the channel would completely fill with pulpwood. Today, the paper companies that own this land have protected the river's border through a series of conservation easements, and the primary human users are now boaters, anglers, and wildlife watchers, who enjoy easy viewing from Route 16, which parallels the west bank of the river. From the edge of the Thirteen Mile Woods, the 170-mile Androscoggin continues south toward Gorham, where it turns abruptly east and winds through Maine's western mountains to its mouth on the coast at Brunswick.

VIEWING

Moose are regularly observed along the margins of Route 16 from April through early fall, particularly near swampy areas and backwaters along the river. In spring they are often attracted to road salt left over from winter. Sightings are quite common early and late in the day, and motorists should pay particular attention when driving during this time. Another reliable area is Success Road east of Milan, where moose are often seen in the muddy wallows along the road (to reach this area, take the bridge over the Androscoggin River at Milan, then turn right on East River Road and continue 1.5 miles to a left on Success Road). White-tailed deer and black bears are common here as well.

Watch for mink and river otters along the edge of the river and its associated wetlands; they periodically even visit fishermen along the riverbanks, motivated by curiosity or the prospects of a free meal. Pairs of common loons, wood and ring-necked ducks, and other waterfowl glide along in the river currents, great blue and black-crowned night herons silently stalk vegetated edges, and sharp-eyed bald eagles, red-tailed hawks, and ospreys seek prey from perches high above the water. Among the fish sought by the various waterfowl, weasels, and anglers are rainbow, brown, and brook trout, smallmouth bass, and Atlantic salmon. Check the spruce-fir forests along the riverbanks for northern birds such as boreal chickadees, pine grosbeaks, white-winged crossbills, and uncommon northern three-toed woodpeckers; the latter venture south into New England at roughly six-to-eight-year intervals.

GETTING AROUND

The river, marshy backwaters, and surrounding woodlands are easily viewed from pullouts along Route 16. For a different perspective, drop a canoe or kayak at one of the boat launches. Within the easement lies the Mollidgewock State Park campground, which offers 47 sites spread along a bend in the river and easy access for canoe campers using the Northern Forest Canoe Trail. Interpretive signs detailing the natural history of the area are posted at the campground and waysides along the road.

Umbagog National Wildlife Refuge

U.S. Fish and Wildlife Service, 603-482-3415,
www.fws.gov/northeast/lakeumbagog
CLOSEST TOWN: Errol
DIRECTIONS: From the junction of NH 16 and US 2 in Gorham follow NH 16 north along the Androscoggin River for 35 miles to the junction with NH 26 in Errol. Continue north on NH 16 for 5.5 miles to the refuge offices and visitor center.

Straddling the border between New Hampshire and the hills of western Maine is scenic 8,500-acre Lake Umbagog (which translates to "clear water"), the southernmost of the interconnected Rangeley Lakes. Along the west shores of this relatively shallow water body, which has an average depth of just 15 feet, are wetland habitats that support one of the state's richest and most diverse wildlife communities. From headwaters at the confluence with the Magalloway River, the Androscoggin River begins its 170-mile journey to the Atlantic Ocean amid a series of floodplain freshwater marshes that are the largest example of this habitat type in New

Hampshire. In 1979 these wetlands were designated as a National Natural Landmark by the secretary of the interior.

Following many years of cooperative work among multiple agencies and landowners, the Umbagog National Wildlife Refuge was established in 1992. Today, the refuge protects more than 16,000 acres along the lake's western and southern shore, supplemented by large tracts that are owned by the states of New Hampshire and Maine. Some 50 miles of shoreline, islands, upland forests, and rivers, swamps and other wetlands offer habitat for a variety of wildlife, including many species that are uncommon statewide.

VIEWING

In 1989 a pair of bald eagles successfully nested at the refuge, becoming the first breeding pair recorded in New Hampshire in 40 years. The lake hosts one of the state's largest communities of nesting osprey and its largest contingent of common loons, more than 20 pairs. Other waterfowl that breed on the lake and its associated wetlands include wood, black, mallard, and ring-necked ducks, common goldeneyes, and hooded and common mergansers. During spring and fall they are joined by flocks of migrating black, white-winged, and surf scoters, Barrow's goldeneyes, and greater scaups. Belted kingfishers, secretive American bitterns, and great blue herons frequent these areas as well. Another uncommon species that resides here is the rusty blackbird, which favors boggy and shrubby wetlands, especially in areas that have not been disturbed by humans.

The spruce-fir woodlands that border the lake support state-listed northern harriers and a variety of boreal species that are uncommon in New Hampshire, including spruce grouse, black-backed woodpeckers, gray jays, and white-throated sparrows. In spring and summer roughly 25 varieties of woodland warblers use these forests for resting or breeding grounds. Vagrants that have been seen here include great egrets, snowy owls, summer tanagers, and northern three-toed woodpeckers.

Anything but uncommon are moose, which are regularly seen throughout the refuge and along Route 16, particularly when feeding on aquatic vegetation and in muddy wallows during the summer months. Other familiar wetland mammals include beavers, river otters, mink, and muskrats, while white-tailed deer, black bears, pine martens, and bobcat roam the forests.

Amphibians include mink, leopard, green and gray tree frogs, and spring, dusky, two-lined, and blue-spotted salamanders; the latter are distinguished by their flecks of blue and white spots on their dark blue-black bodies.

Perhaps the best way to explore this area and see a wide variety of wildlife is by canoe or kayak; the refuge is part of the 370-mile Northern Forest
Canoe Trail, and a car-top boat launch is located on Route 16, 3 miles north
of the refuge office. Several recommended routes that range from 4 to 14
miles in length are detailed on a map that, along with other information, is
available at the office and on the refuge's website. A public boat launch is
located off Route 26 in the town of Cambridge at Sargent Cove just west of
the Maine state line, and there are numerous campgrounds and campsites
along the lakeshore.

As of this writing, there is just one foot trail, a 0.3-mile universally accessible path that begins at a parking area 1 mile north of the refuge office
and leads to a viewing platform along the backwaters of the Magalloway
River, but more are planned for the near future. Moose and other wildlife
can often be seen from Route 16, which follows the edge of the river and
the adjacent Thirteen Mile Woods to the south.

 ## Wapack Range: Pack and North Pack Monadnock Mountains

New Hampshire Division of Parks and Recreation, 603-924-3672;
www.nhstateparks.com/miller (Miller State Park), www.fws.gov (Wapack
National Wildlife Refuge)

CLOSEST TOWNS: Greenfield, New Ipswich

DIRECTIONS: For Pack Monadnock Mountain and Miller State Park, from the
center of Peterborough follow NH 101 east for 3 miles to the park entrance
on the north side of the highway, where a $3 fee is charged. For North
Pack, from NH 101 just west of Miller State Park bear north on Old Mountain
Road for 0.6 mile, then right on East Mountain Road. After 2.4 miles turn
right on Sand Hill Road (which becomes another Old Mountain Road) and
follow the road as it bears left, then right, for 1.5 miles to the Wapack Trail
parking area.

Rising out of southern New Hampshire's uplands is the 21-mile-long
ridge of the Wapack Mountains, a chain of low summits that stretches from
Mount Watatic on the Massachusetts state line to North Pack Monadnock
in the town of Greenfield. Here open overlooks offer long views across central New England to the distant White Mountains and Green Mountains,
the Berkshire Hills, and the tall buildings of Boston across the coastal
plain. Stone walls that mark former sheep pastures testify to the extent

that this region was once cleared for agriculture, even along the heights of these rocky slopes.

At the northern end of the ridge are its two highest eminences, sisters Pack and North Pack Monadnock mountains, 2,290 and 2,276 feet respectively. The former is home to Miller State Park, where an auto road provides easy access to picnic areas, lookouts (including a viewpoint where Mount Washington can be glimpsed on very clear days), and a raptor observation area where migration studies are conducted. The bulk of neighboring North Pack lies within the 1,672-acre Wapack National Wildlife Refuge, which encompasses the only mountaintop habitat within the New England national wildlife refuge network.

While both mountains are home to forests, rocky ridges, and wetlands that benefit a variety of creatures, they are best known among naturalists for what passes above them. During autumn and spring migrations, the range is one of New England's premiere raptor viewing sites, as it lies in the heart of a heavily traveled corridor where hills and low mountains provide abundant thermal lift for migrants.

VIEWING

In terms of sheer numbers, the best raptor viewing is during the height of the broad-winged hawk flights in mid-September, especially on clear days following the passage of a front with a wind from the northwest. Bald eagles, osprey, and sharp-shinned and Cooper's hawks are among the other raptors regularly seen from the open overlooks during this time. Though the overall numbers drop off thereafter, the viewing season continues into November. Even if your visit falls outside the migratory period, you may well see common ravens, red-tailed hawks, and turkey vultures soaring along and above the rocky ledges.

Over the past century, maturing forests have gradually reclaimed the old pastures and today provide food and cover for moose, black bears, white-tailed deer, gray foxes, and fishers, all of which were once nearly eliminated from this landscape but are now thriving in the again-abundant woodlands. Though glimpses of fishers are quite rare, a winter tracking trip may reveal a wealth of tracks and sign along the old stone walls, including buried kills or even a body imprint marking where one jumped out of a tall tree into the snow below. Large, oval-shaped cavities in dead trees mark areas that have been excavated by crow-size red-crested pileated woodpeckers; fresh chips on the ground below indicate a recent visit.

The forests also are used by migratory songbirds, including a number of woodland warblers and other species that breed throughout the late spring and summer months. Dark-eyed juncos, cedar waxwings, white-throated sparrows, pine grosbeaks, and winter wrens are often present in high-elevation spruce groves.

Check the grassy openings along the ridge and trail edges for smooth green snakes, which are named for their light green camouflage that enables them to easily blend into low vegetation. Dragonflies and butterflies favor these sunlit areas as well; watch for swarms of darner and meadow-hawk dragonflies circling overhead during late-summer feeding forays.

GETTING AROUND

Pack Monadnock's 1.3-mile auto road is open from May to early November. The mountain's hiking trails include a segment of the long-distance Wapack Trail that begins at the Miller State Park entrance and reaches the summit in 1.4 miles, gaining roughly 850 feet from the trailhead. The nearby Marion Davis Trail, which is also 1.4 miles long, branches to the right at the parking area and ascends to the east of the auto road, briefly leaving the state park before reaching the summit. These routes are often combined as a loop that takes roughly two hours to complete. A third option is the Raymond Trail, which begins outside the state park on East Mountain Road and makes a 1.6-mile climb up the west slopes. The red-blazed Summit Loop Trail connects all these paths and makes an easy 0.4-mile circuit around the top, passing several lookouts and the raptor viewing area.

The most direct route up North Pack is via the trailhead on Old Mountain Road, where the Wapack Trail rises easily past stone walls and a stream crossing to a rock ledge, then steepens as it ascends to the mountain's partially open top at 1.5 miles. An interesting side route is the blue-blazed Cliff Trail, a 1.2-mile spur that leads to a fine panoramic view from open ledges, then traverses steep, rugged terrain along the east slopes before rejoining the Wapack Trail (those wishing to avoid the lower portion can follow the trail from the summit to the vista, then double back).

Both summits are connected by a 2.3-mile segment of the Wapack Trail, which follows rolling, rocky terrain as it passes through a parcel of land owned by the Nature Conservancy and leads through the heart of the national wildlife refuge. The round-trip hike from the base of Pack Monadnock to North Pack and back is 7.4 miles. From the opposite direction it is 7.6 miles from Mountain Road to Pack's summit and back. Allow four to five hours for either outing.

RHODE ISLAND

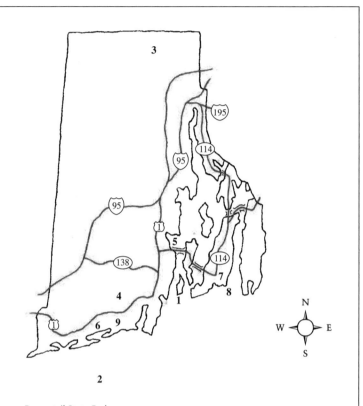

1. Beavertail State Park
2. Block Island
3. Fort Nature Refuge
4. Great Swamp Wildlife Management Area
5. John H. Chafee Nature Preserve at Rome Point
6. Ninigret National Wildlife Refuge
7. Norman Bird Sanctuary
8. Sachuest Point National Wildlife Refuge
9. Trustholm Pond National Wildlife Refuge

RHODE ISLAND

Beavertail State Park

Rhode Island Division of Parks and Recreation, 401-884-2010,
www.riparks.com/beavertail

CLOSEST TOWN: Jamestown

DIRECTIONS: From the junction of US 1 and RI 138 in Kingston take RI 138 east across the Jamestown Bridge (from Newport follow RI 138 west across the Newport-Pell Bridge). After the crossing, take the Jamestown exit and continue for 1.2 miles to a stop sign near the waterfront. Turn right on Narragansett Avenue, then left on Southwest Avenue and follow the latter south to its end at the park entrance, 5 miles from the RI 138 exit.

At the southern tip of Conanicut Island, the second-largest of Narragansett Bay's numerous islands, are rocky bluffs that offer sweeping views of Rhode Island Sound and the south coastal region. In 1749 one of America's first lighthouses was erected here to mark a safe passage through this hazardous area, where many shipwrecks have occurred over the centuries.

Though this structure and other buildings were destroyed by the British during an American Revolution raid in 1779, its successors, including the present Jamestown Lighthouse, have survived numerous storms, including the hurricane of September 1938, which unearthed part of a mid-nineteenth-century shipwreck.

Today, the point and lighthouse are part of 138-acre Beavertail State Park, which is renowned for its wildlife, ocean views, and saltwater fishing. In all seasons a variety of wildlife, ranging from gray seals and harlequin ducks to songbirds, can be observed from the bluffs and beaches. Additional habitats within this compact, easily accessible preserve include a patchwork of open grassy clearings, shrubby areas, and woodlands. A small nature center includes several aquariums, where a variety of native wildlife, ranging from snakes to juvenile dogfish sharks, can be viewed, and the adjacent lighthouse museum is also open during the summer months.

VIEWING

From the top of the bluffs scan the bay carefully for glimpses of marine mammals such as dolphins, dogfish sharks, blue sharks, and harbor porpoises. Among the more conspicuous marine mammals here are gray seals, which even when well offshore are easily identified by their prominent, horse-shaped heads, which are much larger than those of harbor seals. There is abundant tide pool habitat here for sea stars, starfish, crabs, shellfish, sea anemones, and other distinctive creatures. Striped bass and spearfish are among the species sought by saltwater anglers.

These rocky, active waters are ideal habitat for wintering harlequin ducks, and a group of roughly 20 individuals has frequented Beavertail's bluffs and coves since 2000. Other wintering seabirds include razorbills, dovekies, common murres, scoters, common eider ducks, common and red-throated loons, and flocks of purple sandpipers; irregular visitors such as snowy owls and northern harriers may also be seen during this time.

The grassy areas and shrubs are visited by a wide variety of perching birds, including northern flickers, vireos, goldfinches, mockingbirds, eastern towhees, and gray catbirds. White-tailed deer are common here; watch for all-white (albino) or partially white (piebald) individuals that are periodically seen. Ospreys nest near the center of the park, and turkey vultures are frequently spotted overhead during the warm months. Coyotes are relative newcomers to Rhode Island, having reached the state during the late 1970s, but have spread throughout Conanicut Island and the rest of the south coast. The most visible reptiles and amphibians here are milk and garter snakes and painted and snapping turtles.

GETTING AROUND

The park's 1.2-mile loop road, which includes four main parking areas, provides easy access to the bluffs and lighthouse area. Short, unmarked paths from lots 1 and 4 lead through a mix of open and brushy habitats en route to the shore, and the auto road itself can be walked as a circuit. Explorers should use caution along the cliffs and beach and be alert for waves and slippery areas, especially during or after high tides and inclement weather. The park is open year-round; the nature center is open 9 to 5 from April into October, and the lighthouse museum is open during the summer months (call ahead to confirm hours).

Block Island

Various; www.fws.gov (Block Island National Wildlife Refuge)

CLOSEST TOWN: New Shoreham

DIRECTIONS: Block Island is served year-round by ferry from Point Judith and seasonally from Providence, Newport, and New London. The easiest way to get around the island is by bicycle, as the various trailheads can be reached by fairly short rides on town roads; the ferry charges more than $70 per car.

The relatively quiet spring and fall months are ideal for a visit, as the island is much more crowded during July and August.

To reach Rodman's Hollow, from New Shoreham center follow Pilot Road to a right on the Mohegan Trail, then continue for 1 mile past the bluffs to a right on Lakeside Drive. Follow Lakeside Drive for 1 mile, then bear left on Cooneymus Road and continue for 0.7 mile to the parking area on the right-hand side of the road.

For the national wildlife refuge and Clay Head areas, bear right at the ferry terminal and continue to the first stop sign, then turn right on Corn Neck Road. Follow Corn Neck Road for 3.3 miles to a dirt road on the right that leads to the Clay Head parking area, and 4 miles to the refuge parking area at the road's end.

The Kettle Pond Visitor Center in Charlestown serves as the visitor center for the Rhode Island national wildlife refuges; see directions under the Ninigret National Wildlife Refuge listing.

Described by Italian explorer Giovanni da Verrazano in 1524 as "a triangular shaped island full of hills, covered in trees and highly populated to judge by the fires we saw continually burning on the shore" and now designated by the Nature Conservancy as a "Last Great Place," picturesque Block Island lies 12 miles off Rhode Island's south coast. The island has a largely rural character, with a year-round population of 800 and little development outside the town of New Shoreham; nearly one-third of its 11-square-mile landscape of ocean bluffs, beaches, hills, wetlands, and glacial valleys is protected. Great Salt Pond, with an inlet to Block Island Sound on the west shore, nearly divides the island in half, and there are hundreds of smaller freshwater ponds.

Rising as high as 185 feet above the southeast shores are the dramatic Mohegan Bluffs, which are constantly reshaped by wind and surf; because of erosion, the brick Southeast Lighthouse was moved 200 feet inland in 1993. A short distance west of the bluffs is Rodman's Hollow, a brushy glacial depression with abundant arrowwood, bayberry, and shadbush where trails drop below sea level and wind across knolls with fine views. The protection of this 230-acre area by the Nature Conservancy during the 1970s triggered a host of successful conservation projects across the island.

The island's northern tip is part of the Block Island National Wildlife Refuge, whose 127 acres include beaches bordered by 40-foot dunes, thickets of bayberry and beach plum, 105-acre Sachem Pond and other freshwater wetlands, and Sandy Point. First established as a 30-acre transfer from the Coast Guard in 1973, the refuge has steadily expanded to its present size via a series of subsequent purchases and easements. The North Lighthouse presides over Cow's Cove just south of the point. Nearby Clay Head, named for its tall clay ocean cliffs, is another excellent wildlife area with cobble beaches, a salt marsh, and views of a farm pasture.

VIEWING

Thanks to its varied habitats and location on the Atlantic Flyway, the island offers outstanding bird-watching during the fall, when more than 150 species are generally seen on weekend counts. In early October the island comes alive as a rest area for great numbers of southbound migratory songbirds; more than 70 species, on average, visit the wildlife refuge annually. Many of these are younger fliers that stop on the island after overflying the mainland coast. A signature resident of the ocean bluffs is the bank swallow, which lives in narrow holes dug into the soft soils of the cliffs. Threatened piping plovers nest on the sands of the wildlife refuge beaches, which are also the domain of colorful American oystercatchers. Overhead soar birds of prey such as peregrine falcons and uncommon barn owls. In winter watch for snow buntings along the dunes and beaches.

Joining the birds in the cold-weather exodus from the Northeast are throngs of monarch butterflies; the individuals that undertake the journey to the mountains of Mexico are from a hardy, long-lived generation that survives as long as eight months. In some years swarms of migrating common green darners and other dragonflies may also be seen passing overhead. Common throughout the summer months are tiger swallowtails, cabbage whites, and other species.

A much less common insect found here is the American burying beetle; in fact the island hosts one of only two known North American populations of this unique species. Also known as the giant carrion beetle, thanks to its practice of moving and burying carcasses of juvenile birds (such as woodcock and pheasant chicks) and small mammals as part of its reproductive process, American burying beetles were once widespread throughout the eastern and Midwestern states but disappeared from all but a few locations by the 1920s. It is believed that widespread forest fragmentation and suburbanization reduced populations of carrion species and promoted scavengers such as foxes and coyotes, all but eliminating the beetle's reproductive capability. Adults range in size from 1 to 1.4 inches and are identified by their black bodies and wings splotched with red and orange markings.

After being absent since the nineteenth century, white-tailed deer were reintroduced to the island in 1967, when four does and a buck arrived on the ferry. With mild winters, an abundance of brushy habitat, and no predators, the herd rapidly grew to the point that nuisance encounters and Lyme disease were regularly reported. Other mammals include muskrats, striped skunks, meadow voles, shrews, and mice; familiar adaptable species such as coyotes, squirrels, possums, and raccoons are not present. Check freshwater wetlands such as Sachem Pond at the national wildlife refuge and other freshwater wetlands for snapping and painted turtles.

From the ocean overlooks and the ferry, scan the offshore waters for Cory's, sooty, Manx, and greater shearwaters and Wilson's and Leach's storm petrels during the warm months. Of these hardy ocean birds, only the latter breeds in New England, at a handful of locations along the coast, though at least one record exists of a nesting Manx shearwater. In winter watch for waterfowl such as loons, grebes, and scoters. Minke, fin, and humpback whales are present in the waters surrounding the island, while leatherback sea turtles periodically are stranded on the shores.

GETTING AROUND

The main trail at the Block Island National Wildlife Refuge is a one-way beach road that begins at Settlers Rock at the entrance and continues west past Sachem Pond and the dunes along Cow Cove, reaching the lighthouse in 0.5 mile and its end at Sandy Point at 0.75 mile.

A dozen miles of trails wind across nearby Clay Head, many of which are part of an unmarked network appropriately known as the Maze. The Clay Head Trail passes a salt marsh known as Clay Head Swamp and the Littlefield Farm pasture before reaching the shore at 0.3 mile, with fine views of the cliffs. The main route continues north along the shore, passing side trails on the left, before ending at 1.5 miles, though one can continue north to Corn Neck Road just south of Settlers Rock at the refuge.

At Rodman's Hollow several paths form a 3.7-mile circuit that begins along Black Rock Road. This old jeep road leads south, passing a dirt road on the left at 0.8 mile before ending near the bluffs, 1 mile from the trailhead. Backtrack to the dirt road and continue for another mile to a left on the Mohegan Trail, then follow Lakeside Drive for a third mile-long segment that leads past Seneca Swamp, Fresh Pond, and several small ponds. Complete the loop by bearing left at Fresh Pond on the greenway trail, which returns to the entrance in 0.7 mile. A shorter option is a half-mile loop that leads to an overlook with a fine view.

Fort Nature Refuge

Audubon Society of Rhode Island, 401-949-5454,
www.asri.org/refuges/fort-nature-refuge

CLOSEST TOWN: North Smithfield

DIRECTIONS: From RI 146 in Woonsocket take the RI 104 exit and follow RI 104 south for 1.8 miles to its junction with RI 5. Turn north on RI 5 and continue for 0.6 mile to the marked entrance on the left (west) side of the highway.

Less known and visited than the popular coastal region, Rhode Island's quiet interior is home to gently rolling hills, forests, and numerous ponds and wetlands. Well exemplifying this landscape are the 235 acres of the Fort Nature Refuge, which is situated a short distance northwest of the greater Providence area. It has the feel of a much larger place, as backcountry trails explore mixed forests of oak and pine and a series of undeveloped ponds and beaver wetlands that form the headwaters of the Woonasquatucket River. The preserve is named for the Fort family, which operated a large farm on the property during the early twentieth century, then grew Christ-

As winter winds to a close, wood frogs, distinguished by their quacklike call, emerge at woodland vernal pools.

mas trees on the site. Today, stone walls and subtle differences in forest age and composition are the only evidence of the old fields, orchards, and tree farm. The property was donated to the Audubon Society of Rhode Island in 1978.

VIEWING

The Yellow and Red trails offer close-up views of beaver activity along the pond shores, including cut and downed trees of all sizes. River otters, mink, and muskrats are all common in these wetlands, and the muddy pond edges often record the narrow, fingerlike tracks of raccoons. Among the most distinctive of the waterfowl that use the ponds are hooded mergansers; males are easily identified by their large, white, fan-shaped crests. The bulk of the "hoodies" seen in Rhode Island are midautumn and early spring migrants, though the sanctuary lies along the southern extent of their breeding range in New England. Nesting boxes are used by wood ducks, which may be seen at any of the ponds.

In the pine groves along the woodland trails look for areas of disturbed leaf litter or snow that are evidence of deer beds. Evergreens such as pines and hemlock serve a valuable purpose for deer during winter by providing food, cover, and facilitating travel through snow. Groups of deer often sleep or rest with individuals facing in different directions to better detect threats. Also common in the forest are eastern cottontails, eastern chipmunks, and red, gray, and flying squirrels. The latter, which actually glide for distances up to 200 feet, are primarily nocturnal creatures that den in small tree cavities and feed mostly on insects. These small mammals serve as prey species for eastern coyotes and fishers, both of which are relative newcomers to Rhode Island: coyotes arrived during the late 1970s, and fishers have spread south into the state over the past quarter century. Keep an eye out for moose, which are common in neighboring Massachusetts and have also been expanding toward the south coast in recent years. Following the spring thaw, wood frogs and spotted salamanders use vernal pools for breeding grounds; several wet areas are evident along the Blue Trail near the parking area.

In winter watch for flocks of pine siskins, which favor the refuge's mixed and coniferous woodlands. These finches, which are distinguished by their brown-streaked body and their yellow wing bars, are year-round residents in Maine, New Hampshire, and Vermont and are present in southern New England during the winter, when large groups often visit bird feeders. Migratory songbirds arrive in spring; Nashville, blackburnian, and black and white warblers and northern waterthrushes are among the species that thrive in the mixed and moist woods.

The power line clearing north of the junction of the Blue and Yellow trails serves as open meadow habitat that benefits a number of species, including wild turkeys and ruffed grouse, which favor forest-field edges. In late summer, monarch butterflies pause to feed here during the course of their migrations.

GETTING AROUND

The sanctuary's well-blazed trails are suited to wildlife observation and nature study in all seasons, as hunting, dogs, bicycles, horses, and jogging are all prohibited. The Blue Trail is the main loop that provides access from the entrance to the outer Yellow and Red trails. The 3.75-mile outing that combines all three is strongly recommended, as this route offers fine views of the ponds and wetlands in the northern portion of the refuge; if you prefer a shorter outing, any portion of the Yellow and Red trails may be omitted. It takes 2 to 2.5 hours to walk the full route, plus additional time for viewing.

From the entrance follow the Blue Trail to the start of a fork where the loop begins. Bear right to follow the trail through moist woods and vernal pools for 0.5 mile (15 minutes) to a side path that offers a quick detour to the south shores of the first pond. From here the Blue Trail continues northerly past the White Trail cutoff path, then turns sharply left and arrives at the junction with the Yellow Trail. Here you can follow the Blue Loop back to the trailhead or make the detour to explore the ponds and wetlands along the Yellow and Red trails.

From the junction the one-way Yellow Trail leads through a power line clearing, then continues straight (a utility road bears left here) through a hemlock grove to the edge of the middle pond. There are fine views as the path skirts the south and east shores before ending at the start of the Red Trail loop, 15 minutes from the Blue Trail junction. The Red Trail then bears left at two successive junctions. At the second fork bear right off the main loop and follow the one-way path on an easy, quarter-mile detour that offers fine views of the third pond. To complete the outing, backtrack to the Red Trail and go right to complete the loop, then follow the Yellow Trail back to the Blue Trail junction. Turn right and follow the latter as it winds south and east through pine groves and along low ridges back to the junction near the trailhead, then bear right again to reach the nearby entrance.

Great Swamp Wildlife Management Area

Rhode Island Division of Fish and Wildlife, 401-222-6800, www.dem.ri.gov
CLOSEST TOWN: South Kingston
DIRECTIONS: From the junction of RI 2 and RI 138 near West Kingstown village
drive east on RI 138 for 1.4 miles to a sharp right turn on Liberty Lane at a sign
for the refuge. Follow Liberty Lane for 1.5 miles to the refuge headquarters,
bearing left at railroad tracks. From the headquarters continue another 0.5
mile along the dirt road to the parking area and gate.

From ospreys and box turtles to butterflies and dragonflies, wildlife of all
sorts abounds throughout the Great Swamp Management Area, where old
roads and footpaths traverse a mix of diverse habitats. Extensive wetlands
within the watershed of the Pawcatuck River make up roughly two-thirds
of this 3,350-acre preserve, including red maple, cedar, and shrub swamps,
shallow and deep marshes, brooks and streams, and a 138-acre impoundment. These are bordered by 900 acres of upland forests dominated by
oak, maple, and birch, which are interspersed with roughly 200 acres of
brushy, grassy, and agricultural fields of various sizes. This diversity makes
for especially good birding, with abundant waterfowl, grassland birds, and
woodland warblers. The swamp is historically significant as the site of a
fierce conflict during King Philip's War in December 1675 that effectively
ended the local power of the Narragansett tribe.

VIEWING

With its extensive wetlands and fields, Great Swamp is an excellent place
to watch insects. An especially visible butterfly here in the late spring and
summer is the red-spotted purple, which features dark blue wings lined
with lighter bands. Though it was once considered a separate species from
the equally beautiful white admiral, which is common in northern and
western New England, both are now considered variants of a single species known as the red-spotted admiral. Dragonflies such as chalk-fronted
corporals, dot-tailed whitefaces, darners, and meadowhawks are common
along openings and edges from late April into November, and several species of tiny bluet damselflies frequent the vegetation along the shores of
the impoundment.

The large osprey nests atop utility poles near the impoundment's southwest corner are a popular attraction and are easily viewed from the dike
road. In early spring and autumn, migrating waterfowl such as buffleheads,

greater and lesser scaups, mergansers, and ruddy ducks use the wetlands as a rest area while en route to and from northern breeding grounds, while mallards, black ducks, and wood ducks are present throughout the spring and summer. Scan the marshy areas for beavers, raccoons, muskrat, mink, and river otters. Red-winged blackbirds, eastern kingbirds, and tree swallows make acrobatic twists and dives while hunting insects over the wetlands.

In the meadows and woodlands look carefully for the distinctive yellow- or orange-patterned shell of the eastern box turtle, which spends much of its life on land but periodically basks in puddles, vernal pools, and muddy wallows. The odds of a sighting are best early in the morning or after a storm, when the grass is wet. Individual box turtles may live for more than a century.

The upland field-forest mosaic is ideal habitat for white-tailed deer, as well as predators such as eastern coyotes and red and gray foxes, which hunt eastern cottontail rabbits, gray squirrels, mice, and voles in the openings and their associated edges. Game birds here include wild turkeys, bobwhite quail, ruffed grouse, American woodcock, and ring-necked pheasants. The latter is not a native species, as it was introduced from Asia during the nineteenth century. Though some individuals are able to survive in the wild for extended periods, most succumb quickly to hunters and cold winters, and populations are generally sustained by yearly releases at wildlife management areas. Songbirds that benefit from these clearings include indigo buntings, bobolinks, eastern meadowlarks, field sparrows, and tree swallows.

GETTING AROUND

A network of dirt and gravel roads and trails offers easy walking and viewing of the various habitats. Because these paths are unmarked and unnamed, a map is recommended for first-time visitors, particularly those wishing to explore the Worden Pond area east of the impoundment. This area is heavily hunted in late autumn and early winter, and visiting is not advised during this time; check with the refuge office for full details. The office is open weekdays from 8:30 to 4:30.

From the main parking area follow the road beyond the gate, which soon reaches a wetland. Just beyond is the first of two forks; bear right here (the road that eventually reaches the Worden Pond area forks to the left) and continue through a succession of habitats including woods, a small brushy field, large fields, and a power line clearing. The next fork marks the beginning of the loop that encircles the impoundment. Bear right again and follow the road along the edge of the impoundment, with fine continuous views across the water for more than a mile. The road eventually curves around the impoundment's southwest corner, passing close by the utility poles and osprey nests roughly 2 miles from the parking area.

Shortly after leaving the wetland you'll reach a junction where you have the option of bearing left and continuing along the main trail past more fields and forests to the start of the loop (4-mile round-trip from the parking area) or going right to explore the potentially confusing unmarked roads and trails that lead through the woods to the shore of Worden Pond. The latter adds roughly 1.5 miles to the outing; return to the first fork via the aforementioned dirt road.

John H. Chafee Nature Preserve at Rome Point

Rhode Island Department of Environmental Management, 401-846-2577, www.riparks.com/chafee

CLOSEST TOWN: Wickford

DIRECTIONS: From the junction of combined US 1 / RI 4 and RI 138 north of Kingston, follow RI 138 east for 1.8 miles and take the RI 1A exit. Turn left at the stop sign at the end of the ramp and follow RI 1A north for 0.6 mile to the parking area on the right (east) side of the road.

As low tide approaches along the west passage of Narragansett Bay in winter, large groups of harbor seals congregate on a series of rocks a short distance offshore from Rome Point, a small, windswept promontory. Observing the seals is often entertaining, as they gradually position themselves to "haul out," to bask on the rocks after their feeding forays at high tide.

Rome Point lies within the recently created John H. Chafee Nature Preserve, which encompasses 230 acres of forest and shorefront south of Wickford harbor and west of Conanicut Island. Once home to a large population of the Narragansett tribe, this land hosted a large dairy farm, a railroad, and was proposed as the site of a nuclear power plant before being donated to the state by National Grid in 2001. In addition to the seal and shore views, visitors may explore trails along the edge of butterfly-shaped Bissel Cove, mature woodlands with groves of cedar and oak, and a utility clearing that offers brushy edge habitat and a travel corridor for wildlife. A short distance offshore from the point is Fox Island.

Seal-watchers at Rome Point on the west shores of Narragansett Bay in Rhode Island.

VIEWING

The harbor seals begin to arrive in the bay in early autumn, and though viewing is fairly reliable by the end of November, the peak time is from January to mid-April. Check tidal information for Wickford (available in newspapers, weather reports, or online) and time your visit from two hours before to two hours after low tide, when the favored haul-out rocks are exposed. Because the rocks are several hundred yards off the point, bring binoculars or a spotting scope for the best views of individuals. The seals may be less visible on days with gusty breezes from the unbuffered north, east, or south. By mid-May the majority of the seals have dispersed along the coast to the north, though some are present in the bay during the warm months.

Fifteen other marine mammals have been documented in the bay and the adjacent south coast, including gray and harp seals, Atlantic white-sided, bottlenose, and striped dolphins, and harbor porpoises. Leatherback, Kemp's ridley, and loggerhead sea turtles have also been recorded. Starfish (sea stars) are a common sight along the beach and low-tide rocks; look for individuals with various hues of red, purple, and pink. Fish include healthy populations of bluefish, striped bass, scup, and summer flounder from spring to fall, along with black sea bass, winter flounder, weakfish, and tautog.

Nearly half the birds found in Rhode Island use Narragansett Bay and its associated habitats. Double-crested cormorants are among the most visible species now, but as recently as 1980 there wasn't a single nesting pair on record at the bay. A dozen varieties of waterfowl may be seen here in winter, including common goldeneyes, eider ducks, scaups, red-breasted mergansers, and common and red-throated loons. Check Bissel Cove for large flocks of black-backed and herring gulls.

With its brushy tangle of shrubs and evergreen cover, the power line clearing is ideal habitat for coyotes, which are thriving in Rhode Island after arriving in the past quarter century. White-tailed deer and their sign are also often evident along the edges of this corridor. Thanks to the preserve's location along the relatively mild south coast, you may see birds that are absent from much of New England in winter, including hermit thrushes and gray catbirds. Songbird migration is well under way by early to mid-April; among the species that use the forests here are blue-gray gnatcatchers, scarlet tanagers, and black-throated green warblers.

GETTING AROUND

The main gravel road and unmarked footpaths (which are indicated on the map at the entrance as "single track trails") offer easy walking to the shore and through the woods. This is a popular area for dog walkers and boaters, and a midweek or early morning visit may be most enjoyable for wildlife viewers. Even if it seems calm at the entrance and along the trails, be prepared for gusty winds along the shore, especially when planning an extended stop to view the seals.

From the parking area the gravel road leads east for 0.5 mile to the bay, paralleling the power lines and descending at a gentle grade for part of the way. After about 15 or 20 minutes of walking you'll arrive at the rocky beach, with fine views of the Jamestown Bridge on the right and Rome Point to the left. Follow the beach north toward the point; at the narrow neck opposite Bissel Cove you'll see a parallel dirt path on the left that is part of the return route (and offers a more sheltered route to the point on especially windy days).

After exploring the point, find the unmarked but obvious dirt path in the woods adjacent to the shore and follow it through a grove of cedars and oaks and along the edge of Bissel Cove. Shortly after the trail leaves the water it reaches the power lines. Turn left here off the main route and follow paths that roughly parallel the left (east) side of the utility clearing. You'll soon rejoin the main road; turn right and make the 15-minute walk back to the parking area. Allow roughly an hour and a half of walking time for the 2.5-mile round-trip.

Ninigret National Wildlife Refuge

U.S. Fish and Wildlife Service, 401-364-9124, www.fws.gov/ninigret
CLOSEST TOWN: Charlestown
DIRECTIONS: From US 1 in Charlestown take either of the well-marked refuge
entrance roads on the south side of the highway. The Grassy Point Trail and
welcome signs are at the east entrance, while the west entrance provides
access to the Foster Cove Trail. Both parking lots are connected by the
Charlietown Runway Trail.

To reach the Charlestown Breachway, from the junction of Charlestown
Beach Road and Matunuck School House Road follow Charlestown Beach
Road south for 1.5 miles past the town beach parking area to the road's end
at the Breachway state beach and boat launch.

The Kettle Pond Visitor Center in Charlestown serves as the visitor
center for the Rhode Island national wildlife refuges. It is located off US 1 at
50 Bend Road in Charlestown and offers natural history exhibits, educational
programs, a gift shop, and trails. The building is open daily from 10 to 4.

In historical times the land that is now the Ninigret National Wildlife
Refuge was cleared for agriculture and grazed by herds of sheep, then was
home to a navy airfield used to train Hellcat fighter pilots during World
War II. Though artifacts of both uses, including abandoned runways and
taxiways, remain evident today, these 844 acres now encompass a variety
of natural habitats along the northeast shores of Ninigret Pond, including
shrubs, grasslands, salt marshes, a barrier beach, ponds, and upland oak-
maple forests. The westernmost portion of the refuge borders fist-shaped
Foster Cove, where a deer impact study is being conducted in the adjacent
woodlands. Low shrubs and grassy areas are slowly reclaiming the openings
around the old runways, which are now part of the refuge's trail network.

Just outside the refuge is the Charlestown Breachway, one of the four
inlets in this region that connect the ocean to coastal ponds. Motivated in
part by a desire to keep Ninigret Pond open to the sea and thus fit for oyster
cultivation, townspeople authorized the reinforcement of this natural passage into a permanent, wall-lined opening in 1904. Adjacent to the Breachway is Charlestown Beach, a popular destination of the south coast.

VIEWING

The refuge is one of the most productive bird-watching areas along the
New England coast, with 310 recorded species, including more than 20 ac-

cidentals and vagrants. Migratory waterfowl arrive at Ninigret Pond in early spring, followed by piping plovers and semipalmated plovers in April, and dunlins, greater and lesser yellowlegs, spotted sandpipers, black-bellied plovers, willets, and other shorebirds as spring progresses. During hawk migrations watch for merlins, peregrine falcons, and American kestrels over open areas, and sharp-shinned and Cooper's hawks in the woods and along field edges. Double-crested cormorants are familiar inhabitants of the pond; watch for them drying their wings while perched on rocks along the shoreline. Great egrets are easily observed stalking marshy areas and soaring overhead. Much less conspicuous are uncommon black skimmers and roseate terns, which have been seen here in midsummer.

The familiar mammals of the south coast, all of which are adaptable creatures that thrive in mixed habitats and suburban areas, are all found here, including Virginia opossums, eastern coyotes, red and gray foxes, striped skunks, and raccoons; the latter are especially common along wetland edges. White-tailed deer may be seen at any time, especially in fields and the shrubby vegetation along the old runways; watch for mothers with their spotted offspring during the summer months. The antlered bucks are somewhat shier and more of a challenge to get a good look at.

In autumn large numbers of monarch butterflies pause to rest at this well-placed coastal preserve during the course of their southbound migration. Other familiar butterflies include tiger and black swallowtails, red-spotted purples, red admirals, American ladies, and silver fritillaries.

At the Charlestown Breachway and adjacent state beach, watch for common and red-throated loons, surf and white-winged scoters, horned grebes, and long-tailed ducks in winter. With the onset of spring comes the arrival of wading birds such as green, great blue, and black-crowned night herons, great and snowy egrets, and songbirds such as common yellowthroats, yellow warblers, and tree swallows. During the summer shorebird migration scan the mudflats carefully for uncommon species such as Baird's sandpipers, American avocets, white-rumped sandpipers, and red-necked phalaropes. Large colonies of least terns nest at East Beach, which is opposite the Breachway from the state beach.

GETTING AROUND

Easy, level foot trails explore the habitats and old runways; maps are available at the entrance and are posted at trail junctions. If your time is short, the Grassy Point Trail, which begins amid the old runways at the east entrance and leads south past a small cove and beach to fine views across the north shores of Ninigret Pond, is an excellent option. From the west parking area the Foster Cove Trail makes a 1.1-mile circuit through the forest, passing a rest bench with a view of the cove.

Connecting these routes and the two entrances are the Cross Refuge and Charlietown Runway trails, which were once traversed by navy planes and now offer views of grasslands and shrublands. From its junction with the Grassy Point Trail, the former leads southwest along an old runway, then follows a wide grassy path through an extensive area of shrubs and woods. The easy Charlietown Runway Trail follows the old Runway 30 for 0.8 mile along the refuge's north boundary, passing close by adjacent Ninigret Park.

These routes may be combined as an easy 3.5-mile circuit beginning at either parking area. From the east entrance follow the Grassy Point Trail to the point, then backtrack to the beach and bear left on the connecting path that leads to the Cross Refuge Trail junction at a runway. Turn left here and follow the Cross Refuge Trail to its junction with the Foster Cove Loop. Continue straight and follow the outer half of the loop for 0.5 mile to the west parking area, then complete the hike with an easy walk along the Charlietown Runway Trail back to the east lot. Allow two hours to complete this circuit, though you'll want to allow extra time for viewing.

For those with a canoe or kayak, the boat launch just beyond the bridge on Charlestown Beach Road is recommended as a starting point for exploring the Breachway, pond, and mudflats. After putting in, stay to the left and continue through the canal; the mudflats will be visible to the right. At the refuge a launch is available at the east entrance.

Norman Bird Sanctuary

Norman Bird Sanctuary, Audubon Society of Rhode Island, 401-846-2577, www.normanbirdsanctuary.org

CLOSEST TOWN: Middletown

DIRECTIONS: From RI 24 take exit 1 and follow RI 138 south through Portsmouth. Turn left on RI 138A (Aquidneck Avenue) and continue to the first traffic light. Turn left on Green End Avenue and continue to a four-way intersection. Turn right here on Third Beach Road and continue 0.75 mile to the sanctuary entrance on the right. A $5 admission fee ($2 for children 4–13) is charged for nonmembers.

For most people a bird sanctuary along the southern New England coast doesn't conjure images of exposed, windswept ridge trails with sweeping views and stunted evergreens. Indeed, the most distinctive features of the 300-acre Norman Bird Sanctuary, which is situated in the southeast corner of Aquidneck Island a short distance from Newport, are its unique, finger-like ridges of "purgatory conglomerate" rock (commonly known as "puddinstone") that offer fine views to Rhode Island Sound, the Sachuest Point National Wildlife Refuge, and nearby Gardner and Nelson ponds, which lie just outside the sanctuary boundary. The easternmost and most-visited of the ridges is Hanging Rock; across the small valley is Red Fox Ridge.

The sanctuary's other habitats include forests of black cherry, red cedar, black locust, beech, and oak, with red maples and black gums in wet areas. Wetlands include a handful of small ponds, including the Red Maple Pond near the center of the preserve, vernal pools, streams, and salt marshes. Adjacent to the sanctuary entrance and nature center are large wildflower meadows and shrubby fields that are maintained for additional diversity.

VIEWING

The meadows are a colorful spectacle in summer, when wildflowers including asters, thistle, Queen Anne's lace, goldenrod, and jewelweed provide nourishment for ruby-throated hummingbirds and a variety of insects, including tiger swallowtail, monarch, red admiral, and red-spotted purple butterflies. Open grasslands, which were common when much of the region was cleared for agriculture during historical times but have recently been lost to forest regrowth and development, are maintained for species such as bobolinks, eastern meadowlarks, eastern bluebirds (which are often seen here during the winter months), and barn owls. House sparrows, which were introduced to North America during the mid-nineteenth century in a mistaken effort to control pests on crops (they in fact eat few insects), thrive in urban and suburban habitats and often outcompete bluebirds and swallows for nesting boxes.

White-tailed deer, striped skunks, red foxes, and eastern coyotes are among the mammals that frequent areas with mixed woods and clearings. Favored prey of the latter includes eastern cottontails, northern short-tailed shrews, meadow voles, and white-footed mice. Raccoons are common in and near wetlands.

From the open overlooks along the Hanging Rock Trail, scan Gardiner Pond for flocks of canvasbacks, ring-necked ducks, and scaups during spring and fall migrations, and check the marshy areas in the little valley between the ridges for wading birds. Over the ridges soar birds of prey such as peregrine falcons, merlins, and American kestrels.

Red Maple Pond, easily reached via the sanctuary's accessible trail, is home to mallard ducks, mute swans, and green and black-crowned night herons. Other waders found throughout wetland edges are great blue and great egrets. An early spring visit may reveal activity at vernal pools along the Nelson Pond Trail, as frogs and salamanders emerge from winter hibernation to breed. Reptiles often seen at the sanctuary include painted and snapping turtles and northern brown and eastern ribbon snakes, while green frogs and northern two-lined, red-backed, and spotted salamanders represent the amphibians. Along wetland edges and fields look for damselflies such as slender spreadwings, familiar bluets, and meadowhawks, and black saddlebag and eastern pondhawk dragonflies.

GETTING AROUND

The sanctuary grounds and visitor center are open from 9 to 5 daily; the building is closed on Sunday during the winter months. There are seven miles of walking trails that include easy loops through the fields and woods to more rugged one-way paths that traverse the ridges; all are well-marked and detailed in the sanctuary brochure. The Norman Universal (accessible) and Woodland trails explore the forests and Red Maple Pond near the visitor center; the latter is an easy 15-minute walk from the entrance. The aptly named Woodcock Trail makes a half-mile circuit through brushy old fields and clearings, while the nearby Quarry Trail leads through more fields and forest edges to a small pond.

The ridges are explored via the Hanging Rock, Red Fox, and Nelson Pond trails, all of which branch south from the center of the sanctuary. There is little elevation gain along these routes, though hikers should watch their footing while traversing the exposed ledges. The most direct route to Hanging Rock is to follow the universally accessible trail to its junction with the Woodcock Trail, then bear left and follow the boardwalk along Red Maple Swamp and the pond. After crossing a small bridge, turn left on the Hanging Rock Trail, which rises south along the ridge to its end at an overlook, 1.2 miles from the entrance. Backtrack from here to the northern end of the Hanging Rock Trail, where you can either return to the nature center or explore the other ridges.

Sachuest Point National Wildlife Refuge

U.S. Fish and Wildlife Service, 401-847-5511, www.fws.gov

CLOSEST TOWNS: Middletown, Newport

DIRECTIONS: From RI 138 at the Newport Bridge follow Miantonomi Avenue east for 0.6 mile, then continue for another 1.2 miles on Green End Avenue. Turn right on Paradise Avenue and continue for 1.3 miles to a left on Hanging Rock Road, then turn right on Sachuest Point Road for 1.5 miles to its end at the refuge entrance.

For a different perspective of the Sakonnet River, the Audubon Society of Rhode Island's Emilie Ruecker Wildlife Refuge near Tiverton protects 50 acres along the east bank upstream from the wildlife refuge. This is an especially good destination for families, as short, easy trails explore woodlands, a small field, and a pair of small peninsulas with salt marshes where colonies of fiddler crabs, wading birds, shorebirds, and waterfowl are easily observed. To reach the sanctuary, from the junction of RI 24 and RI 77 in Tiverton follow RI 77 south for 4.1 miles to a right on Seapowet Road.

With its long ocean views, colorful beaches, wildflower meadows, and varied flora and fauna (as well as some of the region's best saltwater

Colorful harlequin ducks are visible at the Sachuest Point National Wildlife Refuge and nearby Beavertail State Park during the winter months. Courtesy of Brooks Mathewson.

fishing), Sachuest Point is worth a visit in any season. But it's during winter, long after the warm-weather crowds have departed, that this rocky, windswept peninsula offers unique opportunities to observe uncommon cold-weather visitors, including a large flock of colorful harlequin ducks.

Once the site of a navy communications station, the point is now home to the 242-acre Sachuest Point National Wildlife Refuge, which was established in 1970. It is bordered by Sachuest Bay and the mouth of the Sakonnet River; Gardiner Pond and the ridges of the nearby Norman Bird Sanctuary are a short distance to the north. Easy walking trails and observation platforms offer views across the shores to the water and offshore rocks that are frequented by a number of birds; the rocky beaches offer abundant tidal pool habitat. The interior is mostly open, with grasslands and extensive brushy thickets of bayberry, sumac, and other low shrubs and vines.

VIEWING

The refuge is home to the second-largest flock (after a group that frequents Isle au Haut at Acadia National Park) of wintering harlequin ducks in New England. From November through April they are often easily observed in the coves and pockets along the east side of the peninsula or out on the open water. Other cold-weather visitors to watch for include king eiders, razorbills, surf scoters, long-tailed ducks, American wigeons, northern gannets, and purple sandpipers, and harbor and gray seals. Winter viewing isn't limited to the ocean: watch for northern harriers, snowy and short-eared owls, snow buntings, and horned larks in and above the clearings and grasslands.

More than 200 bird species have been recorded in the various habitats. The refuge was created as a stopover for migrants along the Atlantic Flyway, and during the spring and summer it hosts large congregations of shorebirds such as black-bellied and semipalmated plovers, ruddy turnstones, great cormorants, sanderlings, and common terns, which nest on the Island Rocks off the east shore. American redstarts and palm and yellow-rumped warblers are among the numerous songbirds that arrive in spring. In autumn large flocks of swallows often make for a notable spectacle, and migrating raptors are often visible overhead.

The expansive grassy and shrubby vegetation allows for easy viewing of a variety of butterflies and other insects. In late summer large numbers of southbound monarchs feed on the wildflowers along the trails and in the fields. Colorful red admirals, with distinctive orange and white wing bands, are also prominent. Red foxes and coyotes hunt these clearings in search of eastern cottontails, meadow voles, and other prey; scats may also offer evidence of berries gleaned from low shrubs. Adaptable brown snakes, which are found in a variety of habitats, including fields, forests, and urban areas, are also seen here. Watch for white-tailed deer in the clearings and along Sachuest Point Road near the entrance at dawn and dusk.

As the tides recede, check pools and pockets along the beach and in the rocks for hermit and green crabs, periwinkles, and other distinctive creatures of the intertidal zone.

GETTING AROUND

The refuge's two loop paths follow the perimeter of the peninsula above the shoreline, with long views from overlooks and observation platforms. Short paths offer easy access to the rocky beaches. Both routes, which meet near the Island Rocks lookout, may be walked individually, or combined as a 2.6-mile circuit.

The 1.2-mile, universally accessible Flint Point Trail explores the northern half of the point. At a fork just beyond the parking area, bear left to follow this trail through shrubby vegetation for a quarter mile to the observation deck at Flint Point. (For a quick, direct route to the east shore, the trail to the right reaches the bluffs in an eighth of a mile.) From the Flint Point observation deck the trail curves sharply south and continues to the Island Rocks viewing area, where a mounted spotting scope offers close-up views of the various waterfowl, shorebirds, and seals.

The 1.5-mile Ocean View Trail, which meets the Flint Point Trail at this lookout, explores the southern and western shores, with a short side path that leads to the tip of the peninsula. There are good views of the grasslands and across Sachuest and Easton bays toward Newport along this route.

Be prepared for beach traffic in the vicinity of the refuge during the summer months, and for wind during winter. With the long ocean and meadow views, good binoculars or spotting scopes are especially helpful here.

 ## Trustom Pond National Wildlife Refuge

U.S. Fish and Wildlife Service, 401-364-9124, www.fws.gov/trustompond
CLOSEST TOWN: Charlestown
DIRECTIONS: From US 1 in Charlestown east of the Ninigret National Wildlife Refuge take the Moonstone Beach Road exit, marked with a sign for the

Trustom Pond Refuge. Continue for 1 mile south to a right on Matunick Schoolhouse Road, then continue 0.7 mile to the refuge entrance and parking area on the left-hand side of the road.

The Kettle Pond Visitor Center in Charlestown serves as the visitor center for the Rhode Island national wildlife refuges; see directions under Ninigret National Wildlife Refuge listing.

The last remaining pond entirely free of development along Rhode Island's coast is 160-acre Trustom Pond, which lies a short distance east of the Ninigret National Wildlife Refuge. Primarily a freshwater pond, Trustom has a saltwater content dependent on the tides that are channeled through the narrow inlet, as well as seasonal precipitation. The pond's south shores are barely separated from Block Island Sound by Moonstone Beach, a narrow section of barrier beach that is closed to the public above the high-tide line from April 1 to September 15 during shorebird nesting season.

The pond is the centerpiece of the Trustom Pond National Wildlife Refuge, whose 787 acres provide a large buffer and offer a diversity of habitats for wildlife, including coastal woodlands of scrub oak and maple, thickets of raspberry, honeysuckle, viburnum, shadbush, highbush blueberry, and other shrubs, fresh and saltwater marshes, and a red maple swamp. Old fields and shrublands, which were once part of a farm that operated on the grounds, are now maintained to provide habitat for a variety of wildlife, including grassland birds, butterflies, and field mammals. Viewing platforms are situated at the end of Osprey and Otter points, two small, narrow peninsulas that jut into the pond from its north shores.

The species list here includes nearly 300 birds, 40 mammals, and 20 reptiles and amphibians. The bulk of the refuge was established by a private donation in 1974, and additional land was given by the Audubon Society of Rhode Island in 1982.

VIEWING

Once cleared for agriculture by English colonists, the fields adjacent to the entrance and visitor center are now maintained as open areas for the benefit of field and edge-favoring species such as white-tailed deer, which are common and may be seen at any time of the day. Though more elusive, eastern coyotes, which are fairly recent arrivals to the Rhode Island coast, may also be glimpsed making hunting rounds in these fields, especially as daylight changes at dawn, dusk, and during changing weather. Numerous butterflies feed on wildflowers here during the warm months, including tiger swallowtails, viceroys, red admirals, red-spotted purples, and monarchs, which may be seen moving south during late-summer migrations.

Also ideally suited to the refuge's mix of partially open and marshy wet areas is the purple martin (named for the dark coloration of the male), which is found locally in portions of New England, including a belt along western Rhode Island and adjacent Connecticut. Most people know this member of the overall swallow family best for the large, apartment-style birdhouses that are erected to attract nesting groups from April to September. Other grassland birds to watch for in and above the fields are eastern meadowlarks, bobolinks, eastern bluebirds, northern harriers, and short-eared owls.

Birding is spectacular here during the peak of the spring and fall migrations, as large flocks of raptors, shorebirds, songbirds, waterfowl, and wading birds all use the refuge during the course of their journeys. Threatened piping plovers and least terns arrive in April and May to nest and breed on the barrier beach. Familiar wading birds, some of which arrive as early as February, include great and snowy egrets and great blue and green herons; another species worth checking for is the glossy ibis, which is gradually expanding its range along the New England coast. The most conspicuous of the waterfowl are nonnative mute swans; as many as 200 reside in the pond. In early spring watch for hooded mergansers, northern pintails, and green-winged teal. Breeding ospreys returned to the refuge during the early 1990s; look for their large nests on platforms atop specially constructed poles. Songbirds to watch and listen for include solitary vireos, northern parulas, and Wilson's and prairie warblers; the drawn-out rising call of the latter is one of the more distinctive warbler calls.

Reptiles present include smooth green, brown, garter, and northern water snakes. Painted turtles are the most common of the resident turtles, snapping turtles the largest and most striking; the observation deck at the small Farm Pond near the entrance is a good place to check for the latter.

GETTING AROUND

The refuge offers four easy, level, well-marked foot trails that explore the central portion of the preserve, including two short peninsulas on the north shore of Trustom Pond. From the visitor center and the farm field area, the Osprey Point Trail leads south for 0.8 mile to an elevated observation platform on the pond's north shore, with fine views to Block Island Sound and the barrier beach. The slightly shorter Otter Point Trail offers a 0.6-mile walk from Farm Pond to another viewing area to the east. Connecting these routes is the 0.6-mile Red Maple Swamp Trail, which zigzags across the center of the refuge, passing an old windmill. Closer to the entrance, the Farm Field Loop makes a quick 0.5-mile circuit through the old fields and clearings adjoining the entrance.

These routes are easily combined as a 3-mile circuit that visits both of the points. To make a counterclockwise loop, from the farm field area follow the Osprey Point Trail to its end at the viewing platform, then backtrack to the nearby junction with the Red Maple Swamp Trail. Follow the latter to its end at the Otter Point Trail, then turn right and walk south for 0.5 mile to the observation platform. Complete the outing by backtracking on the Otter Pond Trail for 0.7 mile to the Farm Pond and fields at the entrance.

VERMONT

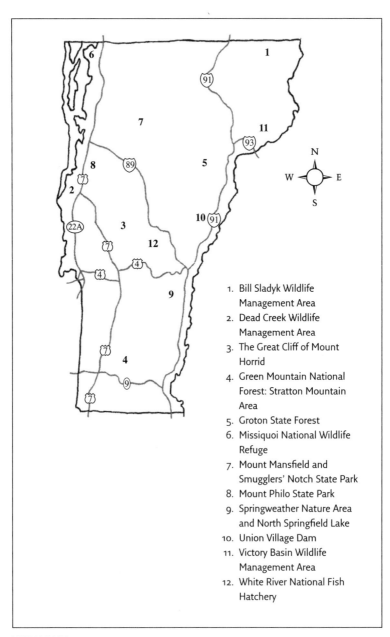

1. Bill Sladyk Wildlife
   Management Area
2. Dead Creek Wildlife
   Management Area
3. The Great Cliff of Mount
   Horrid
4. Green Mountain National
   Forest: Stratton Mountain
   Area
5. Groton State Forest
6. Missiquoi National Wildlife
   Refuge
7. Mount Mansfield and
   Smugglers' Notch State Park
8. Mount Philo State Park
9. Springweather Nature Area
   and North Springfield Lake
10. Union Village Dam
11. Victory Basin Wildlife
    Management Area
12. White River National Fish
    Hatchery

VERMONT

Bill Sladyk Wildlife Management Area

Vermont Fish and Wildlife, 802-748-8787,
www.vtfishandwildlife.com/wma_maps.cfm

CLOSEST TOWNS: Island Pond, Newport

DIRECTIONS: For the Holland Pond entrance, from VT 111 at the Seymour
Lake Lodge in Morgan turn north on Valley Road and continue toward
Holland village. After 4.7 miles, at a junction where the main road curves
left, bear right (straight) on the gravel road and continue for 2.9 miles to a
T intersection. Turn right here on Holland Pond Road and continue for 2.3
miles to the road's end at the boat ramp.

For the Hurricane Brook area, from the junction of VT 114 and VT 111 north
of Island Pond follow VT 114 north for 3.1 miles and turn left on Hurricane
Brook Road (unmarked as of this writing). Follow Hurricane Brook Road
along the edge of Norton Pond and past residences for 2 miles to the
entrance sign.

Those visiting or staying in the nearby Newport area should stop at the
boat launch at the South Bay Wildlife Management Area, which is located
on Coventry Street half a mile from the downtown traffic light. Bald eagles,
osprey, wading birds, kingfishers, and large flocks of migrating waterfowl
are all seen here, as are black terns, which in New England outside of Maine
nest only in far northwest and northeast Vermont. The waterfront of nearby
Lake Memphremagog offers more wildlife and scenic viewing opportunities.

For a remote, wild north woods experience, the Bill Sladyk Wildlife Management Area, named in memory of a former state wildlife forester, protects more than 10,000 acres of forest and wetland habitats at the tip of
the Northeast Kingdom. The preserve stretches from the northern tip of
Norton Pond to the Canadian border, which it abuts for two miles. A classic
northern forest of hardwood birches, beeches, and maples and softwood
spruce, fir, and cedar is the predominant habitat here. Within these expansive woods the state Fish and Wildlife Department has implemented
a variety of management practices for wildlife, including a patchwork of
small clear-cuts north of the Hurricane Brook entrance for ruffed grouse
and clearings with wildflowers such as black-eyed Susan, crown vetch,
goldenrod, and daisies.

Interspersed among the forests is a diverse group of wetlands, including
seven natural ponds, beaver wetlands, swamps, brooks and streams, and
peat bogs. The largest and most accessible of these is 335-acre Holland

Pond on the preserve's northwest boundary. To its north and east just south of the international border are the smaller Beaver, Round, Turtle, and Duck ponds.

VIEWING

The regenerating forest groves offer food and cover for snowshoe hares, which in turn sustain predators such as eastern coyotes, red and gray foxes, fishers, and bobcats. Forest management also benefits white-tailed deer, which are more dependent on disturbances and openings in the deep north woods than in other regions of New England. Moose, of course, thrive in this ideal combination of their favored forest and wetland habitats and unbroken travel corridors. Black bears enjoy abundant beechnuts and wetland vegetation, and plenty of remote denning sites.

Lodges, dams, cut trees, wetlands, and regenerating meadows mark the handiwork of beavers, which are common in the ponds and streams. Also benefiting from these wetlands are river otters, muskrats, mink, raccoons, and amphibians such as spring peepers and leopard, wood, green, and mink frogs. The latter is unique among New England's frogs and toads in that it is found exclusively in the northernmost regions of Vermont, New Hampshire, and Maine. Hidden beneath the numerous rocks and downed trees are dusky, blue-spotted, and red-backed salamanders. Reptiles include painted, snapping, and wood turtles. In spite of their remoteness, these ponds have been stocked with trout.

Common loons are present at Holland Pond during the warm months; boaters should be alert for areas that are closed during the early summer nesting season. Other waterfowl regularly seen, especially during early spring and late autumn migrations, are ring-necked ducks, mallards, wood ducks, mergansers, and goldeneyes.

This is a prime area for boreal forest birds such as black-backed woodpeckers, gray jays, boreal chickadees, and white-winged crossbills. The latter are named for the distinguishing white stripes on their black wings; the male's body is a pale red color, while his mate is a yellowish-brown. During some winters, flocks periodically wander south into central and southern New England. During spring and sometimes in fall you may hear the drumming courtship sound of the male ruffed grouse.

The wildflowers that bloom in the clearings and along the edges of Hurricane Brook Road sustain insects such as grasshoppers, crickets, honeybees, meadowhawk and darner dragonflies, and yellow mustard, monarch, and white admiral butterflies.

GETTING AROUND

This expansive area is traversed by nearly 50 miles of unmarked woods roads and backcountry trails. Those venturing into the interior should obtain a copy of the property map in advance (available at www .vtfishandwildlife.com/wma_maps.cfm); a compass and/or GPS is also strongly recommended.

From the southeastern entrance on Hurricane Brook Road the main dirt road leads north past a boggy wetland, a woods road that forks to the right, and a small wildflower meadow before reaching another clearing at 1.8 miles. This portion is passable by passenger car. From the clearing other trails branch off to explore the center of the preserve.

The other access area is at Holland Pond, where a boat ramp and large parking area are situated at the end of Holland Pond Road. At the north side (left, when facing the water) of the lot is a dirt road that leads past private residences for half a mile to a gate at a small parking area. From here an old road continues through the woods along the north shore of Holland Pond, providing access to trails that lead to the ponds just south of the Canadian border. For a short and straightforward outing you can follow the main route for 0.8 mile to Duck Pond by staying left at several junctions.

 ## Dead Creek Wildlife Management Area

Vermont Department of Fish and Wildlife, 802-759-2397,
www.vtfishandwildlife.com/wma_maps.cfm
CLOSEST TOWN: Addison
DIRECTIONS: From the junction of VT 22A and VT 17 in Addison follow VT 17
   west across the valley for 1.6 miles to the viewing area on the south side of
   the highway. VT 22A is a recommended scenic route to the area, with fine
   farm views, and is easily accessed from US 7, the region's major highway.
      The nearby 53-acre McCuen Slang Waterfowl Area offers easily accessible
   views of Lake Champlain and its marshy margins. It is located at the junction
   of VT 125 and Town Line Road on the Addison-Bridport line, 5.5 miles west of
   VT 22A; the Whitney-Hospital Creek Wildlife Management Area is on the north
   shore of nearby Whitney Creek.

Each autumn, upstate Vermont's bucolic Lake Champlain Valley hosts one of New England's most spectacular wildlife viewing spectacles, when large flocks of snow geese pause to rest and refuel in the region's expansive agricultural fields during the course of their southbound migration from

Migrating snow geese at rest in the fields at Dead Creek Wildlife Management Area in Vermont's Champlain Valley.

Arctic breeding grounds to wintering areas along the mid-Atlantic and Gulf coasts. The valley is an important flyway for other migrants, such as Canada geese, ducks, songbirds, shorebirds, and even monarch butterflies, all of which use the patchwork of fields, marshes, farmlands, and woodlands as a resting area.

The prime area for viewing the geese and other wildlife is Dead Creek Wildlife Management Area, a 2,900-acre mosaic of open fields and wetlands amid the expansive dairy farms east of Lake Champlain's southern tip. Here a series of impoundments along Dead Creek has created large areas of open water and marshes that benefit a variety of wildlife, especially migratory waterfowl. When water levels are lowered in summer, shorebirds benefit from exposed mudflats. The wetlands are bordered by shrubby thickets, open fields, and a lowland forest community of white, swamp white, and red oaks, shagbark hickory, and white pine.

VIEWING

The autumn snow goose migration occurs from mid-October into early November; during its peak, 20,000 individuals pass through the valley each week. Watch for large groups resting in the fields near the observation area along Route 17 and passing overhead in flight above the backdrops of the nearby Adirondack and Green mountains. While viewing the vast flocks, keep an eye out for the rare Ross's Goose, which periodically tags along and hybridizes with snow geese. It is distinguished from the snow geese by its smaller size and lack of a "grinning patch," or subtle black markings next to its beak. Large numbers of Canada geese are often seen during this time as well.

After the migrants have passed through and winter sets in, watch for snowy owls, rough-legged hawks, and other winter raptors, as well as horned larks and flocks of snow buntings. During the warm months check the marshes for elusive Virginia rails, black-crowned night herons, American and least bitterns, soras, and marsh wrens. This is a prime area for viewing waterfowl, particularly during early spring and autumn migrations; species regularly seen include blue-winged teal, northern pintails, black ducks, mallards, wood ducks, and Canada geese. Birds of prey include American kestrels, northern harriers, red-tailed hawks, and great horned and screech owls; bald eagle restoration efforts have been conducted here in recent years. Forest-field edges are frequented by wild turkeys, ruffed grouse, and American woodcock. Check open areas for grasshopper sparrows, which are listed as endangered or threatened in the New England states and breed in areas with no trees or shrubs.

Mammals of these wetlands include river otters, mink, and muskrats, which feed on the stems of abundant cattails. A familiar creature of mixed upland/aquatic habitats is the raccoon, which dens in hollow trees and may be seen scampering along wetland edges. Reptiles include northern water, garter, and milk snakes, and painted, snapping, and musk turtles. The latter, also commonly known as "stinkpots," thanks to their often musky odor, are near their northernmost limit in New England here, as they are primarily a species of low elevations. They are somewhat harder to observe than some of the other turtles, as they spend much of their time hidden amid mucky wetland edges.

GETTING AROUND

The observation area along Route 17, which is a short drive west of Addison center, is the main area for viewing the geese. This large pullout offers fine views across the fields of the valley to Snake Mountain and the distant ridges of the Adirondack and Green mountains. Geese and other wildlife may also be observed by driving the roads that branch off of Routes 17 and 22A. There is no public access to the south in the posted areas bordering the pullout.

From north to south, public boat launches are located at the end of West Road in the town of Panton just north of the Addison town line, off Goodrich Corner Road on the Addison-Panton town line, at the convergence of the East and West branches west of the observation area, and along Nortontown Road west of its junction with Route 22A south of Addison center. These are clearly marked on the management area map, which is available at www.vtfishandwildlife.com/wma_maps.cfm. Boaters should use caution when waterfowl are nesting in spring and be aware of hunters in autumn.

The Great Cliff of Mount Horrid

U.S. Forest Service, Green Mountain National Forest, 802-767-4777, www.fs.fed.us/r9/forests/greenmountain

CLOSEST TOWN: Brandon

DIRECTIONS: From the junction of VT 100 and VT 73 in Rochester follow VT 73 north for 9.7 miles. The overlook pullout is on the right (north) side of the road just before the height-of-land; the Long Trail parking area is a few hundred feet beyond on the left (south) side.

With its steep, exposed face that contrasts sharply with the surrounding rolling hills, the "Great Cliff" is one of the most distinctive natural areas of the Green Mountains and is home to a number of endangered and uncommon plant and animal species. Mount Horrid, whose forested, 3,126-foot summit lies just over a half mile by trail from the ledges, forms the east wall of Brandon Gap, one of several scenic mountain passes in the Green Mountains. Here Route 73 crosses the windswept height-of-land at an elevation of 2,170 feet. Predominant on these slopes are northern hardwood forests of maple, birch, and beech that are characteristic of the Green Mountains. At the base of the cliff lies a wildlife-rich beaver pond that is bordered by shrubby thickets and a ring of spruce trees. A roadside pullout offers a fine overview of both the cliffs and pond, allowing visitors to search for wildlife ranging from peregrine falcons to moose.

VIEWING

The Great Cliff is classic peregrine falcon habitat and has long hosted breeding pairs. They were absent from the late 1950s to the early 1980s following the DDT epidemic but were successfully reintroduced here in 1981. The viewing period runs from their arrival during early spring to August, though activity generally decreases from midsummer onward. The cliff is one of 38 known nest sites statewide as of 2009.

Abundant beech trees and rocky jumbles along Mount Horrid's slopes offer ideal food and denning habitat for black bears. Other tracks and sign to watch for along the trails include fishers, porcupines, snowshoe hares, and bobcat. Watch for white-tailed deer both in the woods and at the edge of the beaver pond. Migratory songbirds such as vireos, thrushes, veeries, and woodland warblers arrive in mid to late spring and use the forests for breeding or as a rest stop during their journeys north.

The beaver pond is a good moose-viewing site, especially early and late in the day or during the changing light of a passing storm. Watch the shrubby thickets carefully, as a moose may be nearly hidden amid the tangle of vegetation; muddy wallows along the wetland edge also may offer evidence of recent activity. Drivers should use caution in this area, as there are active moose crossings along Route 73. Beavers are also most active at the margins of daylight; bring binoculars for a close-up view of their large lodge. Listen for the loud laughing calls of pileated woodpeckers, the guttural caw of common ravens, and the much less conspicuous and higher-pitched *zee* of cedar waxwings, which feed on emergent berries in mid to late summer. Tree swallows feed on the ubiquitous insects here. All the smaller birds are potential prey for the falcons, which may reach speeds nearing 200 miles per hour on hunting dives.

GETTING AROUND

The Great Cliff and the beaver pond are easily viewed from the roadside pullout just east of the height-of-land where the Long Trail crosses Route 73. Though the cliff looks imposingly high when viewed from the road, the hike to the top is relatively easy, as it reaches the ledges in just 0.6 mile after climbing 620 feet from Brandon Gap. From the parking area at the gap's height-of-land, the Long Trail crosses the highway, then winds on a moderate ascent through groves of white birch, maple, and beech trees. After a steep but short climb over rock steps, the blue-blazed Great Cliff Trail branches to the right and soon reaches the vistas, where there are dramatic views of the gap and the surrounding Green Mountains and a bird's-eye perspective of the beaver pond. Backtrack from here for a round-trip that can be completed in as little as one hour, or continue north on the Long Trail for another 0.6 mile to Mount Horrid's wooded summit.

Like other areas that host nesting falcons, the Great Cliff Trail is closed from mid-March to early July during the breeding season, though it may open earlier if a nest proves unsuccessful. Updated trail conditions and restrictions are available at the Vermont Fish and Wildlife Department website (www.vermontfishandwildlife.com), or call 802-229-0650.

 ## Green Mountain National Forest: Stratton Mountain Area

Green Mountain National Forest, 802-747-6700,
www.fs.fed.us/r9/forests/greenmountain

CLOSEST TOWN: Stratton

DIRECTIONS: From the junction of VT 9 and VT 100 in Wilmington follow VT 100 north to West Wardsboro. After passing the town line, turn west on the Stratton–Arlington Road, also known as Kelly Stand Road. At 6.2 miles from VT 100, Grout Pond Road (FS 262) branches south and leads 1.2 miles to the day-use parking area at Grout Pond. At 6.8 miles is the parking area for the Long Trail at Stratton Mountain; the Stratton Pond trailhead is another 0.9 mile to the west.

The highest summit of the southern Green Mountains, 3,940-foot Stratton Mountain rises high enough above the surrounding mountain ridge to be considered a monadnock, or isolated peak, within the chain. In 1840 famed statesman Daniel Webster gave a well-attended speech in a meadow at its base, and in the early twentieth century, visits to the mountain helped inspire Green Mountain Club founder James P. Taylor and noted conservationist Benton MacKaye to conceive the ideas for the Long Trail and the Appalachian Trail respectively. Stratton's 70-foot summit observation tower offers views of many familiar New England peaks, including Mount Equinox and the Taconic Mountain ridge, Bromley Mountain, Mount Snow, Mount Ascutney, Mount Greylock, Mount Monadnock, Killington Peak, and, on a clear day, the tip of Mount Washington some 120 miles to the northeast. Several lakes and ponds are also visible, the largest of which is the Somerset Reservoir to the south, which serves as the headwaters for the Deerfield River.

Stratton Mountain lies within the southern division of the Green Mountain National Forest, which protects more than 350,000 acres along the chain. Three trail miles below its summit is Stratton Pond, a picturesque tarn at an elevation of 2,555 feet that is the largest and most popular water body visited by the 265-mile Long Trail. A short distance east of the mountain is Grout Pond, which offers easy trails and access to boaters. Areas of the surrounding national forest, including old orchards and clearings that

Bear-claw marks on a downed beech tree near Grout Pond in the Green Mountain National Forest southern division.

are holdovers from the area's agricultural past, are managed and maintained for the benefit of wildlife, including game species such as deer, black bear, wild turkeys, and ruffed grouse. The variety of trails and roads here makes the area a fine destination for those looking to sample the nature of the southern Green Mountains in all seasons.

VIEWING
Black bears enjoy abundant beechnuts in the forests, apples in the old orchards, and blueberries along the pond edges; evidence of their activities includes claw marks dragged into the bark of smooth-trunked beech trees and logs. On all the pond and mountain trails watch for moose and their sign, which includes droppings and incisor and antler rubs on trees; the odds of a sighting are greatest early and late in the day, when moose are most active. The trill-like call of the red squirrel is a familiar sound in conifer groves, while eastern chipmunks scamper in and out of holes and along downed logs and branches. In winter watch for tracks and sign of eastern coyotes, bobcat, fishers, pine martens, porcupines, and white-tailed deer; the latter are often seen in clearings and old orchards.

The northern hardwood-spruce forests are inhabited by many songbirds, including a number of species that generally favor northern regions of New England. Warm-weather migrants include blue-eyed vireos and blackpoll, blackburnian, and Nashville warblers, while hardy year-round residents include boreal chickadees, white-throated sparrows, and red-breasted nuthatches, which are slightly smaller than their white-breasted relatives and prefer conifer forests. This area lies within the southernmost breeding range in New England of the uncommon Bicknell's thrush; the nearly identical Swainson's thrush is also found here. From the summit viewing tower look for ravens and turkey vultures riding wind currents. Other birds of prey include northern saw-whet, great horned, and barred owls. Ruffed grouse are quite common, and walkers will likely flush at least one individual out of cover along the trails.

At Stratton and Grout ponds, common loons are present during the warm months, along with other waterfowl. Dragonflies and damselflies frequent low vegetation along wetland edges; a good place to observe them is the short boardwalk at the south end of Grout Pond. Here nesting boxes provide homes for colorful wood ducks, which have recovered strongly from declines caused by historical forest clearing and unregulated hunting.

GETTING AROUND

Grout Pond and its trails and boat launch are easily accessed from the day-use parking area. The pond's 2.7-mile loop trail begins near the entrance as a wide path that leads past the campsites along the north shore, then narrows and follows a series of log bridges over wet areas. A beaver lodge is visible at a small opening where the trail crosses the pond's outlet, and a short boardwalk traverses a boggy area. At 1.6 miles the trail meets the East Loop and Hill trails at a four-way junction; turn right here and follow the path above the southwest shores. At another junction with several paths, bear right and continue past cabins to the entrance road, then follow the road for 0.2 mile to the parking area. Other trails explore the surrounding woods and hills, including a route that leads southwest to the nearby Somerset Reservoir.

Stratton Mountain and Stratton Pond may be explored individually, or by a full-day circuit of 11.7 miles. The route to Stratton Mountain's summit is relatively gentle by the standard of other New England mountains of similar heights, as it gains 1,730 feet over 3.8 miles. From the trailhead on Kelly Stand Road the combined Long and Appalachian trails climb easily for 1.4 miles to a crossing of Forest Service Road 341, then make a steeper ascent up the southeast slopes to the summit observation tower. Here hikers have the option of backtracking or continuing the long loop by descending 3.2 miles to Stratton Pond. During the summer and fall months gondola rides to the summit are available at the ski area (contact the resort at 800-787-2886 for more information).

The Stratton Pond Trail begins on Kelly Stand Road at a trailhead 0.9 mile west of the Stratton Mountain Trail. This blue-blazed route rises easily through mixed woods for 3.9 miles to meet the Long/Appalachian trails near the pond's southeast corner. The pond can be fully circled by following the Long, Lye Brook, and North Shore trails along its perimeter; doing so adds an extra 1.5 miles to the outing. From the latter, boardwalks allow views of the pond's boggy and marshy edges. Designated campsites and a shelter ($6-a-night fee) are available at the pond.

Groton State Forest

Vermont Department of Forests, Parks, and Recreation, 802-241-3655, www.vtstateparks.com

CLOSEST TOWN: Groton

DIRECTIONS: From the junction of US 302 and VT 232 two miles west of Groton turn north on VT 232 and continue for 5 miles. Turn right on Boulder Beach Road to reach the nature center trails and the state parks adjacent to Lake Groton. For the Owl's Head, continue north on VT 232 for another 2.6 miles and look for the marked access road on the right.

At the southern edge of the Northeast Kingdom between the Connecticut River Valley and the Green Mountains lies the Groton State Forest, one of Vermont's largest and most diverse natural areas. Among the many attractions of this 26,000-acre expanse is kidney-shaped Peacham Bog, a 200-acre raised black spruce and tamarack bog with peat domes and unusual flora such as northern pitcher plants, sheep laurel, and leatherleaf. Surrounding the bog, which is one of the largest examples of this habitat in the state, is a 750-acre natural area that serves as a buffer for this fragile environment. The largest of the other wetlands is finger-shaped, 423-acre Lake Groton, the shoreline of which is mostly privately owned. Smaller ponds include Kettle Pond along the western boundary, Osmore Pond, which includes a picnic area and boat rental, and Ricker Pond below Lake Groton; all offer fine trout fishing.

Rising above these wetlands are rolling hills and low mountains that are geologic extensions of the nearby White Mountains. Thanks to an auto road that provides easy access to summit views, the most popular of these is the 1,953-foot Owl's Head, which offers fine views, from Lake Groton below to the profile of Camel's Hump along the ridge of the Green Mountains. The nearby Big Deer and Little Deer mountains, 1,992 and 1,760 feet respectively, offer more vistas.

The forests here, which include groves of maple, birch, beech, spruce, fir, and pine, have recovered from centuries of human and natural disturbances. The area was extensively logged through the 1920s, especially following the opening of a railroad in 1873. Several large fires, ice storms, and the hurricane of 1938 have also impacted these woodlands, though a 25-acre pocket of old-growth hemlock and hardwoods on the slopes of Lord's Hill has survived all these disturbances. The forest is now managed for multiple purposes, including wildlife habitat, human recreation, and sustainable forestry.

VIEWING

During the warm months watch for moose feeding along wetland edges, in ponds, and in clearings (they sometimes use the boardwalk at Peacham Bog). They are somewhat less visible in winter, when they spend most of their time in wooded areas at higher elevations feeding on hardwood and softwood trees. White-tailed deer are common in the forest, especially in areas that offer softwood cover and young hardwood sprouts as a food source. One of the favored food trees for both deer and moose is striped maple, an understory tree that is also known as moosewood. Black bears and bobcat are also present but more elusive. From the pond trails, scan the water and shoreline for beavers and muskrats; raccoon tracks are often evident along muddy edges. In winter, tracks of fishers, river otters, and mink reveal the high activity levels of these energetic weasels.

All the trails have fine birding potential, as more than 100 species have been recorded in the various habitats. Some familiar residents include red-breasted nuthatches, winter wrens, common ravens, and golden-crowned kinglets, whose soft, high-toned whistle can be a challenge for some birders to hear. Northern species such as boreal chickadees and black-backed woodpeckers inhabit groves of evergreen spruces, firs, and pines. The first experience of flushing a well-camouflaged ruffed grouse can be rather startling, as they often wait until humans are almost on top of them before scattering in a jumble of sound. In late spring and early summer the forests offer habitat for many migratory songbirds, including more than 15 wood warbler species, 5 varieties of flycatchers, and hermit and wood thrushes. Watch for common loons at Kettle Pond and Lake Groton. Red-tailed and broad-winged hawks and barred owls are among the birds of prey that nest on the grounds, and in late summer and early fall Owl's Head and the other mountain summits offer fine views of migrating raptors.

GETTING AROUND

The state forest offers trails of all lengths for a variety of recreational users. A detailed park map and informative natural history pamphlets and interpretive guides are available at contact stations. Within the overall preserve are small state parks that administer the various camping and swimming beach areas.

Several trails originate from the nature center parking area on Boulder Beach Road, including the 4.5-mile circuit that visits Peacham Bog. This is a good route in late spring and early summer, when songbirds and moose are active and forest and bog wildflowers are in bloom. This well-marked, mostly easy trail, which gains roughly 450 feet, branches off the Little Loop and Coldwater Brook trails near the entrance and winds east through the woods, reaching the bog boardwalk and viewing deck at 2 miles. It then curves west near the park boundary to begin the return leg, which leads back to Coldwater Brook Road. Allow from three to three and a half hours for the full circuit.

For those looking for a shorter outing in this area, the 0.9-mile Little Loop follows a ravine above a stream to views of another boggy wetland, then traverses gently rolling terrain through the woods as it returns to the parking lot.

At Kettle Pond a universally accessible path at the day-use parking area offers a short walk to shore views from a boat portage. From here the pond's 3-mile loop trail continues along the north shore over periodically wet and rocky terrain. After a short boardwalk, it traverses drier ground, then becomes rocky again as it curves to follow the south shore. After leading through a jumble of moss-covered boulders it continues east to its end at the group camping area; a short walk along the access road and Route 232 leads back to the trailhead. Other pond circuits include a scenic 2-mile loop around Osmore Pond that begins at the picnic area (canoes and rowboats are also available for rental here), and a shorter trail at Noyes Pond in the southwestern corner.

The summit of Owl's Head is easily reached in season via a dirt state forest road that climbs to a parking area just below the summit; from here it's a steep but short, 0.2-mile walk to the vistas at the top. From Boulder Beach Road there is a scenic view of wetlands along Stillwater Brook.

Missisquoi National Wildlife Refuge

U.S. Fish and Wildlife Service, 802-868-4781,
www.fws.gov/northeast/missisquoi

CLOSEST TOWN: Swanton

DIRECTIONS: From Interstate 89 north of Burlington take exit 1 and follow VT 78 west for 2 miles to the refuge headquarters at the junction with Tabor Road. The parking area at Louie's Landing is roughly 2 miles east of the visitor center, on the north side of VT 78.

Encompassing more than 6,500 acres of floodplain, wetland, and upland habitats along the delta where the Missisquoi River discharges into the northeast finger of Lake Champlain near the Canadian border, the Missisquoi National Wildlife Refuge is one of Vermont's richest wildlife areas. The refuge is a key piece of the network of preserves along the Champlain Valley corridor of the overall Atlantic Flyway that provides crucial habitat

Leopard frogs are a familiar sight along the shores of the Missisquoi River near its confluence with Lake Champlain.

for migratory waterfowl, songbirds, shorebirds, wading birds, and monarch butterflies. The unique and diverse features here include the state's largest great blue heron rookery, an uncommon silver maple floodplain forest, and a complex of wetlands including some 5,000 acres of natural marshes supplemented by an additional 1,200 acres of impoundments that are managed primarily to benefit waterfowl. Large open fields are also maintained to provide additional habitat diversity for grassland birds and a variety of other species that favor openings and edges.

VIEWING

Among the refuge's most visible inhabitants are northern leopard frogs, which are abundant to the point of often being underfoot along the Jeep Road Trail. These semiterrestrial amphibians, which are common in both aquatic and field habitats, are distinguished from the similar pickerel frog by their rounded spots and green-brown coloration. Walkers along this seasonally muddy route will also likely see the tracks of mammals such as moose, white-tailed deer, and raccoons and enjoy a loud chorus of migratory songbirds in late spring and summer.

The wetlands here are used by more than 20,000 ducks annually. Look for large flocks of mallards, green-winged teal, black and ring-necked ducks, and pintails, especially during the height of autumn migration. Wood ducks, hooded mergansers, black ducks, and common goldeneyes all breed throughout the preserve. An uncommon species that favors freshwater marshes and other wetlands is the black tern, whose range in New England outside of Maine is limited to the far northwest and northeast corners of Vermont.

The great blue heron colony, which is one of the largest in the Northeast, is located on Shad Island at the refuge's far northern tip, where several short branches of the Missisquoi River meet Lake Champlain at an area known as the Bird's Foot Delta. This area can be viewed only by boat (setting foot on the island is strictly prohibited); bear right at a fork in the river and follow the Middle Branch to the island.

The open fields along the Old Railroad Passage are frequented by field sparrows and bluebirds, as well as bobolinks and eastern meadowlarks in late spring and summer. Here red and gray foxes, eastern coyotes, and birds of prey such as northern harriers, red-tailed hawks, and American kestrels hunt mice and voles, while white-tailed deer emerge from the surrounding forest to graze in early morning and evening. This is prime woodcock habitat; watch and listen for twilight courtship flights from March through

May and look carefully for well-camouflaged individuals and family groups near field and wetland edges.

A beaver lodge and wetland are easily observed via a short trail and observation deck on Tabor Road, and more sign is evident along Maquam Creek and the other waterways. River otters, mink, and muskrats may be seen at any time in these wetlands, while raccoons, which are a significant predator on waterfowl nests, are most active by night.

GETTING AROUND

The refuge offers several well-marked trails that explore the various habitats. Maps and interpretive guides are available at the visitor center on Tabor Road. Mac's Bend Road and the Jeep Road Trail offer the best views of the river and floodplain and the longest hike, a round-trip of 7 miles if the entire route is walked from the parking area at Louie's Landing to the trail's end. From the landing, this route follows the west bank of the river north for 1 mile to the parking area and boat launch at Mac's Bend, which is open seasonally. From here the Jeep Trail continues along the river for another 2.5 miles to Missisquoi Bay. Be prepared for seasonally muddy areas here.

Shorter routes include the one-way Old Railroad Passage, which begins at the open fields along Tabor Road and leads southeast to explore southwest corner of Maquam Bog before ending at the north shore of Maquam Bay. On the opposite side of the road the Stephen Young Marsh Trail makes a 1.25-mile loop along a freshwater wetland. In the southwesternmost corner of the refuge, Black and Maquam creeks are explored by a 2.5-mile trail that winds through several habitats, including open fields, forested lowlands, and wetlands along both waterways. Be prepared for lots of bugs here in warm months, especially near the wetlands.

For those exploring the river and adjacent portions of Lake Champlain by water, the boat launch at Louie's Landing is open year-round, while the ramp at Mac's Bend, which is roughly a mile to the north, is open from September to November. Boaters should be alert for signs marking areas that are closed to protect wildlife.

A common raven at rest in the alpine ridge of 4,393-foot Mount Mansfield, Vermont's highest summit.

Mount Mansfield and Smugglers' Notch State Park

Vermont Department of Forests, Parks, and Recreation, 802-241-3655, www.vtstateparks.com/htm/smugglers

CLOSEST TOWN: Stowe

DIRECTIONS: From Interstate 89 take exit 10 and follow VT 100 north to Stowe. From the village center follow VT 108 north for 5.5 miles to the auto road entrance, 8.5 miles to the Long Trail trailhead, and 10.2 miles to the height-of-land at Smugglers' Notch.

The summit ridge of Mount Mansfield, Vermont's highest peak, is one of Vermont's unique environments. Thanks to its unbuffered exposure to prevailing winds and storms that keep forests from growing above 4,000 feet, it is home to a 250-acre open alpine area that is one of only three such communities in the state; the others are much smaller zones atop Camel's Hump and Mount Abraham to the south. A handful of high-elevation peat bogs are dispersed in depressions along the ridge, where hardy alpine flowers include diapensia and mountain cranberry. The various peaks are often described as resembling the profile of a human looking skyward; the 4,393-foot summit is known as the "Chin" and other prominent humps are known as the "Adam's Apple," "Nose," and "Forehead." The mountain's lower slopes are covered in northern hardwood forests that transition to evergreen spruces and firs below the summit. The 37,250-acre Mount Mansfield State Forest protects the bulk of the mountain and its forests, while the alpine zone is managed by the University of Vermont. The popular Stowe ski resort operates on the mountain's west face.

At the base of Mount Mansfield's east slopes is the narrow, V-shaped pass known as Smugglers' Notch, so named for its long and colorful historical use. It has served as a route to and from Canada for contraband smugglers following a trade embargo during the early nineteenth century, for slaves escaping the country in the years before the Civil War, and for locals importing alcohol illegally during Prohibition. Today, the notch is part of a popular state park where visitors explore rock caves and towering cliffs reached by a narrow, winding scenic highway.

VIEWING

Among the handful of hardy mammals present in the high elevations are red-backed voles, which thrive in moist mountain environments, and deer mice. Snowshoe hares periodically emerge from high-elevation forest cover to browse the low vegetation; watch for their large, often well-spaced tracks in dense conifer groves. During the summer months look for black bears or their droppings near blueberry patches. Ever-unpredictable moose occasionally ramble through these heights as well; they have been observed atop Mount Mansfield and the Presidential Range in New Hampshire. Rocky ledges and outcroppings provide den habitat for bobcats, porcupines, bears, fishers, and coyotes. At lower elevations white-tailed deer use evergreen spruce, pine, and hemlock for cover during the winter and feed on low shrubs.

Befitting their status as wilderness symbols, common ravens are often the most visible birds in and around the alpine zone; a small breeding population nests in trees below the summit and in the rock ledges of Smugglers' Notch. Juncos and white-throated sparrows nest amid the low alpine vegetation during the warm months. A migratory songbird that favors high-elevation forests is the blackpoll warbler, which has a black head patch similar to that of the familiar black-capped chickadee. The spruce groves offer habitat for uncommon Bicknell's thrushes, which were designated as a separate species from gray-cheeked thrushes as recently as

1995 and breed in northern New England's high mountains. Outside the Green Mountains their only other Vermont nesting sites are in the rugged Northeast Kingdom. Some colorful northern birds to watch for at lower elevations include pine siskins, red and white-winged crossbills, evening grosbeaks, and yellow-bellied sapsuckers.

The cliffs and ledges of Smugglers' Notch have long been a nesting area for peregrine falcons, which return to favored sites for generations. After an absence during the mid-twentieth century as the result of DDT contamination, peregrines returned to the notch in 1987 and bred successfully in 1989. Potential viewing areas include the information booth parking area and the Elephant's Head cliffs on the east side on the notch.

GETTING AROUND

The shortest, most direct, and often most sheltered hiking route to Mount Mansfield's summit is via the Long Trail from Smugglers' Notch north of Stowe. From the trailhead below the road's height-of-land, this path climbs at a moderate-to-steep grade up the east slopes, reaching the Taft Lodge at 1.7 miles and the summit at 2.3 miles, gaining 2,800 feet along the way. A longer but especially scenic route is the spectacular Sunset Ridge Trail, which begins at Underhill State Park and follows the open Sunset Ridge above the trees for nearly a mile before reaching the summit at 3.3 miles after climbing 2,600 feet.

Open from spring to fall, the privately operated auto road climbs for 4.5 miles to a visitor center at the site of an old inn below the summit at the "Nose" ($24 toll per car). From here a mostly easy 1.5-mile segment of the Long Trail leads to the summit, traversing some rocky areas and offering good views of the alpine zone. Visitors should be prepared for changing weather, wind, and possible ice along the exposed ridge and must stay on marked trails to avoid damaging sensitive alpine plants, which are well adapted to survive extreme weather at these heights but not human footsteps. Hiking is not recommended during early to mid spring due to erosion.

Smugglers' Notch is easily accessed and explored via scenic Route 108, which winds steeply to the caves at the road's height-of-land. The upper portions of the road are not maintained during winter but are open to recreation, including walking, snowshoeing, and skiing during this time.

 Mount Philo State Park

Vermont Department of Forests, Parks, and Recreation, 802-425-2390,
www.vtstateparks.com/htm/philo

CLOSEST TOWN: Charlotte

DIRECTIONS: From the junction of US 7 and Ferry Road in Charlotte drive south
on US 7 for 3 miles and turn left (east) on State Park Road. Follow the road
to its end at the parking area and ranger booth at the reservation entrance.
An entrance fee of $2 is collected from Memorial Day through Columbus Day.

Some 10,000 years ago a visitor to Mount Philo would be standing on
a rocky island within glacial Lake Vermont, which once filled the present
Champlain Valley. Today, this beehive-shaped eminence, the slopes of
which bear scars left by cutting waves, rises alone above the valley and offers, from its summit at 968 feet, an often-photographed panoramic vista
across farm fields, barns, and woodlots to Lake Champlain, the Adirondack
Mountains, and Mounts Abraham and Ellen along the Monroe Skyline of
the Green Mountains. Its rich soils host a variety of plant life, including
abundant showy trilliums, New Jersey tea, barren strawberry, huckleberry,
whitewood aster, and magenta fireweed. Thanks to its location along the
Champlain flyway corridor, the mountain is one of the region's finest
hawk-watch sites.

VIEWING

Though broad-wings dominate the species count—they accounted for all
but 100 out of 2,900 birds counted on one particular mid-September day
in 2009—other raptors to watch for include bald eagles, red-tailed, red-
shouldered, sharp-shinned, and Cooper's hawks, and northern harriers.
In October watch for flocks of snow geese flying along the valley; many
will stop to rest in the fields in and near Dead Creek Wildlife Management
Area to the south, which is easily combined with a visit to Mount Philo in a
single day. In flight, the snow goose flocks are distinguished by their wavy,
changing formations, which contrast with the well-defined V of familiar
Canada geese.

Migratory songbirds to watch for during spring and summer include
rose-breasted grosbeaks, hermit thrushes, great-crested flycatchers, blackburnian warblers, and American redstarts. Other residents include yellow-
bellied sapsuckers, barred owls, and ruffed grouse.

Tracks, sign, and occasional sightings of all the region's characteristic woodland mammals, including moose, black bears, white-tailed deer, bobcat, porcupines, and coyotes, may be found along the trails here.

GETTING AROUND

Established as Vermont's first state park in 1924, Mount Philo State Park, which is open from Memorial Day through mid-October, includes a 10-site campground and picnic area at the summit and a seasonal auto road that winds from the entrance to the top. The House Boulder Trail begins near the ranger station and winds up the west slopes at a moderately steep grade, passing a series of glacial erratics before reaching the summit at 0.9 mile. Many hikers make a 2.2-mile circuit by incorporating the auto road, which offers views of wildflowers along the road's edge.

 ## Springweather Nature Area and North Springfield Lake

U.S. Army Corps of Engineers, 802-886-2775, www.nae.usace.army.mil; Ascutney Mountain Audubon Society

CLOSEST TOWNS: Windsor, Springfield

DIRECTIONS: From the center of Springfield follow VT 106 north for 3 miles to a right on Reservoir Road. Enter the park and follow the road across the dam, then turn left (north) on Reservoir Road and continue for 0.7 mile. After passing the recreation area parking lot, turn left at a sign for the nature area. Bear right at a sign marking historic Old Reservoir Road and park in the lot next to the picnic area.

Nearby 3,144-foot Mount Ascutney, the highest point along the Connecticut River Valley, is a fine spot for viewing migratory raptors and songbirds such as blackpoll and Tennessee warblers. Its rocky slopes are home for a variety of wildlife, including black bears, white-tailed deer, porcupines, and snowshoe hares. The auto road, which winds nearly 4 miles to a parking area half a mile below the summit, is open seasonally from May to October, and there are several base-to-summit hiking trails. To reach the mountain, from Interstate 91 take exit 8 and follow US 5 north to its junction with VT 44A at a sign for Ascutney State Park. Bear left here on VT 44A and continue for 1 mile to the park entrance and auto road on the left.

In the shadow of pyramid-shaped Mount Ascutney, the 40-mile-long Black River winds toward its confluence with the Connecticut River in southeastern Vermont. A short distance upstream from its mouth it flows through 100-acre North Springfield Lake, a shallow reservoir formed by the

The easy trails at Vermont's Springweather Nature Area offer views of wetland, field, forest, and stream habitats.

construction of the North Springfield Dam in 1960. The dam, which is part of the Connecticut Valley flood control network, has saved area communities an estimated $60 million in damages after storms in 1927 and 1938 devastated the region.

The lake and its surrounding habitats are part of a 1,370-acre preserve that is managed by the Army Corps of Engineers. On its east shore is a 70-acre parcel known as the Springweather Nature Area, which is leased to and managed by the Ascutney Mountain Audubon Society. This compact preserve features a fine mix of habitats, including grassy fields, woodlands of oak, birch, maple, pine, and hemlock, brooks and a cascading stream, and a large agricultural field. Several overlooks offer fine views of the lake and its marshy margins. Thanks to this variety and the preserve's proximity to the Connecticut Valley, nearly 160 bird species have been recorded here.

VIEWING
The fields along the Blue Trail host colorful indigo buntings, tree swallows, bluebirds, eastern meadowlarks, and bobolinks, all of which favor open areas. Small mammals include woodchucks, short-tailed shrews, and meadow jumping, deer, and white-footed mice, all of which are prey species for red foxes, eastern coyotes, fishers, and bobcats. In warm months

watch for tiger swallowtail, viceroy, yellow mustard, and monarch butterflies, as well as widow skimmer, darner, and meadowhawk dragonflies. Along the grassy path that follows the edge of the adjacent cornfield, check the muddy edges for the tracks of mammals such as white-tailed deer, which may also be glimpsed hiding in the vegetation that borders the field (listen for their coughlike warning grunts).

From the overlooks along the Blue, Red, and Green trails scan the lake and marshes for great blue herons, green herons, and secretive American bitterns. During migrations, ruddy ducks, buffleheads, northern pintails, green and blue-winged teal, and other waterfowl use the lake as a stopover and resting ground. Check swampy wetland edges for river otters, beavers, muskrats, and painted and snapping turtles. Sustaining many of these creatures is the lake's fish community, which includes yellow perch, rainbow, brown, and brook trout, blacknose dace, and chain pickerel.

Also present here are much less conspicuous wood turtles, which are uncommon to rare throughout New England. This partly terrestrial species favors pristine, unpolluted stream banks, as well as fields and forests during the summer months; its pattern and color allow it to blend in remarkably well with rocky river and stream bottoms. Northern two-lined, red-backed, and spotted salamanders take cover beneath rocks and logs adjacent to streams and brooks. Other reptiles and amphibians include pickerel, northern leopard, and wood frogs and smooth green, garter, and eastern red-bellied snakes.

Birds of prey include American kestrels, merlins, and barred and great horned owls; during spring and fall watch for migrating raptors from the dam and lake overlooks. Bald eagles built nests near the lake in 2002 and 2005, but breeding proved unsuccessful; in both instances great horned owls took over the abandoned nests the following year.

GETTING AROUND

The easy walking trails here, which are divided into three color-blazed networks, are especially good for families. From the main trailhead across the road from the picnic area at the entrance, the Blue Trail explores a small ravine with a cascading stream, then emerges at a large grassy field at post B10. Here mowed paths lead across the fields to a narrow footpath that follows the east bank of the lake, where there are abundant summer wildflowers and views across the water. The trail then loops back into the forest and returns to the field at post B7. This circuit can be completed in 35 minutes.

When exploring the Red and Green trails it's easiest to combine them as a loop, as both routes are fairly short and are interconnected. The Red Trail begins at the same trailhead as the Blue and leads north (right) past several junctions to a picnic area in a small clearing with a scenic elevated view across the valley. At post R9 the Red Trail bears right to loop back toward the trailhead, offering the option of a short round-trip, while the Green Trail continues straight and follows along the edges of the cliffs and an old pine plantation, with views of Mount Ascutney through the trees. Shortly after turning sharply right, the trail reaches a junction at post G4, where you can make a detour left to explore a seasonal stream and old mill site. From G4 the main Green Trail continues through a clearing, then ends as it rejoins the Red Trail at post R10. From here it's a short walk back to the trailhead. This loop can be completed in an hour or less.

Though it's not part of the nature area, the North Springfield Lake boat ramp provides access to the reservoir from the west banks. From the end of Maple Street in Perkinsville turn right and follow the road past the old Grout Cemetery to the ramp. Canoes and kayaks are often best suited to the shallow water here.

Union Village Dam

U.S. Army Corps of Engineers, 802-649-1606, www.nae.usace.army.mil
CLOSEST TOWN: Thetford
DIRECTIONS: From the junction of US 5 and VT 132 follow VT 132 north for 2.5 miles. After passing a sign for the dam and the Hogwash Farm, bear right and continue to an intersection at the historic Union Village covered bridge. Bear left here and continue to the nearby park entrance, 3 miles from US 5.

In the quiet rolling hills of east-central Vermont is another productive wildlife area centered on a flood-control impoundment in the Connecticut River Valley. Here the 1,100-foot-long Union Village Dam was completed in 1950 to mitigate flood flows along the Ompompanoosuc River a short distance upstream from its confluence with the Connecticut River.

Because the dam was built entirely for flood control, there is no large lake behind it, but instead a diverse section of the river with extensive marshy areas and colorful wildflowers, rocky cascades, pools, a swimming beach, and beaver ponds. Bordering the river are mixed forests of red oak, white pine, red and sugar maple, birch, hemlock, aspen, and ash, and clearings and shrubby areas on old farm sites.

From atop the dam there are long views from 170 feet above the valley, while the adjacent grassy fields offer additional habitat diversity. Like much of New England, this area has a long history of use over the years: along the riverbanks are the remains of a woolen mill that was part of an industrial village, while nearby stone walls and old-field pines are evidence of past agricultural clearings.

VIEWING

From the park road and the Mystery Trail, scan the river, marshy areas, and beaver ponds for river otters, beavers, muskrats, and mink. Like other weasels, mink regularly travel long distances in search of prey, which includes fish, frogs, small mammals, and even birds. They are active year-round but spend bad-weather periods in dens along wetland banks. In late spring look carefully for newborn white-tailed deer fawns hidden in the grassy and shrubby fields. The best chance for encountering a bear might be when fruiting shrubs are at their peak during late summer. The woods and field edges are the domain of fishers, bobcats, coyotes, and foxes, which hunt chipmunks, squirrels, and other prey during forays along the old stone walls; you might also see sign of the occasional moose.

The wetlands and fields offer plenty of habitat for butterflies, dragonflies, and damselflies. A common early-season dragonfly is the chalk-fronted corporal, which is often seen in groups resting on and circling above rocks. As the summer progresses, look for twelve-spotted skimmers, common whitetails, meadowhawks, and Canada and green darners, large groups of which may be seen circling and snapping up insects in late summer swarms. Flowers along the river and the large meadow attract and nourish a variety of butterflies of all sizes and colors, including pearl crescents, common ringlets, eastern commas, and black, tiger, and Canadian swallowtails.

The varied habitats and proximity to the Connecticut Valley flyway attract a wide diversity of birds. Bluebirds, indigo buntings, bobolinks, field sparrows, and swallows all breed in open areas; the abundant wildflowers and flowering shrubs nourish ruby-throated hummingbirds. Ruffed grouse, wild turkeys, and American woodcock are most often seen along edges where these openings and recently cut areas border the woods. Bald eagles, osprey, great blue herons, mallard and wood ducks, and kingfishers hunt the pond and river; other birds of prey include broad-winged and red-shouldered hawks and northern harriers. Shorebird migrants seen long the river and wetland edges include spotted, least, and solitary sandpipers, while a wide range of songbirds use the forests as resting and breeding grounds, including least, willow, and olive-sided flycatchers.

GETTING AROUND

The trailheads, picnic areas, and other attractions of the recreation area are easily reached via the park road, which parallels the Ompompanoosuc River for 2.8 miles from the end of the dam to the gated entrance near Thetford Center. From the sharp left turn at the brick house at the end of the dam, it leads to the Forest Management Demonstration trail at 0.8 mile, cascades and a pool at the "Chute" at 1.8 miles, the Mystery Trail parking area at 2 miles, and a large wildflower meadow at 2.3 miles.

The interpretive Mystery and Forest Management Demonstration trails offer an excellent introduction to the preserve's natural and cultural history, habitats, and management. The three-quarter-mile Mystery Trail crosses the river on a wood bridge, then bears left to start a loop at post 2 (turn right here for a direct route to the beaver pond) and follows the bank of the river. After passing an old mill site, the trail leaves the river and rises into a brushy clearing with fruiting shrubs, wildflowers, and regenerating young pines. It then bears left to make a short loop past another brushy area and old pines on an abandoned farm site, then leads left to views of a beaver pond. A short detour left at post 13 leads to a clearing along the water, and then the trail returns to the parking area.

The 1.6-mile Management Trail leads through a variety of forest habitats, including groves of northern hardwoods, white pine, and aspen and an old clear-cut and experimental planting site. A yellow-blazed trail branches off the main route near the trailhead and offers a shorter, 0.9-mile loop. An informative pamphlet details the various management practices and tree species.

Victory Basin Wildlife Management Area

Vermont Department of Fish and Wildlife, 802-748-8787,
www.vtfishandwildlife.com/wma_maps.cfm
CLOSEST TOWNS: St. Johnsbury, Victory
DIRECTIONS: From the junction of US 2 and Victory Road in North Concord, which is 11.5 miles east of the center of St. Johnsbury, follow Victory Road (which becomes River Road) for 3.2 miles to the reservation boundary and 5.5 miles to Damon's Crossing.

Other nearby preserves with similar habitats include the 1,993-acre Wenlock Wildlife Management Area on VT Route 105, in the town of Ferdinand, which is 5.5 miles east of Island Pond. Here a short trail leads to Moose Bog, a fine example of a boreal peatland. There are also privately owned areas that are open to the public. Visitors exploring these areas should use caution and yield to logging trucks and be aware that it's quite easy to get lost in the maze of unmarked roads.

Vermont's Northeast Kingdom region has a rugged, remote character that contrasts with the bucolic rolling mountains and valleys that characterize the rest of the state. Here moving glaciers left behind extensive deposits of rock and sand, the legacy of which is a vast network of swamps and bogs nestled below low granite mountains and hills. Because of its poor soils and harsh climate, this region has historically been lightly populated, with little agricultural activity, though it was heavily logged. It is now home to an extensive wildland conservation network that protects more than 200,000 acres of boreal forest and wetland habitats along the watersheds of the Victory and Nulhegan rivers.

Fifteen miles northeast of St. Johnsbury lies the 4,970-acre Victory Basin Wildlife Management Area, where Victory Bog and a network of streams and brooks form the headwaters of the Moose River. The state of Vermont purchased this land in 1969 from a power company, averting a plan by the company to dam the river and inundate the basin. Roughly 60 percent of the preserve is forested with groves of northern hardwoods and spruce-fir, and the remainder is largely wetlands associated with the Moose River and its tributaries, which include Rogers, Bog, Hay Hill, and Cold brooks. A 20-acre northern bog includes characteristic flora such as northern pitcher plants, Labrador tea, and leatherleaf, and other communities include beaver wetlands, floodplain forests, swamps, and marshes. The topography is relatively level, with elevations ranging from 1,100 to 1,400 feet.

VIEWING

As you might expect at a preserve that is bisected by the Moose River, moose are common in this mix of wetlands and woodlands. They may be seen along River Road in the early morning and evening, and there are active crossings in the wetlands that border Route 2 east of St. Johnsbury (use caution when driving in this area). A walk along the old logging roads will likely reveal plenty of moose sign, including large heart-shaped prints in muddy areas. Snowshoe hares also frequent the margins of these paths, especially near groves of young, regenerating softwoods; signs of their presence include low vegetation nipped at a 45-degree angle by their sharp incisors, and subtle nests, known as "forms," in thickets. The hares and other small mammals are prey for bobcats, coyotes, foxes, and fishers. In 2007 a wildlife biologist discovered tracks of Canada lynx here; it was the first evidence of the species in Vermont since 1968. The basin is an important wintering area for white-tailed deer, which "yard up" beneath softwoods in large groups. Black bears may be seen in any of the habitats in search of food, particularly in late summer when fruits and berries are at their peak.

Playing an integral role as active "managers" of the property are beavers, who have engineered an extensive network of ponds and wetlands. Numerous species benefit from their efforts, including mink, river otters, and muskrats. As these areas gradually thaw as spring progresses, reptiles and amphibians emerge from their long winter hibernation; watch for mink, pickerel, leopard, and green frogs, snapping and painted turtles, and northern spring and red-backed salamanders.

More than 130 species of birds have been recorded throughout the preserve. With the spring thaws also come waterfowl such as mergansers and nesting wood and black ducks, along with waders such as green and great blue herons. Possible boreal species include spruce grouse, black-backed woodpeckers, gray jays, boreal chickadees, white-winged crossbills, and migratory olive-sided flycatchers and Cape May warblers. During summer watch for American bitterns amid marshy vegetation. Other species that favor these boggy habitats and beaver wetlands include alder and willow flycatchers and rusty blackbirds.

On late spring days look for congregations of tiger swallowtail butterflies along the muddy roads and trails. Another especially beautiful butterfly found here from June to early September is the white admiral, easily identified by its black, white, and blue coloration and white wing bands.

GETTING AROUND

River Road leads through the heart of the preserve for 5.5 miles, paralleling the Moose River and its associated wetlands. This public road is open year-round but may be muddy or rough in early spring. As is the case at most wildlife management areas, there is no blazed trail network, but there are approximately five miles' worth of unmarked old logging roads for visitors to explore. These may be accessed at parking areas along River Road. One path begins at Damon's Crossing and follows the edge of wetlands associated with Bog Brook near the preserve's western boundary. After a mile it meets a trail that leads west for 0.6 mile to Bog Pond in the adjacent Victory State Forest. Waterproof footwear is strongly recommended for those venturing on these trails, especially in spring. One of the best ways to watch for wildlife here is to drop a canoe or kayak in the Moose River and drift quietly along the vegetation.

White River National Fish Hatchery

U.S. Fish and Wildlife Service, 802-234-3241, www.fws.gov/whiterivernfh
CLOSEST TOWN: Bethel
DIRECTIONS: From Interstate 89 take exit 3 and follow VT 107 west for 3 miles to Bethel, where the road makes a sharp left and crosses an iron bridge. From the turn continue to follow VT 107 for another 2 miles to the hatchery entrance on the right. The facility is open from 8 AM to 3 PM year-round.

Located in a pleasant setting amid the hills of the scenic White River Valley, the White River National Fish Hatchery serves as the primary center for rearing and restoring Atlantic salmon to the Connecticut Valley. Visitors here have the opportunity to view salmon and lake trout of various ages and sizes and learn about the life history and restoration process. Some eight million eggs are incubated here annually, provided by stock from the area as well as other hatcheries throughout New England. After spending the winter at the hatchery, the eggs are released as "fry" into waters of the Connecticut River basin. New England's first fish hatchery was established at Craig Brook in Maine in 1862, and today many other facilities operate throughout the region.

Adjacent to the hatchery building are four rows of concrete pools, which are covered by igloo-shaped tents that protect the fish from exposure to sun, snow, ice, and other elements. The fish are grouped by age, with large, mature Atlantic salmon visible in a handful of the pools; a color-coded map posted above the guest register indicates where each age class can be viewed. The visitor center includes informative displays, aquariums, and views of the incubation tanks. Allow an hour or so for viewing the pools and indoor exhibits.

From headwaters on Battell Mountain in the central Green Mountains, the White River flows 56 miles across east-central Vermont to its mouth at the Connecticut River at White River Junction. It is especially significant for salmon restoration in that it is the largest undammed tributary of the Connecticut River. Salmon were present in the White River until the early nineteenth century, when they were extirpated as a result of dam construction on the Connecticut and industrial pollution.

NEW ENGLAND WILDLIFE SPECIES PROFILES

The following profiles identify characteristic wildlife commonly (or in some cases, rarely) seen in New England and describe where and when sightings are most likely. This list concentrates on the region's iconic and charismatic fauna and is by no means exhaustive. The profiles are sorted by family and are arranged by primary habitat, although many of these creatures can be seen in a variety of environments around the region. For many, histories of their population changes over time are included.

Woodland

The history of New England's forests is intricately tied to and as dynamic as that of its wildlife.

Over the past four centuries, the region's landscape has undergone a remarkable cycle as the fields that were largely cleared during colonial times have reverted to forest.

The general forest types in New England are distributed by geography and climate. They include northern hardwoods (birch, beech, maple) in the high-elevation northern and western regions, spruce and fir in harsh high-elevation and boggy environments, oak-hickory in the milder southern locales, scrub oak–pitch pine along the coast, and a central transition zone.

The following profiles of some of the region's characteristic forest species include large animals such as moose and black bear that favor undeveloped areas, along with others species you are likely to observe along woodland trails, including six-spotted green tiger beetles, red efts, and hermit thrushes.

BLACK BEAR (*Ursus americanus*)
Probably no creature, save perhaps the moose, better symbolizes the New England wilderness or inspires more excitement or emotion when sighted than black bears. Though they are increasingly common throughout much of the region, bears can be remarkably elusive, and it is possible to spend years exploring the wild without actually seeing one.

Black bears are most common in the hills and forests of interior Maine, north-central New Hampshire, Vermont, western Massachusetts, and northwest Connecticut, but they are also highly adaptable (their diets range from deer fawns, insects, fish, and frogs to berries, crops, and human garbage) and have expanded their range toward the populated coastal regions of southern New England, including the greater Boston area. They spend winters in a deep sleep, as opposed to a true hibernation, sheltered in secluded caves, large hollow logs, rock ledges, and brush piles, which they may line with bark, leaves, moss, and grasses. As the climate warms in early spring they become active again, as many a New Englander who has cleaned up a smashed bird feeder in March or April can attest.

As with many of New England's familiar species, the present abundance of black bears is a relatively recent phenomenon that belies their absence from much of the region in the not-too-distant past. During historical

Black bears have made a strong comeback and are expanding into more populated regions of New England, where encounters like this one regularly occur.

times, unregulated hunting and widespread clearing of forests for agricultural use had a profound effect on most of the region's wildlife.

This is well exemplified by Vermont, where the bear population reached its lowest point around 1850, when 75 percent of the state's woodlands had been cleared. Today, this percentage has been almost exactly reversed, and forests have reclaimed 80 percent of the landscape. In turn, the bears have strongly recovered, and an estimated 3,000 to 5,000 now reside in the state, mostly in the Green Mountain and Northeast Kingdom regions. It's a similar story in neighboring New Hampshire, where the population has risen from a low of fewer than 1,000 at the onset of the twentieth century to some 5,000 today. Though interior Maine has supported a generally healthy bear population over the years, they were extirpated from the southern region following widespread forest clearing in colonial times and have been somewhat slow to reclaim this area.

Bears are also thriving in southern New England. In 1982 only 500 were estimated to reside in Massachusetts, but this figure is now believed to exceed 3,000. Most live in the hills west of the Connecticut River Valley, which along with Interstate 91 has served as a dual barrier impeding their movement east. Nevertheless, they are well established in the rural central hills and have been reported with increasing regularity in the eastern counties not far from Boston.

After more than a century's absence, breeding black bears were first observed in Connecticut during the early 1980s. Their numbers rapidly increased over the next 25 years; in one recent 12-month period, 1,800 sightings were reported to the state Department of Environmental Protection. Though bears have been largely absent from neighboring Rhode Island since the American Revolution, a number of sightings and encounters have recently been reported statewide in towns as far south as the Narragansett Bay region.

MOOSE (*Alces alces*)

Endearing to some, ungainly to others, moose are one of New England's preeminent wilderness symbols. Anyone who spends time hiking, paddling, fishing, or just driving in the north country will eventually have stories to tell of encounters with the region's largest land mammal.

Though moose are northern creatures best suited to the wetlands and forests of the cool boreal mountain regions, as their population has flourished throughout northern New England, they have rapidly expanded their range into the more southern states. They have benefited from the regrowth of forests, which provide cover and travel corridors, and also from timber harvests that provide an abundant food source of young hardwood sprouts. The return of beavers has also been important, as moose use these wetlands to feed on aquatic plants, cool off, and escape biting insects.

In Maine, moose were common at the time of European settlement but were steadily reduced by unregulated hunting. Even after a closed hunting season was mandated by the state in 1830, the population continued to dwindle for the next 100 years, as white-tailed deer expanded into the northern and central regions and spread a brain-worm disease that is fatal to moose. In 1935, after moose bottomed out at fewer than 2,000 individuals, the state enacted year-round protection from hunting. The ban, combined with the recovery of large timberlands that had been clear-cut, allowed the population to steadily recover to 25,000 by the 1980s and roughly 30,000 today, an estimate that many believe is too low.

By 1840, moose were largely eliminated from Vermont and New Hampshire, and it wasn't until the 1970s that the population began to truly recover in both states. However, from 1996 to 2005 Vermont moose population rapidly increased from 2,000 to more than 5,000 individuals, prompting the state to increase hunting permits. Fewer than 15 individuals were estimated to reside in New Hampshire during the mid-nineteenth century, but today a visitor to the Connecticut Lakes and White Mountains regions may well see that many during a single trip; the overall state estimate is 6,000.

Moose were extirpated in Massachusetts by the close of the 1800s, save for a brief private reintroduction attempt in the Berkshires. From the early 1930s onward, there were periodic sightings of vagrant individuals, mostly young bulls, as populations increased in northern New England. By the mid-1990s, reports of mothers with calves became as frequent as individual bulls, confirming the existence of a resident breeding population. Today, roughly 700 to 1,000 moose roam the Bay State, a figure that is estimated to grow at 100 individuals per year.

Whether or not moose were ever common in Connecticut in precolonial times is unknown. As was the case in Massachusetts, vagrants were reported through the mid-1990s, with mothers with offspring confirmed by 1998. Most of the present estimated 100 animals inhabit the northwest hills, but individuals have recently been reported in the coastal region.

With these robust numbers has also come an inevitable increase in motor vehicle collisions, which kill an average of 700 and 250 moose, respectively, in Maine and New Hampshire alone annually. As such incidents continue to occur in Massachusetts and Connecticut, public demand for a hunting season to control numbers in these states will increase.

FISHER (*Martes pennanti*)

For those willing to travel off the beaten path and negotiate stone walls and forest debris, fishers are especially interesting and dynamic creatures to track. These energetic and active weasels (the commonly used term "fisher cats" is a misnomer) have large home territories that may extend as far as 15 miles. Their search for prey leads them over downed logs and snags, across stone walls, through dense shrubs, and up tall trees; one of the more unusual signs of a fisher's passage is a body imprint in snow made by its jumping off a high branch. Actual sightings are uncommon, but fortunate observers who encounter one in the wild may see it shoot up and down tall trees or dash across a field or stone wall at a remarkable speed. One identifying trait is their head, which is almost bearlike in appearance.

Fishers are effective but also opportunistic predators that feed on a wide variety of prey, ranging from squirrels, chipmunks, raccoons, and snowshoe hares to frogs and insects; they will also eat berries. Along with mountain lions, they are the only species that actively hunts porcupines; they cleverly avoid a smattering of quills by attacking their victim's head, then turning the kill over and feeding on the exposed belly. They will also cover, cache, and mark their kills, which they return to feed on over time.

As creatures that favor large blocks of mature forest, fishers suffered considerably from historical land clearing, and they were nearly eliminated throughout their North American range by hunting and trapping for their pelts, which had high market values. However, with the return of extensive woodlands throughout much of New England, fishers have rapidly reclaimed much of their former range and are quickly spreading across the south coastal regions and far down-east Maine. When snow levels are high, coniferous or mixed forests are advantageous to fishers, as they are easier to negotiate.

CANADA LYNX *(Lynx canadensis)*

A sighting of either of New England's midsize feline predators is something to treasure, as both are highly secretive and rarely seen. Especially uncommon are Canada lynx, whose range is restricted to the far reaches of northern New England, in contrast to their bobcat cousins, which are fairly common throughout most of the region. There are several subtle differences between the two, as lynx have longer ear tufts, larger feet with hairy bottoms, and slightly shorter tails; they also favor areas with deep snow.

Lynx are part of an especially strong predator-prey interrelationship, as snowshoe hares constitute three-quarters of their diet. As hare populations fluctuate, so too do lynx, and periodic reports of individuals outside their standard range in New England are likely vagrants seeking food during lean hare years. Because young forest sprouts are a significant food source for snowshoe hares, timber harvests and regenerating clear-cuts also indirectly benefit lynx. This is part of an interesting dichotomy among conservation managers and landowners, as many people are opposed to widespread forest cutting in spite of the fact that it creates favorable conditions for certain species.

Maine hosts the largest population of lynx in the eastern states, an estimated 500 individuals in a band encompassing the northeasternmost third of the state. Though lynx were reported in small numbers in New Hampshire through the 1960s, the only confirmed reports since that time are a roadkill specimen from the 1990s and a set of prints that were discovered by professional wildlife trackers in Jefferson in 2006. The following year a Vermont wildlife biologist found tracks in the Victory Basin region; this was the state's first verified account since the late 1960s. Little is known about how far south they may have ranged in precolonial times.

MOUNTAIN LION (*Felis concolor*)

Though mountain lions (also know as cougars, pumas, and catamounts) and eastern timber wolves have been officially considered extirpated from the New England states since the late nineteenth and early twentieth century, they are the subject of considerable intrigue and debate today. Continual sighting reports from throughout the region offer the possibility that they might someday join the aforementioned species that have returned to reclaim old territories. The absence of these top predators has had a profound effect along the food chain, as evidenced by large populations of deer and other prey species in many areas. Though eastern coyotes are close in size and genetic makeup to wolves, they tend to be more opportunistic, generalist feeders that have relatively minor impact on deer.

The last confirmed mountain lion reports occurred in Massachusetts in 1858, Vermont in 1881 (though bounties were offered as late as 1894), New Hampshire in the 1920s, and Maine in 1938. In recent years hundreds of reports of sightings and sign have been registered throughout all regions of New England. While the majority of these reports have been erroneous accounts of deer, coyotes, bobcats, foxes, and even house cats, some have been made by credible sources and/or confirmed by DNA tests. In the late 1960s a professional wildlife photographer and a university graduate student provided detailed accounts of separate sightings of a mountain lion in the same area at Quabbin Reservoir. At Craftsbury, Vermont, in 1993, an adult with young was observed, and a scat with hair was subsequently recovered. In 1997 a professional wildlife tracker from central Massachusetts discovered a large scat at Quabbin Reservoir next to the remains of a beaver; the scat that was subsequently confirmed by DNA tests as mountain lion. In 2003 a scat collected in the Ossippee Mountains in New Hampshire's lakes region also tested positive for mountain lion.

Though some of the reports may be of released pets, and there is a consistent lack of follow-up reports or sign, many wildlife professionals believe that the confirmation of breeding mountain lions in New England is inevitable. The abundance of white-tailed deer in many areas provides a potential food source for lions; of note is that several reliable sighting reports at Quabbin Reservoir occurred when the reservation had an abnormally high deer density before hunting was allowed in the early 1990s. Given the recovery of other species detailed here, it's not unreasonable to believe that mountain lions and wolves will be officially confirmed in the wilds of New England in the not-too-distant future. After all, reports of moose, coyotes, beavers, and even deer were once considered unusual in many areas.

WOOD FROG (*Rane sylvatica*)

On mild late-winter and early spring days, a walk in the woods may reveal an early sign of the changing seasons: the short, quacklike calls of wood frogs congregated at seasonal pools. After spending the winter months in a torpor beneath wood and leaves along the forest floor or mud at wet meadow edges, wood frogs emerge from their hibernation before bullfrogs, green frogs, and their other relatives in the true frog family and are in fact often active while ponds and pools are still partially frozen.

Wood frogs, easily distinguished by their dark mask that stretches from their eyes to their ears, are found throughout New England in moist woods with small, fishless ponds that serve as their breeding habitat. They owe their name to their terrestrial nature, as the forest floor provides their habitat and cover. At 2¼ inches, they are roughly half the size of bullfrogs, and in turn twice as large as tiny spring peepers. Wood frogs have a relatively short life span of roughly three years, and local populations are especially susceptible to dry periods or being cut off from water.

The presence of wood frogs, spotted salamanders, and other amphibians underscores the overall importance of woodland vernal pools. These seasonal and often overlooked wetlands, which may be a matter of feet in width and depth and hold water for only two to three months, offer essential breeding habitat and food resources for a variety of organisms, including spotted and blue-spotted salamanders and fairy shrimp. Even when the pools themselves are protected, their surrounding habitats often remain susceptible to disruption by disturbances such as development, logging, and fragmentation, which impedes or restricts the ability of amphibians to move to and from the pools and robs them of adjacent habitat.

SPOTTED SALAMANDER (*Ambystoma maculatum*)

As temperatures begin to moderate toward 50 degrees Fahrenheit on early spring nights, one of the most striking spectacles of the natural year begins. On select evenings—known to naturalists as "big nights"—at fishless vernal pools formed by snowmelt and spring rains, hundreds of otherwise solitary and elusive spotted salamanders congregate to form large mating groups known as congresses. The female lays an average of 100 to 125 and

A tennis-ball-size salamander egg mass in a vernal pool in early April.

as many as 250 eggs, which hatch within one to two months. Those that survive to reach adulthood may live as long as 20 years or more. The salamanders return to the same pools annually, assuming the pools haven't dried up or been disturbed.

These brief mating-season forays are the only extended periods that spotted salamanders spend aboveground. Common throughout New England, they favor moist deciduous and mixed forests, especially along rocky hillsides. Here they spend much of their time hidden beneath rocks, fallen logs, and boards. Active from the onset of the breeding season in March through October, they spend the winter months hibernating on land.

Undeniably among the most conspicuous of New England's 15 salamander species, spotted salamanders are easily distinguished by, and named for, for the twin rows of yellow or orange spots on their rather plump black bodies, which at seven inches long are considerably larger that most of their relatives. Like other amphibians, they are vulnerable to habitat loss, destruction and fragmentation of vernal pool habitats, acid rain, and absorption of other chemicals and pollutants. Their large size and distinctive color patterns also make them a popular subject for collectors.

RED-SPOTTED NEWT (*Notophthalmus viridescens*)

When walking New England's forest trails during the warm months, keep an eye on the forest floor. Chances are you'll glimpse a tiny, bright orange red eft scampering or hiding amid fallen leaves, logs, stumps, rocks, and plants, and if it's been raining or you're close by a wetland, you may well see them by the dozen.

The red eft is the terrestrial, midlife stage of the red-spotted (or eastern) newt, so named for the row of spots along its back that are evident in all life stages. This cycle begins in wetlands where newly hatched juveniles spend their initial three to four months in a larval aquatic form. They then emerge, with the fresh orange skin that serves as a warning to potential predators, to begin the land-based phase, which lasts from two to seven years (four to five is the norm). After doing a year's worth of feeding during the summer months, the efts survive their handful of land-based New England winters by burrowing beneath the forest floor. Not every population undergoes all three phases; some groups skip the eft stage.

For their third and final phase, the efts return to wetlands such as vegetated ponds, lakes, and stream backwaters, where they fully mature into adults; the males make a final color transformation from orange to green. Here the females attach as many as 375 eggs to aquatic plants, and after three to five weeks the cycle begins again. In all their forms, red-spotted newts are adaptable eaters whose diet includes insects and their larvae, frog eggs, and snails and minnows.

HERMIT THRUSH (*Catharus guttatus*)

Many consider the song of the hermit thrush to be the most beautiful and distinctive of all birdcalls and the highlight of the chorus of songbirds each spring and summer. Though somewhat visually drab compared with other migrants such as scarlet tanagers, northern orioles, indigo buntings, and the woodland warblers, hermit thrushes more than compensate for this with their melodious, flutelike song of ascending and descending notes. They are also among the last species heard singing as the forests go quiet in mid to late summer.

Hermit thrushes are closely related and visually similar to wood thrushes, which have a similarly melodious but slightly higher-pitched and faster call. They nest on the ground in coniferous and mixed forests and near wetlands, where they feed primarily on insects. They spend a longer period of time in New England than other migrants, as they arrive early in the spring and linger into November; some even overwinter along the south coast.

What motivates hermit thrushes and other seemingly fragile songbirds to undertake their energy-sapping journey north from the tropics each year? The northern latitudes offer abundant breeding habitat with reduced competition, and a food resource of insects, plants, and seeds that makes the trip worthwhile. The birds generally concentrate their movement through the Northeast along the Atlantic coastal flyway, resulting in outstanding viewing at preserves such as Hammonasset Beach in Connecticut, Rhode Island's coastal wildlife refuges, the Parker River National Wildlife Refuge in Massachusetts, and Maine's Monhegan Island. Other key corridors within the flyway include major rivers and lowlands, including the Connecticut, Housatonic, and Champlain valleys. There are numerous issues and complexities related to songbird conservation, including the loss of tropical forest habitat and development and fragmentation of potential rest areas along the flyways. Another concern involves collisions with towers atop mountains and hills, which have killed a significant number of migrating birds.

BROAD-WINGED HAWK (*Buteo platypterus*)

During the late spring and summer months broad-winged hawks assume a fairly low profile as they breed throughout the woodlands of New England. In contrast to many other birds of prey, broad-wings eschew open and mixed habitats in favor of more secluded forest groves and wetlands, where they nest in mature deciduous trees.

All this changes during a window of roughly 10 days in mid to late September, when individuals take to the skies and form large flocks that migrate to wintering grounds as far south as Peru. They are often observed riding and circling along thermal currents in groups that are known as kettles. On days with a wind from the north or northeast, viewing can be remarkable: some single-day totals in New England include 31,988 and 30,500 individuals at Quaker Ridge in Greenwich, Connecticut, on, respectively, September 15, 1995, and September 14, 1986, and 20,000 at Wachusett Mountain in central Massachusetts on September 13, 1983 (note the consistent timing of these dates). The broad-winged migrations tend to be concentrated, and sightings outside the peak movement are uncommon. The average total of broad-winged hawks observed annually at Quaker Ridge, which is one of New England's best hawk-watch sites, is more than six times that of sharp-shinned hawks, which are the second-most-numerous species.

As a species that favors older trees in dense forests, broad-wings have benefited from the regrowth of forests in New England over the past century. Though there are several varieties of color and plumage among the various juvenile and adult phases, one characteristic to watch for in individuals in flight is prominent black-and-white tail bands. In spite of their name, their wing proportions are equivalent to other related raptors and aren't a distinguishing feature. At 13 to 19 inches, their size, which is roughly the same as a large crow, is small relative to other birds of prey.

SIX-SPOTTED GREEN TIGER BEETLE (*Cicindela sexguttata*)

Like red efts, six-spotted green tiger beetles are familiar creatures of the forest floor that are commonly viewed along trails and old roads. Befitting their name, these colorful and distinctive beetles are readily identified and named for their bright green metallic bodies and legs and U-shaped series of tiny white dots along the edge of their back. Their legs also are bright green, though some have a darker purple sheen. They are most common in the vicinity of dry, sandy areas.

The large range of green tigers includes all New England and the eastern states and as far west as South Dakota. They are easily distinguished from their numerous relatives in the overall tiger beetle family by their color and preference for both shaded forest openings and open areas. The others, including the much less common brown tiger, generally are present exclusively in sandy areas that receive full sunlight. A visually similar relative, the Barrens tiger beetle, has only 50 known colonies worldwide, including one near Plymouth, Massachusetts. Other subspecies, including the white beach tiger beetle, inhabit areas of the southeastern states.

Adding to the visibility of six-spotted tigers is their long period of activity; they are among the first large insects on the move in April and remain active throughout the warm months into October. They are active predators that use the openings in the forest as hunting corridors, where they feed on a variety of other insects, including spiders. Tiger beetles will quickly hop along when shadows are thrown over the forest path but can easily be observed and photographed by those who move slowly.

LUNA MOTH (*Actias luna*)

Arguably the most beautiful, and certainly among the most conspicuous, of New England's moths is the luna, so named for its pair of spots that resemble a half moon. This four-inch-wide, pale green member of the overall giant silkworm moth family has received its share of publicity, as it has been the subject of field guide covers, a postage stamp, and television commercials.

Luna moths are common throughout the eastern states west to Texas and North Dakota, mostly in habitats with broadleaf trees. Hickories are among their favored host trees throughout their range, though they often use white birches and beeches in the northern regions. Though their flight season is limited from May to July in the Northeast, they are active and visible year-round in the milder southern states. Luna moth caterpillars, which are also green, with yellow stripes, grow as large as $2\frac{3}{4}$ inches as they mature toward the winged phase. In all stages they are vulnerable to predators, including similarly nocturnal owls and other birds and insects, though their color provides a level of camouflage.

Both moths and butterflies belong to the overall Lepidoptera (or "scale winged") order. There are a handful of differences between the two groups, as moths have slightly different antennae, areas of distinctive markings, and are active by both day and night. Other distinctive species to watch for in New England include the large and gaudily colored cecropia and polyphemus moths, bee-shaped hummingbird moths, eight-spotted foresters, and less welcome gypsy and tomato hornworm moths.

HEMLOCK WOOLLY ADELGID (*Adelges tsugae*) and ASIAN LONGHORNED BEETLE (*Anoplophora glabripennis*)

While the forests of New England are seemingly thriving today, they remain susceptible to a variety of natural and human threats. With the advent and popularity of intercontinental travel in recent centuries has come another problem: the spread of pathogens and disease from other regions of the world to which native trees have no evolved resistance. A well-known example was the loss of the American chestnut, one of the Northeast's most significant species from both an ecological and economic perspective, to a fungus that was introduced to North America in the early twentieth century.

In recent decades New England's eastern hemlock trees have been adversely impacted by the hemlock woolly adelgid (HWA), an aphid that was brought into the mid-Atlantic states from Asia in the mid-1920s. After being swept into southern Connecticut by a large storm in the mid-1980s, HWA has gradually spread north through the region and caused extensive mortality to hemlocks in certain areas of southern New England. The tiny adelgids, which are largely spread by birds, feed on hemlock needles and gradually kill individual trees over several years. Though studies are ongoing, the advance of HWA into northern and central New England may be checked to some degree by colder winter temperatures. Options for treating individual trees include spraying with oil and injecting chemicals into roots. The presence of HWA is easily identified by tiny white egg sacs on the hemlock needles.

A significant threat to the region's hardwood species emerged during the summer of 2008, when the Asian longhorned beetle was discovered in Worcester, Massachusetts, having likely reached the region in a wooden shipping pallet. Easily distinguished by the white bands on their long antennae and white spots on their back, these beetles can infest and kill many common and important tree species, including birches, maples, ash, and willows. Because there are currently no countermeasures, the only option for controlling the beetle's spread was to remove some 15,000 trees. A quarantine banning the transport of wood out of the region was declared for a 60-square-mile zone encompassing Worcester and four surrounding towns, which are within a densely forested part of Massachusetts.

Mixed Habitats: Forests and Fields

Many animals benefit from a mixture of forests and clearings. Areas where these habitats meet offer food, cover, and breeding habitat. The animals here, many of which are thriving today, favor woodland-field mosaics, which can include backyards and suburban areas.

WHITE-TAILED DEER (*Odocoileus virginianus*)
As beautiful as they are common, white-tailed deer are the region's most familiar game species and the first large mammal encountered in the wild by most New Englanders. Because they are thriving in all the region's states and are sometimes considered nuisances, it is hard to imagine that not long ago there were many places in New England where one had little or no chance of seeing a deer in the wild.

In terms of sheer numbers and visibility, no mammal better exemplifies the fluctuations that have characterized New England's dynamic wildlife history. Prized for their venison and hides, deer were hunted for market by early European colonists and deprived of food and cover by widespread forest clearing. So rapid was their decline that hunting seasons were enacted in Massachusetts and Connecticut by the 1690s, and a full three-year ban was implemented in the Bay State in 1718. By the onset of the twentieth century, deer were largely absent from southern New England, save for holdouts in isolated areas of the Berkshire Hills and Cape Cod; Connecticut's deer population was estimated at an even dozen in 1896. In Vermont, deer were essentially eliminated from the region south of Middlebury by 1800.

Whitetail dynamics in interior Maine and north-central New Hampshire have an interesting history relative to other areas of New England. In the precolonial era, the deer population in both states was likely concentrated along the coast and in river valleys, with lesser numbers in the interior uplands due to the harsh winters, predators, and lack of food availability in mature old forests. However, as colonists cleared the forests, they created a mosaic of mixed habitats and an abundant food source of hardwood saplings, and removed wolves and mountain lions, all of which benefited deer and allowed an expansion of their range north and west. One consequence of the spread of deer into the north woods was the aforementioned brainworm disease, which has killed many moose.

From mid-twentieth century onward, deer populations have rapidly increased throughout much of New England. An estimated 160,000 individuals have reclaimed Vermont, 150,000 are reported in Connecticut, and the Massachusetts population is approaching 100,000. Rhode Island hosts 16,000, up from fewer than 700 in the mid-twentieth century. Maine provides habitat for more than 255,000 whitetails, though harsh winters in the interior can cause mortality rates as high as 10 to 30 percent. These estimates are a testament to the regrowth of forests over the past century, years of carefully managed hunting seasons, a handful of reintroduction efforts, and the prolific reproductive capacity of the species. The elimination of top predators is an important factor as well, as coyotes and black bears are generally opportunistic predators on fawns or injured or aged individuals and have little impact on overall populations, compared with long-lost wolves and mountain lions.

EASTERN COYOTE (*Canis latrans*)

A now-familiar denizen of habitats ranging from deep mountain forests to sandy beaches and urban neighborhoods, the remarkably adaptable eastern coyote has successfully colonized much of New England's diverse landscape over the past half century and is now the region's top predator. Much larger than their western counterparts, eastern coyotes are fairly close in size and genetic makeup to wolves.

In contrast to species such as white-tailed deer, wild turkeys, beavers, and moose, all of which are reclaiming their original ranges in the Northeast, coyotes are believed to be a newcomer to New England's landscape, having migrated into the region from the western states. Chief among the reasons for their success in the East was the elimination of wolves and mountain lions, which allowed coyotes to fill their niche without competition. The recent reintroduction of wolves to Yellowstone National Park demonstrated how wolves kill coyotes and drive them from their territories. Land clearing and suburban development also created ideal travel corridors that allowed coyotes to move eastward, as they thrive in brushy clearings associated with second-growth forests. Coyotes reached Michigan during the 1920s and the northern Adirondacks by the late 1930s. In New England the first reports were 1942 in Vermont, 1944 in New Hampshire, 1955 in Connecticut, 1957 in Massachusetts (one was trapped in Amherst in 1936, but there is some question if it was a released individual), the late 1960s in Maine, and 1978 for Rhode Island.

The coyote's rapid population growth and spread throughout New England have inevitably resulted in conflicts with humans. Shortly after the animals arrived in the area during the 1960s, farmers in western Massachusetts suffered losses to livestock. In 1999 a coyote that had become acclimated to people bit a young child in a backyard on Cape Cod, while another managed to find its way into a home in the town of Hatfield, giving the owner an early morning surprise. In early 2001, following a series of attacks on domestic animals, parents in a Plymouth, Massachusetts, neighborhood sent children to school bus stops armed with baseball bats. Nevertheless, problem coyotes are the exception rather than the rule, and people are infinitely more likely to be attacked by a domestic animal.

MILK SNAKE (*Lampropeltis triangulum*)

For those unfamiliar with New England snakes, an encounter with a milk snake can be unsettling: they are roughly comparable in size, coloration, and general body pattern to copperheads, and shake their tails in a manner similar to rattlesnakes. However, the only threat these large but even-tempered snakes pose to humans are nonvenomous bites for those who try to handle them.

Unlike the poisonous relatives that they mimic, milk snakes are common and widespread throughout much of the region, though they are absent from most of northern and central Maine and northern portions of New Hampshire and Vermont. They inhabit a wide variety of natural habitats where a level of woody or brushy cover is available, including rocky hillsides, wetland edges, meadows and old fields, and forests. A likely place to spot milk snakes may well be your own backyard, as they are often found around homes, lawns, farm fields, barns, old wells, and garages. They are mostly active by night, spending days hidden beneath the various cover sources.

Though small mammals are their favored food items (one study indicated that mice constituted nearly three-quarters of their diet), other prey includes amphibians, earthworms, insects, birds, and other, smaller snakes.

While their adaptability bodes well for their long-term survival in New England's ever-changing landscape, the continued loss of open and brushy field habitats to forest regrowth and development may affect milk snake populations to some degree.

WILD TURKEY (*Meleagris gallopavo*)

Though Benjamin Franklin's supposed advocacy of the wild turkey as the national emblem of the United States may have been overstated, he nevertheless viewed it as a "true original Native of America . . . a Bird of Courage [that] would not hesitate to attack a Grenadier of the British Guards who should presume to invade his farm yard with a red Coat on." Unfortunately, Franklin's affection for this distinctive game bird didn't stop many of his fellow Americans from extirpating it from most of its original range. From an estimated 10 million individuals in precolonial times, the country's overall wild turkey population bottomed out at a mere 30,000 at the onset of the twentieth century, following three centuries' worth of hunting and forest clearing.

However, by the close of the century, wild turkeys were once again common in New England, thanks to successful reintroduction efforts, the return of forests, and their prolific reproductive capacity. In Vermont a group of 30 birds that was released in 1969 grew to more than 600 within four years, allowing a hunting season to be declared in 1973. After their numbers held steady at 9,000 to 12,000 individuals through the 1980s, mild winters and limited hunting allowed the state's turkey population to swell to the present 35,000, a total roughly equivalent to the nation's cumulative population in 1900. Reintroductions in New Hampshire from the mid-1970s onward also were successful; the state's turkey population is currently 25,000.

Twenty-nine of Vermont's turkeys were sent to Exeter, Rhode Island, in 1980 as part of the Ocean State's first reintroduction project; over a span of 30 years this group has grown to nearly 6,000. In Massachusetts, following several unsuccessful attempts from 1910 onward, breeding turkeys were successfully returned to the Berkshires in 1972. Portions of this population were subsequently relocated to the rest of the state, and flocks are common to abundant in most areas. Neighboring Connecticut has provided birds for similar efforts in Maine, Louisiana, North Carolina, and Texas.

Throughout their range, wild turkeys favor areas where hardwood forests are interspersed with fields and clearings. They are less common in the northern New England mountains because of the harsh winters, deep snow, and reduced habitat diversity. They often form groups of 20 to 30 individuals with distinct social hierarchies, though larger flocks with as many as 200 birds have also been observed. During the spring breeding season, males stage showy courtship displays to attract potential mates.

VIRGINIA OPOSSUM (*Didelphis virginiana*)

How distinctive is the Virginia Opossum? Some 335 species of marsupials, or mammals with pouches where the mother carries her young, are distributed worldwide. Of these, roughly 100 are found in the American continents, but only one—the Virginia opossum—lives in North America. From South and Central America these opossums first reached the southern United States in the early seventeenth century, and arrived in New England around the start of the twentieth century. Over the past 100 years they have gradually become established throughout southern New England and the mild regions of Vermont, New Hampshire, and Maine. The harsh winters of the northern mountains, a world apart from the tropics where they originated, restricts their range limit. Possums don't hibernate during cold periods, but they do reduce their activity levels significantly; it's not uncommon for individuals to lose ears or tails to frostbite.

Virginia opossums are highly adaptable in both habitat and diet. Their preferred homes are moist woods near wetlands such as streams and swamps, but they are also common around buildings and suburban areas. In spite of their frequent proximity to humans, they are rarely seen, as they are primarily nocturnal creatures. So varied is their diet, which includes insects, fruits, nuts, eggs, and even carrion, that their scats are difficult to identify.

One to three times per year, the mother opossum gives birth to a litter that can range from 1 to 14 newborns; the average litter is 9. Born blind, roughly the size of a honeybee or bean, and weighing a fraction of an ounce, the juveniles remain to wean in the pouch for 50 to 65 days. After roughly 60 to 80 days they are mature enough to leave the pouch and often ride along on their mother's back, and after three more weeks they reach full independence.

Perhaps the best-known characteristic of Virginia opossums is their behavior of playing dead (hence the phrase "playing possum") to deter attackers such as predators and domestic dogs; an individual can maintain this comalike state for up to six hours.

LITTLE BROWN BAT (*Myotis lucifugus*)

The hunting prowess of bats is truly remarkable: during the course of a single hour, one individual may consume 600 or more insects, without the benefit of daylight. Using an aptly named process known as "echolocation," bats emit an ultrasound pulse through their nose and listen for return echoes, which indicate the location of mosquitoes, midges, moths, beetles, termites, and other potential prey. The only mammals that actually fly (flying squirrels are gliders), bats reside in a wide variety of habitats, including fields, lakes, ponds, forests, and backyards—essentially anyplace where there's a good stock of insects. They spend daylight hours in treetops and other dark places, which often include barns, attics, and other dwellings.

Of the United States' 45 bat species, 9 are present in New England, the most familiar of which is the little brown bat (also known as the little brown myotis). Though most of the region's species migrate south during the winter months, little brown bats spend this time hibernating in caves in groups that once were as large as 300,000 individuals. During warm-weather days, females roost in maternal communities, while males generally seek isolated, cooler locations such as mountain or hillside slopes and wetland valleys. These prolific eaters generally fill their stomachs within an hour or so of hunting during forays after sunset and before dawn and are in turn targeted by owls and other birds of prey, snakes, and even mice.

Sadly, in recent years brown bat populations throughout New England and the Northeast have been decimated by the spread of white-nose syndrome (WNS), a fungus that causes individuals to prematurely deplete their energy reserves when they would normally be hibernating during winter; starved individuals have been observed flying during daylight in the middle of winter. WNS was first discovered by a caver in upstate New York in February 2006, and it has subsequently been confirmed in all the New England states except Maine, with mortality rates as high as 90 to 100 percent; at one old mine in Chester, Massachusetts, the population has rapidly dropped from 10,000 to fewer than 50. Because bats have a low reproductive rate of one pup per year, it will take a long time for affected colonies to recover. Investigations to better understand this new and unfortunate disease are ongoing.

BLACK FLY (*Simulium*)

From behind a computer screen it's easy to extol the virtues of black flies as an integral link in the food chain and a reliable indicator of pure, clean rivers and streams. From along a forest trail, campground, or riverside it is of course a different story, as almost anyone who has spent time outdoors fending off late-spring swarms can attest.

The term "black fly" is actually a general moniker that encompasses more than 2,000 closely related species worldwide, only 10 percent of which actually seek out and feed on human blood. Some 255 of these are found across North America, including 40 recorded varieties in the Maine woods alone. Black flies favor areas with active rivers and streams, and the Northeast, with its high annual precipitation and variable topography, offers an abundance of this habitat. In these waterways females deposit as many as 500 eggs. Both males and females rely on nectar from plants to sustain their activity; the females seek blood from birds and mammals to nourish their eggs.

New England's black fly season generally lasts from mid-May to the end of the breeding season in early July, though variations occur annually, depending on temperature and precipitation. In areas with little suitable habitat, they may be nothing more than an occasional nuisance, though other biters such as mosquitoes, which thrive in areas with calm, stagnant water, and deerflies are often present. Attracted by carbon dioxide, the flies often swarm the head of their target and target any exposed skin. While individual bites rarely result in anything more serious than nuisance itching and swelling, more serious reactions are possible in rare instances, and concentrated attacks from large swarms have killed livestock and other animals throughout the world.

As annoying as they can be, thriving black fly populations reflect the health of their associated waterways, as contaminated rivers and streams make for untenable breeding areas. Black fly populations dropped during the height of pollution from sewage and mill waste (some ill-advised early control efforts included dumping chemicals in rivers) but have recovered since the passage of the Clean Water Act in 1972. Several revitalized rivers in Maine have recently supported black flies for the first time in many years.

Mountains

Carved and scoured by glaciers, New England's landscape features highly variable topography. The Appalachian Mountains cross all the region's states except Rhode Island. Nearly 70 mountains in New England exceed 4,000 feet, capped by 6,288-foot Mount Washington, the Northeast's highest peak. A handful of these high summits in northern New England have open alpine areas with vegetation characteristic of Labrador. There are also a number of isolated mountains, known as "monadnocks," and innumerable low rolling hills. The following hardy species generally favor rugged, often isolated mountains, ridges, and hills.

EASTERN TIMBER RATTLESNAKE (*Crotalus horridus*)

Many people are surprised to learn that poisonous snakes such as rattlesnakes and copperheads inhabit New England. After all, the "dangerous" wild creatures such as wolves and mountain lions that once inhabited the region have long been extirpated. However, in remote, isolated pockets, a few holdout populations of both these snake species cling to a tenuous existence.

Historical evidence indicates that eastern timber rattlesnakes were once fairly widespread throughout New England; snake bounties were once issued in 20 Connecticut towns. However, overall habitat loss, combined with hunting, motivated largely by the general public's fear and perceptions of poisonous snakes, and excessive gathering by collectors, reduced this eastern rattler's range to a handful of areas.

Documented populations of rattlesnakes currently exist in Connecticut in 10 towns in the northwest hills and the central Connecticut River Valley. The northwest population extends into the southern Berkshire Hills of neighboring Massachusetts, and that state also hosts dens in Hampden County and the Blue Hills near Boston. Since 1980, rattlesnakes have been reported in 11 Vermont towns, most of them clustered in the state's west-central region. In New Hampshire only a single population of roughly 25 individuals in the southern hills is known.

Rattlesnakes emerge from hibernation in April and are active through October, primarily by day during cool months and by night during the heart of summer. They inhabit areas with south-facing hillsides, rocky outcroppings, and ridges that allow them to easily bask in the sun and dense forest cover, where they hunt prey such as squirrels, chipmunks, mice, voles, rabbits, weasels, birds, and amphibians.

The odds of encountering a rattlesnake along a trail are extremely low, as they favor secluded areas and are quite sensitive and easily able to detect footsteps from long distances. Nevertheless, hikers should use caution and back away slowly should one be spotted. In the extremely unlikely event of an actual bite from any poisonous snake, victims should remain still, or if required to move should limit motion of the afflicted area as much as possible to slow the spread of the venom. Medical assistance should be sought immediately, though the bites are rarely fatal.

PEREGRINE FALCON (*Falco peregrinus*)

Few species can match the hardy qualities of peregrine falcons. Fabled worldwide for centuries for their hunting prowess, they often reach speeds as high as 200 miles per hour while diving in pursuit of avian prey ranging from shorebirds and waterfowl to woodland songbirds. During the warm-weather breeding season pairs nest in steep, rugged areas where there is minimal exposure to predators and a elevated view to scope out potential prey, such as the Great Cliff of Mount Horrid and Smugglers' Notch in Vermont, Champlain Mountain in Acadia National Park, and even tall buildings in cities. Once they establish a favored nest site, generations will return to it faithfully for centuries. As winter approaches, these stout fliers undertake long migratory journeys to destinations as far south as South America, though a few overwinter along New England's south coast.

Unfortunately, none of these attributes afforded peregrines protection from the DDT insecticide contamination that also decimated bald eagles and osprey during the mid-twentieth century. In 1948 the Massachusetts state ornithologist noticed that a peregrine nest at Quabbin Reservoir had broken eggs; this was one of the first indications of what turned out to be a worldwide epidemic. By 1955, when the last falcon was seen at Monument Mountain in the Berkshires, the state's 14 pairs were gone, mirroring the national trend.

Throughout the 1980s, reintroduction programs helped restore peregrines to the New England states, and roughly 100 nesting pairs are now known throughout the region. Nearly 100 individuals were released in Vermont from 1982 to 1987, and in 1984 a pair colonized a site on the cliffs of Mount Pisgah for the first time since 1970. Counts in 2008 indicated 38 pairs in Vermont and 18 more in New Hampshire. Some 150 falcons were released throughout Maine, with the first success noted in Oxford County in 1987. The following year peregrines reclaimed a well-known site in Acadia National Park, and as of 2009, 23 breeding pairs were known statewide. In Massachusetts a pair successfully nested atop a tall building in Boston in 1987, and over the next 20 years the population grew to 14 pairs, matching the pre-DDT count. In Connecticut, peregrines nested atop high-rises in Hartford and Bridgeport during the late 1990s.

While the recovery of peregrine falcons from DDT is considered one of the nation's best-known wildlife success stories, a recent study indicated some falcon eggs contained high concentrations of chemicals known as PBDES, which are used as fire retardants in a variety of household products. Though tests on lab animals have shown that PBDES may cause neurological and physical problems, no adverse effects have yet been documented in falcons.

COMMON RAVEN (*Corvus corax*)

Common ravens have a well-earned reputation as wily, clever creatures with humanlike traits, including adaptability, the ability to work cooperatively when hunting, and the lifelong bonds formed by mating pairs. For many people, they are a wilderness symbol on par with bears, moose, and loons, thanks to their propensity for wild, rugged places such as high mountain ridges, remote rocky ledges, and areas with extensive mature forests. They are a revered spirit for Native Americans and the subject of many legends and fables.

At 24 to 26 inches in length, ravens are the country's largest perching bird. They are generally half a foot longer than the familiar American crow, their relative in the overall crow and jay family, and sport a discernibly larger, heavier beak than their counterparts, which enables them to exploit a variety of food sources ranging from carrion and human garbage to fruiting shrubs and even other birds. They are also easily identified by their somewhat primordial guttural call, which is discernibly lower than the crow's.

Historically, ravens were among the many species that suffered from the combined effects of hunting and the widespread clearing of large areas of forest. With the regrowth of forests, they are again well-established year-round residents throughout northern New England and have steadily expanded their range into Massachusetts and Connecticut over the past 40 years. As recently as the 1970s there were only a handful of scattered reports of nonbreeding individuals in Massachusetts, but in 1980 a nesting pair was recorded at Mount Watatic in the north-central region, and within a decade roughly 15 nests existed statewide, mostly in wilderness areas such as Mount Greylock and the Quabbin Reservoir.

AMERICAN PIPIT (*Anthus rubescens*) and
ROCK VOLE (*Microtus chrotorrhinus*)

It's almost inconceivable to think that any creature would specially favor the alpine zones of New England's highest mountains as their home and breeding grounds. After all, these peaks and ridges are subject to, and open because of, exceptionally harsh weather that allows only well-adapted alpine plants, characteristic of regions such as Labrador, and stunted, crooked spruce and fir trees to grow.

Nevertheless, this environment is home to a handful of hardy, well-adapted species that tolerate these conditions. A recent arrival to several high-mountain sites in Maine and New Hampshire is the American pipit, a sparrow-size songbird that nests exclusively in alpine terrain throughout its range. Pipits have been known to nest on Mount Katahdin since the mid-1980s, and in 1991 a pair established a nest in an open meadow at an elevation of 5,400 feet on Mount Washington. Their largely gray and white plumage is unremarkable but provides excellent camouflage in their nesting habitat, which includes rocky burrows and fields where a level of shelter exits from the wind and storms. Once the breeding season ends, southbound migrants are common throughout New England, especially along the coast and in fields and marshes.

Rock voles are true boreal creatures that even breed beneath packed snow. Throughout their range, which stretches from Canada in scattered populations to the southern Appalachian Mountains, they nest along cool, wet rocky slopes, often at elevations above 3,000 feet. In the alpine zone of Mount Washington and the Presidential Range, they have been reported at 5,300 feet. Bunchberry wildflowers are among their preferred foods, and other staples of their diets include insects, flowering berries, roots, grasses and green plants, and mushrooms. They travel in narrow pathways between rocks, and one sign to watch for are caches of vegetation near waterways. They are similar in appearance to the much more widespread meadow voles, which tunnel through and under fields throughout New England.

Freshwater Wetlands

Fed by an average annual precipitation of 45 inches, New England's freshwater wetlands are as diverse as the rest of the region's landscape; they include lakes, ponds, rivers, streams, brooks, swamps, bogs, artificial reservoirs and millponds, and ever-changing beaver wetlands of all sizes. All provide habitat and breeding grounds for a wide variety of creatures, including reptiles, amphibians, and insects.

BEAVER (*Castor canadensis*)

It's hard to overstate the impact that beavers have on their environment. The wetlands created by North America's largest and most industrious rodent offer habitat for a long list of creatures, including moose, river otters, raccoons, and other mammals, waterfowl, wading birds, frogs, turtles, and dragonflies. The standing dead trees killed by flooding are used by nesting great blue herons, wood ducks, woodpeckers, and other birds. In the long term, after beavers abandon an area and the dams break down, the once-flooded wetlands revert to meadows that support a whole new suite of species, including bluebirds and insects that feed on wildflowers.

Beavers mate for life, forming colonies of up to a dozen adults, new-borns, and yearlings. They feed on tree bark, with a strong preference for hardwood species, as well as grasses and plants. As the local food source dwindles, they move on to new territories; one indicator that they may be about to relocate is when hemlock trees, which are not one of their favored items, are being gnawed.

Though beavers are common in New England today—it's hard to go for a late-day paddle or walk at a wetland and *not* be greeted by a sudden loud, territorial tail-slap—such was not the case a century ago, to the detriment of the many species that benefit from their wetlands. Beaver pelts have long been prized, to the extent that the exploration and settlement of large portions of North America, and several associated wars, were motivated by trappers and traders eager to tap the continent's substantial population, which may have exceeded 60 million individuals in precolonial times. By the start of the twentieth century, beavers had been largely eliminated throughout much of North America, though a small population persisted in interior Maine.

During the early to mid-twentieth century, beavers were successfully re-introduced throughout New England, setting the stage for a remarkable recovery. Vermont passed legislation protecting beavers in 1910, and the reintroduction of individuals from surviving colonies in Maine and New York allowed the state's population to slowly recover through the 1950s, when enough existed to allow a limited trapping season. Half a dozen animals were introduced to New Hampshire from 1926 to 1930, and within just 30 years they successfully reclaimed their historic range throughout the state.

A 1928 sighting in the Berkshire town of West Stockbridge was the first record of a beaver in Massachusetts since 1750; successful reintroductions were subsequently made at the nearby Pleasant Valley Wildlife Sanctuary during the 1930s. From 1952 to 1972, another group that was introduced at the Quabbin Reservoir produced 44 colonies. In Connecticut, beavers were introduced in the town of Union in the state's northeast region in

1914. By 1950 there were 20 confirmed colonies, and half a century later an estimated 5,000 to 8,000 individuals were at work reshaping the state's numerous rivers, streams, and brooks. The return of beavers has inevitably resulted in human conflicts—in one recent year Maine alone had more than 900 active damage-control projects—but it has also greatly benefited creatures such as moose and great blue herons, which have thrived in recent years.

RIVER OTTER (*Lutra canadensis*)

Like fishers, their relatives in the weasel family, river otters are active travelers, proficient hunters, and offer an endless repertoire of tracks and sign. However, the odds of actually observing an otter, as opposed to the elusive fisher, are much better: though sometimes secretive and uncommon, river otters are often visible swimming, hunting, feeding, playing, or just resting in wetlands and along riverbanks. They are perhaps easiest to find in early and late winter, when they often stake out and venture in and out of openings in ice, which they sometimes create themselves.

River otters are intelligent and efficient hunters that have been known to work together and even herd prey fish into accessible areas. Fish are their preferred food item, but depending on what's available, they also consume

River otters are familiar residents of wetlands throughout New England. In winter, watch for them feeding at holes and openings in ice.

crayfish and other invertebrates, turtles, snakes, small mammals, birds, and insects. Their hunting prowess leaves them plenty of time to travel about and engage in seemingly playful behavior among family groups. In winter they often belly-slide down a river or pond bank to the water or ice below, and will sometimes do so when traversing level ground. Other evidence of their activities along wetland edges includes areas of disturbed vegetation known as rolls, and piles of fish remains at feeding areas. Otters are often curious and will occasionally approach or tolerate the presence of humans, though people who come upon one by surprise are apt to receive a scolding of angry, raspy barks or a quick, splashy departure.

As a result of widespread trapping, river otters suffered significant declines from colonial times onward; some estimates indicate that they were reduced to as little as one-third of their original range. Though they have made a strong recovery in New England and the Northeast, they have only recently been reintroduced to some of the Midwest states. They remain vulnerable to development of wetland habitats and contamination from pollutants such as mercury, PCBs, and dioxins. Indeed, the presence or absence of these chemicals in otters is a reliable indicator of the water quality of our rivers and wetlands.

SNAPPING TURTLE (*Chelydra serpentina*)

Whether viewed basking on rocks, logs, or beaver lodges or swimming below the surface of a shallow wetland, snapping turtles are a striking, and sometimes startling, sight. With a shell as large as 20 inches long (three to four times that of New England's other freshwater turtles), snappers can weigh as much as 75 pounds, though most adults weigh between 10 to 35 pounds.

With this size also comes a somewhat aggressive and nasty disposition that can result—as the occasional human handler can attest—in a powerful bite with serious injury (these generally occur when the turtle is out of the water, and there is little danger to swimmers). These powerful jaws, which snap very quickly, allow snappers to consume a varied diet that includes fish, frogs, snakes, juvenile turtles, and even small mammals and waterfowl that unwarily venture into their grasp, as well as organic plant matter. Though speed when traveling over land obviously isn't one of their primary traits, snappers compensate for this by blending into their environment and assuming the size, shape, and color of a medium-size rock.

Snapping turtles are common throughout New England in a variety of wetland habitats with shallow water and mucky, debris-laden bottoms,

A giant snapping turtle at the edge of a beaver pond.

including beaver ponds, lakes, streams, swamps, and even coastal estuaries. Though they are largely an aquatic species, individuals may travel for considerable distances over land in search of suitable nesting habitat. Each June, adult females come ashore to lay an average of 20 to 30 eggs in nests along wetland edges and dry open areas such as fields, backyards, and cemeteries. Assuming the nest survives the ever-present threat of predation, juveniles are hatched roughly three months later, just before the onset of cold weather. It is during these land forays that snappers are in danger of being run over by motor vehicles; their size and slow gait make them especially vulnerable.

Along with their relatives in the overall reptile family, snappers hibernate during the winter months. They spend this time amid the muck and debris of wetland bottoms and edges and will use muskrat lodges and submerged logs if available. Though little is known about their activities during this time, snappers have been periodically seen moving about beneath frozen ice.

PAINTED TURTLE (*Chrysemys picta*)
Painted turtles are certainly among the most visible of New England's wetland wildlife. A sighting of one of their smooth, dark shells as these creatures bask atop exposed rocks, fallen logs, and aquatic vegetation inev-

itably leads to many more sightings, and even the smallest wetlands such as old mill, ice, and beaver ponds may host large groups. These "sun turtles" are familiar residents of ponds, slow-flowing rivers and streams, and swamps throughout the region, save for the high mountains, and are especially conspicuous in places with quiet, shallow water with weedy vegetation and muddy bottoms, where they hibernate during the winter months. The seemingly nonchalant basking behavior actually serves an important purpose for cold-blooded reptiles, as it speeds up their metabolism and creates energy for daily feeding forays. The diet of young painted turtles is largely carnivorous, but as they mature through their 20-to-30-year life span they tend more toward vegetarian.

During the breeding season in May and June, females travel out of the water in search of nesting sites, where they deposit an average of five to eight eggs, favoring areas with sandy soils with some sunlight exposure. Unlike other turtle species that leave their nests to travel to wetlands for winter hibernation, juvenile painted turtles often remain at their birth site until their first spring, hibernating in narrow chambers excavated by their mothers. Sometimes an independent adventurous hatchling will leave its siblings behind and make an autumn journey that may range from a matter of minutes to several days to the wetland where it will spend the rest of its life. Those young turtles that are fortunate enough to survive the constant threat of predation will take 6 to 10 years to fully mature as adults.

GREAT BLUE HERON (*Ardea herodias*)

With its six-foot wingspan and primordial croaking call, the great blue heron almost seems like a holdover from a prehistoric era. These large wading birds are now a familiar sight at wetlands throughout New England, where they are easily observed staking out favorite sites in search of the fish, reptiles, amphibians, and even small mammals that constitute the bulk of their diet. In areas where there is suitable habitat, they form large "rookeries," or colonies of nests, in tall dead standing trees.

The fact that many people take blue heron sightings for granted today is a blessing, as these birds have staged a remarkable population recovery and expansion in recent years. From colonial times through the late nineteenth century, herons were eliminated or greatly reduced through their entire range, in large part by hunters seeking feathers to adorn women's hats. By the 1920s the only known colony of great blues in Massachusetts resided in a grove of tall pines at Harvard Pond in Petersham, and until the early 1970s only a handful of scattered colonies were reported in the state's west and central regions. It wasn't until 1984 that nesting pairs were confirmed in Rhode Island at a wetland in the town of Burrillville.

The great blue heron's abundance in most of New England over the last 30 years also demonstrates its strong interrelationship with beavers, which have also made a prolific recovery over the past half century. With the return of beavers have come thousands of acres of new beaver ponds and wetlands, which in turn offer abundant nesting trees and food sources for the great blues. Because beaver populations and wetlands are ever-changing, the dynamics of great blue heron populations will likely shift and fluctuate as well; in one recent instance at the Wachusett Meadow Wildlife Sanctuary in central Massachusetts a large colony quickly abandoned its rookery after a 100-acre wetland abruptly drained following the failure of a beaver dam.

The region's largest colony of great blue herons is an island within the Missisquoi National Wildlife Refuge in northern Vermont that hosts more than 500 nests and has been active since the 1940s. The Maine coast from Casco Bay to Machias Bay is another important area that is home to one-quarter of the entire breeding population along the entire Atlantic coast. Though most migrate to warmer climates for the winter, some overwinter along the mild southern New England coast.

COMMON LOON (*Gavia immer*)

For naturalists, hikers, campers, and vacationers alike, the distinctive, laughlike tremolo call of the common loon, which often echoes loudly across remote lakes and mountain valleys as the sun sets, is one of the hallmarks of the New England outdoors. Indeed, loons rank along with moose and bears as one of the region's iconic wilderness symbols, as evidenced by their presence on innumerable gift items and tourism publications.

Undeniably contributing to the appeal of loons is their preference for many of New England's most scenic and pristine lakes and ponds during the summer breeding season. They require no less than a quarter mile of open water to take flight, a much larger space than other waterfowl. It is believed that a large flock of dead loons discovered at New Hampshire's Lake Winnipesaukee during a recent winter landed in the area seeking open water, then were unable to take off from the frozen lake. In winter they head for open water at bays and inlets along the coast and may be seen in groups from March through June and August to December; in some years groups of several hundred individuals have been observed near Rockport,

Massachusetts. They are adept fishers that have been documented diving as deep as 200 feet.

Like many other species, loons suffered significant declines from hunting in historical times. Though protected since 1918 by the Migratory Bird Treaty, they remain vulnerable to a number of threats, including development of lakes and ponds, the abundance of raccoons, coyotes, and other nest predators, collisions with boats, and entanglement in fishing lines and other garbage. They are also susceptible to high mercury levels resulting from industrial pollution, which affects their reproductive capacity and can even kill individuals outright; recent studies have indicated significant mercury content in 30 percent and 52 percent of the loons in Maine and New Hampshire respectively. As consumers of fish, loons are good indicators of water quality and lake ecosystem integrity, and loon reproductive and mortality problems are indicators of potential consequences for humans and other wildlife. Following studies that indicated that nearly half of all adult loon deaths were caused by ingesting lead fishing sinkers, New Hampshire became the region's first state to ban the use of lead weights in 2000.

With its numerous remote lakes and ponds, Maine hosts a healthy breeding loon population, though efforts are made annually to count and monitor their numbers throughout the state. Thanks to recent conservation efforts, Vermont's loon population has grown from fewer than 10 known pairs in the mid-1980s to 60 today, many of which inhabit the state's northeast region.

In southern New England, loons have benefited from the construction of the Quabbin and Wachusett reservoirs in central Massachusetts during the early to mid-twentieth century. Individuals arrived at Quabbin while it was still filling in 1943, and today it hosts half the state's estimated 25 breeding pairs, while several more call the smaller Wachusett Reservoir home. All told, at least 14 Bay State lakes and ponds have hosted resident loons in recent years.

BALD EAGLE (*Haliaeetus leucocephalus*)

Though the bald eagle was officially proclaimed the nation's national emblem in 1782, little was done to safeguard the welfare of this majestic bird of prey over the next 200 years. After suffering historical declines caused by sport hunting, industrial river pollution, and logging of nesting trees, bald eagles faced an even greater menace during the mid-twentieth century, when use of pesticides such as DDT was widespread. These chemicals caused the eggs of eagles, osprey, and other birds to thin and break prematurely, killing the unborn chicks. By the early 1960s a mere 415 nesting pairs were reported throughout the 48 contiguous states.

Fortunes began to change for eagles with the efforts of Rachel Carson, whose research and pathbreaking book *Silent Spring* ultimately led to the banning of DDT use in 1972. In 1978, bald eagles were afforded full protection by the Endangered Species Act, and populations began to recover throughout North America, aided by reintroduction efforts of both the eagles and Atlantic salmon, one of their favored foods.

Relatively little is known about historical bald eagle populations in New England, but sighting reports appear in the records of Samuel de Champlain and other explorers. Maine, with its long coastline and numerous inland lakes, offers extensive eagle habitat and was the only New England state where these birds weren't entirely extirpated by DDT. Even so, the state's population declined to just 21 pairs by 1967, but quickly recovered to 175 pairs by the close of the century. The first breeding pair to return to New Hampshire did so at Lake Umbagog in 1989, some 40 years after the state's last sighting; another pair nested unsuccessfully at Nubanusit Lake in the Monadnock region 10 years later. For a time Vermont was the country's only state (with the exception of Hawaii) not to host nesting eagles, a distinction that was happily removed during the spring of 2006, when a pair nested in the Connecticut River Valley. This was the first confirmed report since 1940, when a pair was observed at Lake Bomoseen; prior to 2006, unsuccessful nesting attempts were made at the Somerset Reservoir and North Springfield Lake.

In Massachusetts only a handful of reports exist prior to the twentieth century, and breeding pairs were unknown statewide from 1900 until the late 1980s. From 1982 to 1988 more than 40 chicks were hatched at the Quabbin Reservoir, and in 1989 two pairs successfully raised a total of three young. In 1992 one of the Quabbin pairs made their way to a lake in Litchfield County in northwest Connecticut, becoming the state's first reported pair in decades. There are currently 28 known pairs in Massachusetts, and half that number in Connecticut. In Rhode Island a single pair has nested in the town of Scituate since 2000.

In addition to the breeders, migrating and wandering individuals may be observed throughout the year in New England. They are often seen at hawk-watch sites during spring and autumn migrations. Some favored wintering sites include Great Bay in southeastern New Hampshire and the Quabbin Reservoir and the Merrimack River in Massachusetts; an estimated 100 individuals visit Connecticut alone annually.

Thanks to the widespread use of nesting boxes, the unmistakable wood duck is once again a familiar sight in New England.

WOOD DUCK (*Aix sponsa*)

With its multicolored plumage and unmistakable helmet-shaped crest, male wood ducks are the most distinctive of New England's freshwater dabbling ducks. Befitting their name, "woodies" are creatures of freshwater wetlands with forested edges, including swamps, marshes, and beaver ponds. Their nest sites include trees along the shore or in the woods up to a mile from the water, where they built nests that may be as high as 30 feet above the ground. They suffered significant declines in historical times when forests were cleared, hunting was unregulated, and beavers were extirpated, and were further affected by twentieth-century storms such as the hurricane of 1938, which destroyed many of the region's recovering forests.

Over the past half century, wood ducks have benefited significantly from the widespread use of specially designed nest boxes, which replicate cavities in big trees and have provided safe havens for thousands of hatchlings annually. Though the increase of mature trees in recent decades has lessened the need for these boxes, they continue to serve as useful sites that offer a high nesting success rate with protection from raccoons and other predators.

Wood ducks are now a familiar sight throughout much of New England during the summer breeding season, save for far northern Maine. They are also an increasingly common winter resident in southern New England and portions of New Hampshire and Vermont where there is open water. Those that depart the region during this time overwinter on the southeast Atlantic and Gulf coasts and in Cuba; during migratory periods in March and October and November, large flocks of as many as 200 itinerant individuals may join permanent residents at resting grounds. In the field, listen for the female's squeaking *oo-eek* and the male's high-pitched *ter-we-we* calls.

COMMON GREEN DARNER (*Anax junius*)
Though still largely unknown and overlooked relative to other wildlife, dragonflies and damselflies, collectively known as odenates, are a pleasure to observe for many reasons: they are active from the onset of warm weather in midspring through the close of the foliage season, are most visible during the middle of bright sunny days, actively feed on nuisance insects such as mosquitoes and deerflies, and feature colorful names such as violet dancer, eastern pondhawk, and dragonhunter. Roughly 170 odenate species occur in New England, each of which has a specific flight season and range of habitats. The earliest fliers emerge in mid to late April; the peak time, when the greatest numbers of individuals are active, is from mid-July to mid-August; and when conditions permit, the viewing season lasts into mid-November or even December, when the tiny but hardy yellow-legged meadowhawk is the last species on the wing.

Common green darners are arguably the most visible and familiar of New England's odenates. Unlike other species that may be glimpsed for only a matter of days or weeks, they are generally the first dragonfly on the wing in midspring and remain active throughout the warm months into October. Each sex has a distinctive, bright color—electric blue for the male, and green for the female—and both feature a large bull's-eye spot atop their head that makes them easily identifiable even at a distance.

Common green darners are also among a handful of North American dragonfly species that migrate from late July to October; during some years great swarms of nonresidents may be observed passing south over New England, especially during August and September. These movements are often most visible along the coast, though they can be apparent farther inland as well. In general, relatively little is known about these migrations.

AMERICAN RUBYSPOT (*Hetaerina americana*)
Damselflies differ from their dragonfly relatives on several fronts. Most obviously, they have smaller, narrow bodies and are weaker, less active fliers; they also perch with their wings folded parallel to their bodies, while drag-

The American rubyspot is one of the most distinctive damselflies found along New England wetlands during the warm months.

onflies spread theirs horizontally. They are no less abundant or colorful, as in summer the edges of ponds and wetlands are alive with a variety of species including bluets, forktails, and ebony jewelwings. There are roughly 20 species of bluets alone, many of which are so similar that it is difficult to distinguish them visually.

Perhaps the most distinctive, and certainly among the most beautiful, of New England's damselflies is the American rubyspot, which is active during the mid to late summer. Finding rubyspots is often a challenge, as they are relatively uncommon in the Northeast (they are more widespread in the southern states) and live primarily in low vegetation along moderately flowing streams and rivers such as the Penobscot in Maine, the West in southern Vermont, and the Millers and Deerfield in western Massachusetts, often in areas accessible only by canoe or kayak. For those fortunate enough to come across an individual or colony, the bright red thorax (the body segment between the head and the long abdomen) of the male and distinctive red wing patches make for a striking sight. While not quite as showy as her partner, the female features bright green coloration on her thorax.

Because relatively little is known about the abundance and distribution of rubyspots in the New England states, groups affiliated with the Millers River Environmental Center in Athol, Massachusetts, are compiling sighting information. See rubyspot.net for more information.

ATLANTIC SALMON (*Salmo salar*)
Renowned for the great distances they travel between their spawning and ocean feeding grounds, Atlantic salmon are symbols of wild, free-flowing

rivers and streams. These silver-colored, 30-inch-long members of the overall trout family are among a handful of "anadromous" species present in New England, spending most of their lives in salt water but migrating inland to spawn; others include alewife, American shad, blueback herring, and rainbow smelt.

An individual Atlantic salmon begins its life in freshwater rivers and streams, where it feeds on aquatic insects and in turn is vulnerable to predation by waterfowl, kingfishers, and other fish such as trout and pickerel. During this time the scent of these home waters, known as "spawning grounds," becomes imprinted. After two to three years, when the fish reach sufficient size to migrate, they head for ocean waters off Labrador, Newfoundland, and west Greenland, traveling anywhere from 10 to several hundred miles along the way. Here they grow rapidly, sustained by a diet that includes sand lances, zooplankton, and herring; predators include sharks, seals, bluefish, halibut, and tuna.

After one or two years in salt water, salmon follow their homing scent upstream back to their native grounds. Spawning takes place in late October and November, when females lay as many as 15,000 eggs in nests (known as "redds") scraped into gravelly wetland bottoms; hatching takes place during the following March and April.

Many New England Atlantic salmon runs have long been extirpated, due largely to the widespread construction of dams along large rivers such as the Connecticut and Merrimack, industrial pollution, and overfishing. Another factor in their decline is shrinking ocean populations, possibly resulting from overfishing and water temperature fluctuations. In June 2009, federal officials announced plans to classify Atlantic salmon populations in Maine's Androscoggin, Kennebec, and Penobscot rivers as endangered. The latter has served as a successful salmon run, with more than 2,000 individuals counted in 2008.

Fields, Meadows, Thickets

As forests have reclaimed the Northeast, fields and thickets, and the wildlife that favor such environments, have inevitably declined. The species that live exclusively in these areas, including bluebirds and other grassland birds, monarch butterflies, and rapidly declining New England cottontails, are now largely dependent on human management. Some fields are managed as open grasslands, while others are brushy and interspersed with shrubs and thickets.

NEW ENGLAND COTTONTAIL (*Sylvilagus transitionalis*)

From field observations alone, it is almost impossible to distinguish a New England cottontail from its much more common and widespread sibling, the Eastern cottontail. The differences between the two species, which include ear length and subtle stripes and spots, are nearly imperceptible and not always reliable. In the past, wildlife biologists have looked for subtle differences in skull specimens, and today DNA testing of droppings offers a more accessible and palatable alternative.

The story of the New England cottontail is the reverse of many of the region's presently thriving species. As recently as the 1960s, healthy populations existed throughout much of the Northeast, including all of southern New England and southern portions of Vermont, New Hampshire, and Maine. Since that time, populations of New England cottontails have declined by as much as 85 percent, and they now exist in only a handful of isolated pockets; the species has not been reported in Vermont since 1961, and fewer than 300 individuals are believed to exist throughout all Maine.

The overlying reason for this marked shift is the loss of early successional thickets to forest regrowth. New England cottontails are almost wholly dependent on this habitat, which was widespread following farm abandonment in the early twentieth century but has become increasingly rare. During this time, they have also faced increased competition from introduced eastern cottontails, which have sharper instincts to avoid predators such as foxes and coyotes and the ability to colonize a greater variety of habitats than their native counterparts. The prolific increase in deer, which also compete for food in the same brushy habitats, and the introduction of exotic, unpalatable shrubs such as honeysuckle, also have adverse effects on New England cottontail populations. Other factors include habitat fragmentation and suburban development, which increases their exposure to foxes, coyotes, and other predators that thrive in disturbed habitats, and the likelihood of being run over by vehicles.

In response to the scarcity of New England cottontails, several agencies, including the National Fish and Wildlife Foundation and the New Hampshire Fish and Game Department, have initiated projects to monitor and restore them to their range throughout the Northeast. Finding and maintaining increasingly rare brushy habitats in areas with low eastern cottontail populations will be the key for these rabbits' long-term prospects.

AMERICAN WOODCOCK (*Scolopax minor*)

As snow gradually recedes from brushy open fields and clearings each March, one of the earliest and most striking rituals of spring begins. At dawn and dusk, a series of loud, nasal *peent* or *beep* calls, repeated at varying intervals, indicates a male American woodcock calling to attract the attention of prospective mates. After calling, he performs a distinctive courtship flight, taking off and circling over his territory as the wings produce a loud, twittering sound that allows observers to track the bird's silhouette against the fading light. The flight continues for several minutes, then the sounds abruptly stop as the bird rapidly descends to the ground to begin the cycle again. These flights, which generally last until dark but may continue well into the night when there is a full moon, continue until the end of May. They may be viewed at open fields, meadows, parks, farm fields, and even suitable backyards that offer open space for the displays and a measure of protective cover.

Also known as "timberdoodles," woodcock are distinctive among inland birds with their teapot-shaped bodies and long beaks. Superbly camouflaged and often seen only after moving, they blend in with the forest floor at the edge of moist fields and wetlands, where they nest and hunt for earthworms and insects. Their overall range is the eastern United States, and they are year-round residents from Connecticut southward. After the courtship season ends, individuals and family groups can often be observed near moist areas and forest-field edges.

Though New England populations have remained generally healthy, woodcock habitat has declined throughout the eastern United States as maturing forests and housing divisions have increasingly reclaimed and occupied former old-field sites in recent decades; other threats include wetland draining and large timber harvests. The Moosehorn National Wildlife Refuge in Maine is one of several conservation areas that manages extensive portions of its land specifically for woodcock by creating and maintaining brushy habitat.

EASTERN BLUEBIRD *(Sialia sialis)*

Few New England birds are as beloved as eastern bluebirds, thanks to the distinctive blue, white, and red-rust coloration of the males and their propensity for bucolic meadows and fields.

Relatively uncommon in the precolonial era, bluebirds increased in number and peaked across New England when much of the region was cleared for agriculture in the nineteenth century. As the fields were abandoned and the forests grew back, the population of these birds correspondingly declined. Two other developments that further affected bluebirds were the introduction of house sparrows and European starlings, both of which reproduce prolifically and compete for similar nesting areas, and the temporary extirpation of beavers, whose wetlands created nesting trees and openings in the forest.

As a result, many conservation groups now maintain open fields and nesting boxes for bluebirds and other species that are dependent on open or disturbed habitats, such as bobolinks, eastern meadowlarks, indigo buntings, and a variety of mammals and insects. These efforts have helped sustain breeding populations of these species throughout New England, in spite of the recent prominence of forests. Nesting populations of bluebirds are present in all regions of New England, and they are increasingly common year-round residents in the warmer climes of Connecticut, Rhode Island, and southern Massachusetts.

For those who wish to maintain a nesting box, a premade box, metal pole, and mounting brackets can be purchased inexpensively. The box should be set up by April, 5 to 6 feet off the ground in an open field, ideally at least 100 feet from trees and shrubs. A thin pole (no more than half an inch in diameter) and/or baffle is recommended to prevent predators such as raccoons and snakes from climbing up the pole and raiding the nest.

MONARCH BUTTERFLY *(Danaus plexippus)*

It's hard to imagine that an insect weighing a matter of grams could successfully complete a journey of several thousand miles, but each year millions of monarch butterflies undertake a long migration across North America to milder wintering grounds in Mexico and California. As summer transitions into autumn, southbound individuals are regularly observed flitting over fields and even low mountains.

Monarchs are members of the overall brushfoot family of butterflies, which includes many of the Northeast's largest and most colorful species. They are distinguished from the similarly colored and patterned viceroys by their larger size, later flight season, and lack of a black line on their hind wings. The emergence of monarchs in fields and meadows is one of the signs of midsummer; these clearings take on a colorful appearance as the various insects feed on milkweed, goldenrod, clover, and other wildflowers. The loss of this pollinator plant habitat to human development, pesticide use, and invasive species is an issue of concern, as some insects have had notable population declines over the past half century.

While the typical life span for an adult monarch is four to five weeks, each season produces one special generation that lives seven to eight months, the equivalent of a human surviving 500 years. As the summer progresses and day length and temperature begin to change, the migrations begin. While New England's monarchs head for the mountains of central Mexico, those west of the Rockies journey to the central California coast. Though it varies by latitude and climate, the movement generally reaches its peak from late August to late September and continues until the first midautumn frosts. The southbound individuals don't survive long enough to make the return trip, and those that journey back to the Northeast have normal life spans and make the passage over one or two generations.

SNOW GOOSE (*Chen caerulescens*)

The movement of snow geese through the Champlain Valley of Vermont each fall is one of New England's most striking wildlife spectacles. Though these distinctive, orange-beaked geese don't breed in the region and are rare winter visitors, they make extensive use of open fields as rest areas while migrating to and from their breeding grounds in the Arctic. Their name has nothing to do with their presence during winter or the imminent arrival of snow; it instead refers to the resemblance that large flocks of resting geese have to patches of snow on the ground when seen at a distance.

The geese are most visible in the region from October to early November, when large southbound flocks pause to rest in agricultural fields and marshes along migratory corridors. In the Champlain Valley an estimated 20,000 individuals pass through the area each week during the height of the movement. Those that overwinter in the East gather in large groups at marshy areas, fields, and lakes along the Gulf and Atlantic coasts as far north as New Jersey, while others venture west to the valleys of California. In early spring they begin the return journey north and are often visible in the Connecticut River Valley and western New England, especially when grounded by the often inclement weather.

Not all snow geese are all white; once considered a separate species, the "blue morph" form features a bluish or gray-brown body and white head and neck. The blue form may actually be increasing relative to the white, as the latter is less well camouflaged to predators, including human hunters, at both its breeding and wintering grounds. Within the overall flocks, the white and dark forms tend to segregate, though periodic interbreeding occurs. Another similar species is the smaller and much rarer Ross's goose, which occasionally tags along with snow geese and is much sought by bird-watchers.

FIREFLY (*Photinus*)

On peak early summer evenings in open fields, lawns and gardens, and forest clearings, the displays of courting fireflies make for a striking spectacle that often lasts deep into the night. From organs in their abdomen that combine oxygen with a chemical called luciferin, fireflies emanate a yellow-green flash that is repeated every two to three seconds. Though the height of activity may last just a matter of days at a given area, lesser numbers of individuals continue their displays throughout the summer months.

More than 2,000 species of fireflies, which are actually members of the beetle order and are also commonly known as lightning bugs, exist worldwide, particularly in humid regions. Most common in New England and the Northeast is the Pennsylvania firefly, which, thanks to the efforts of schoolchildren, was the nation's first designated state insect. To avoid mating confusion, each of the various species has adapted a distinctive flash pattern. The males generally display while airborne, while females indicate their availability from the ground. Lighting isn't limited to courtship, as it also occurs in eggs and larvae (these are the glows one often observes in grassy margins as the summer winds down) and may deter predators from this insect's less-than-palatable taste.

While enjoying a summer display, one tends not to think of fireflies as predatory creatures, but the diet of juveniles in the larval form includes earthworms, slugs, and snails, which they may immobilize by spreading a paralyzing chemical from their mandibles. Once on the wing, adults feed on pollen and nectar from wildflowers and shrubs in the fields and openings. Cannibalism even occurs in a few species, practiced by females that mimic courtship displays.

Coastal : Ocean

When measured more or less in a line, New England's coast is roughly 575 miles long. But factor in all the various coves, peninsulas, bays, and islands, and this figure swells to nearly 5,500 total miles. From Connecticut to central Maine, sandy beaches and dunes are common, while from central Maine northward the shoreline assumes a rockier and more rugged character. Like their inland counterparts, many of the creatures that inhabit the region's offshore waters, including whales, seals, and seabirds, are recovering from past losses to hunting, predator control, and habitat loss.

GRAY SEAL (*Halichoerus grypus*) and
HARBOR SEAL (*Phoca vitulina*)

Often seen "hauling out" in large groups on rocks, beaches, and sandbars and fishing offshore waters and harbors, gray and harbor seals are among the most visible of New England's marine wildlife. Though they periodically socialize in mixed groups, the two species are easily distinguished, as gray seals are much larger (males can reach nearly 900 pounds) and have large, horse-shaped heads that contrast strongly with their smaller, torpedo-shaped counterparts. In fact, juvenile gray seals are sometimes mistaken at a distance for adult harbors.

As evidenced by popular boat tours that operate from Bar Harbor to Cape Cod, New England's seal populations are thriving; but as is the case with so many other species, these seals' fortunes have fluctuated greatly over the past century. During the late nineteenth century, bounties were placed on seals, which were believed to consume commercially valuable fish and which periodically damaged fishing nets. While Maine rescinded the law in 1905, hunting continued in Massachusetts until 1962, and gray seals in particular suffered substantial declines during this time.

The subsequent passage of the Marine Mammal Act in 1972 afforded protection to both species and set the stage for their rapid recovery over the past 35 years. During the early 1980s, gray seals returned to a historically favored site at Muskeget Island, which is a short distance from Nantucket Island, and five pups were born in the area in 1988. In 1993–94, surveys indicated 2,035 gray seals at Muskeget and the barrier islands of the Monomoy National Wildlife Refuge at Cape Cod's elbow, with another 500 to 1,000 in Maine waters. In 2001 another count recorded a healthy total of 7,200 along the entire New England coast. Today, Muskeget Island is home to the largest gray seal colony in United States waters, an estimated 3,000 individuals.

HUMPBACK WHALE (*Megaptera novaeangliae*)

With their hefty size of 40 to 60 feet, breaching acrobatics, and reliable visibility, humpback whales are the star attraction of wildlife viewing cruises from Rhode Island to Maine. Indeed, many tour operators guarantee sightings, which is a welcome development in light of past abuses this and many other marine species have suffered.

Humpbacks are distributed throughout the world's oceans, with an estimated total population of 80,000 in several distinct groups, most of which migrate from the equator to high-latitude summer feeding grounds. The

North Atlantic group is present in New England waters from April to November; the rich waters of Stellwagen Bank off Massachusetts are an especially favored area. The fish that they consume during this time sustain them for the rest of the year, as they live off fat reserves in winter.

Belying their body weight, which averages close to 30 tons, humpbacks frequently breach the ocean waters in acrobatic leaps, with as much as two-thirds of their body rising above the surface. They are best known for displaying their tail flukes as they dive; each tail has unique patterns that allow individuals to be easily identified and cataloged by researchers. These antics make humpbacks, along with fin and minke whales, the species that whale-watchers are most likely to observe from cruises or shore vistas.

Because of losses to commercial whaling, the worldwide humpback population is believed to have declined by as much as 90 percent by 1966, when a hunting ban was implemented. The North Atlantic population reached a low of only 700 individuals before recovery began.

NORTHERN RIGHT WHALE (*Eubalaena glacialis*)

It's unlikely that any tour operator will guarantee right whale sightings in the near future, as the species is one of the world's most endangered animals, with an estimated present population of only 300. Indeed, such is the concern for them that news and marine weather radio stations broadcast reports of known individuals in an effort to avert boat collisions.

Right whales were among the first mammals to suffer notable population declines during colonial times, as significant decreases were evident by the mid-eighteenth century. Indeed, their name stems from the fact that they were the "right" (that is, easiest) whale to hunt on several counts: they are generally found closer to the shore than other whales, are slow swimmers, hold copious amounts of whale oils, and floated for easy recovery after being harpooned. In contrast to many species that have strongly rebounded from historical declines, the low reproductive rate of right whales has resulted in only minor population increases, in spite of full protection since the 1930s, and it is quite possible that they came precariously close to becoming extinct.

Most right whales that visit New England spend the heart of summer at feeding grounds near Grand Manan Island and the Bay of Fundy off the far eastern Maine coast. During migrations in the spring and from September to November, they are most common around Stellwagen Bank off Massachusetts. During the midsummer months, one place worth visiting for potential sightings from shore is Maine's Quoddy Head State Park, where high bluffs provide views across the Grand Manan Channel. At 40 feet long, right whales are roughly the size of humpbacks; distinctive physical characteristics to watch for are their massive heads, which constitute fully one-third of their overall size, and lack of a back fin.

BASKING SHARK (*Cetorhinus maximus*)
You might expect one of the world's largest sharks to be a scourge of the ocean waters, devouring marine creatures of all sizes unfortunate enough to venture into its path. However, the basking shark is more of a gentle giant that feeds on tiny zooplankton. Individual basking sharks average 20 to 30 feet in length, but some may grow as long as 40 feet and weigh as much as 8,500 pounds. Along with the tropical whale shark (which is a rare visitor to New England's waters), they are the world's largest fish.

As they cruise the surface of New England's coastal waters from spring through autumn, basking sharks are often identified by their large, dark, triangle-shaped first dorsal fin that protrudes above the water; their smaller tail fin may also be evident. This visibility and behavior earned them their name, though in reality they are constantly searching for and filtering food. They are somewhat harder to find when below the surface, thanks to their gray-brown coloration and white mouths that blend with ocean water. Other distinctive characteristics include their rounded snouts, which contrast with the sleeker, pointed noses of other sharks, and small, rounded teeth that are used to filter food from the sea.

All told, roughly 15 varieties of sharks are present along New England's coast during the warm months. During the summer of 2009, great white sharks, which are uncommon visitors this far north, made much-publicized appearances off Chatham and the Monomoy National Wildlife Refuge, where there is an abundant food source of harbor and gray seals. A number of dead seals were found during this time, ocean beaches were closed to swimming, and a handful of sharks were tagged for research tracking. Though documented attacks are extremely rare, other species that are a potential threat to humans swimming well offshore include blue sharks and shortfin makos.

BOTTLENOSE DOLPHIN (*Tursiops truncatus*)
Few animals have as colorful a life history as the bottlenose dolphin: among many distinctions, this most common and best-known of the overall dolphin family has been trained by the United States and Russian navies to detect mines and enemy divers, been a star attraction at aquariums, served

as the namesake and mascot of an NFL franchise, and been the subject for the popular television series *Flipper*, as well as numerous books and movies.

Named for their elongated, beaklike snouts, bottlenose dolphins owe their charisma to their considerable intelligence, curiosity, and periodic affinity for humans and other creatures. Numerous instances of their co-operative behavior have been documented worldwide: they often form closely knit groups that work together by herding groups of fish to feeding areas, and have even been known to form mutually beneficial relationships with fishermen by driving large schools of fish into nets, then feeding in the confusion as the nets are hauled in. They have also been documented assisting injured or stranded fellow dolphins, whales, and humans, and even protected lifeguards from an imminent shark attack off New Zealand in 2004 by forming a tight circle and escorting them to shore.

Bottlenose dolphins reach a maximum length of 8 to 12 feet and are often seen leaping as high as 16 feet above the surface while riding boat waves. They consume as much as 30 pounds of food daily, favoring tuna, mackerel, and other ocean fish. Although they occasionally are prey for the largest sharks, schools of bottlenose dolphins are quite capable of fending off, and even killing, predators. Though their worldwide populations are healthy, threats include collisions with boats in high-traffic areas, entan-glement in fishing nets, declines in local food sources, marine pollution, and viruses. The overall dolphin family consists of 35 species worldwide; other members that frequent New England's offshore waters include At-lantic white-sided, saddle-backed, and white-beaked dolphins, and harbor porpoises.

LEATHERBACK SEA TURTLE (*Dermochelys coriacea*)

Among the least known of New England's marine creatures are the five species of sea turtles that visit the region's coastal waters. The largest of these are the leatherbacks, which boast a number of unique characteris-tics. Biologically, they differ from other turtles in that their shells, or car-apaces, are not bony, but instead are composed of a thick leathery skin, hence their name. They are also considerably more warm-blooded than other reptiles. Though leatherbacks that weigh more than 800 pounds are uncommon, some individuals as heavy as 1,500 to 2,000 pounds have been documented. In spite of their heft, adults migrate great distances to feed-ing grounds annually; one tagged individual traveled more than 20,000 underwater miles from Indonesia to the United States. During the course of their journey, they swim as fast as 22 miles per hour, the quickest speed on record for reptiles.

The Atlantic leatherback population nests at sandy beaches in Africa, Central America, and at one locale in Florida. It is at these sites where females make brief forays to lay eggs on the shore, which is the only time when either sex leaves the water. Little is known about the lives of juveniles, but very few survive to full adulthood. Not surprisingly given their size, those that do make it face little threat from predators, though they are susceptible to entanglement in fishing nets. The Atlantic group generally heads for Arctic waters during the warm months, where they enjoy abundant stores of jellyfish, one of their favored foods.

New England's other sea turtles include loggerheads, which are fairly common and well-distributed along the Northeast coast. Much rarer are the diminutive Kemp's ridley, which nests on only one beach in Mexico and is a species of special concern worldwide, green sea turtles, and hawksbills, only two records of which are known in New England.

ATLANTIC PUFFIN (*Fratercula arctica*)

With their outsize, multihued bills and white faces, Atlantic puffins are undeniably among the most endearing and popular denizens of the New England coast. Each summer, tour boat operators ferry thousands of birdwatchers and tourists to view this distinctive seabird, whose appearance and antics have earned nicknames such as "sea parrot," "bottlenose," and "sea clown." It is during these months that these normally ocean-bound birds make their only foray on land, when they come ashore to hatch and raise chicks in protected burrows on rocky islands, including Machias Seal Island off the down east Maine coast, which hosts some 3,000 pairs annually.

While never endangered worldwide, puffins and other Atlantic seabirds suffered significant declines along the Maine coast south of Machias Seal during the 1800s as a result of unregulated hunting, development, and the introduction of dogs, cats, foxes, and rats to breeding areas. Though they historically nested on at least five other islands along the Maine coast, including Eastern and Western Egg Rock, Large Green, Matinicus, and Seal islands, by 1900 only a single pair remained at Matinicus Rock in the midcoast region.

In 1973, in an attempt to restore puffins to the Maine islands, the National Audubon Society initiated Project Puffin, and over the next 13 years nearly 1,000 individuals were relocated from Newfoundland's Great Island (where more than 150,000 pairs breed annually) to Eastern Egg Rock. In 1981 four pairs returned to the island to nest, and this has grown to 90 as of 2007. Similar efforts at Seal Island from 1984 on have resulted in 300 pairs colonizing the island. The Matinicus Rock population has rebounded to 150 pairs, thanks to protection efforts that started with that last remaining pair.

Puffins are uncommon to fairly regular visitors to the southern New England coast from October to April, particularly following winter storms. They are common in the offshore waters during this time, and vagrants periodically wander down the eastern seaboard as far south as Maryland. One exceptionally unusual inland sighting was an individual that somehow turned up in the town of Lee in the Berkshire Hills of Massachusetts during November 1970.

HARLEQUIN DUCK (*Histrionicus histrionicus*)
Observing harlequin ducks in New England entails a visit to windswept, rocky coastal headlands in the dead of winter, but it's worth it for the views of one of the region's most distinctive birds. As beautiful as they are uncommon, harlequins are distinguished by their blue bodies, chestnut sides, and white head and wing stripes and spots. After spending the warm months nesting in Canada, scattered groups migrate south to overwinter along the Atlantic coast. Here they favor rocky areas with heavy surf and active water, where their preferred foods such as snails and crustaceans are readily available, ripped away from bluffs and ledges by the active tides. In their Arctic summer breeding grounds they also seek flowing water, such as mountain streams.

Because of historical declines caused by hunting and egg collection, fewer than 2,000 harlequin ducks are estimated to visit the entire eastern seaboard from October to early May; they are uncommon in Maine, Massachusetts, and Rhode Island and rare off Connecticut. However, they regularly return to favored sites, such as the ledges off Maine's Isle au Haut, where New England's largest winter colony has resided for the past century. Other reliable, similarly rocky areas include Cape Ann in Massachusetts and Beavertail State Park and Sachuest Point National Wildlife Refuge on Rhode Island's south coast; the latter hosts the region's second-largest colony. While they generally are present along the New England coast from late October to early May, a handful of summer sightings have been recorded over the years.

Other waterfowl that breed outside of New England but are present in the region during winter include surf, white-winged, and black scoters, buffleheads, long-tailed ducks, Barrow's goldeneyes, canvasbacks, king eiders, horned and red-necked grebes, and red-throated loons.

DOUBLE-CRESTED CORMORANT (*Phalacrocorax auritus*)

Though now one of the most conspicuous and easily viewed birds of the New England coast, the double-crested cormorant has had a tenuous relationship with humans since as far back as colonial times. It wasn't so much the volume of fish these modest-size seabirds consumed—swallowing and digesting a single medium-size prey fish can be a bit of a challenge for their long, thin necks—but rather their habit of breaking up schools of fish at weirs that was the bane of early fishermen. In more recent years, cormorants also have been a nuisance at fish hatcheries, where they have raided salmon stock.

From 1880 to 1925, cormorants were essentially absent from coastal Maine, though at least one record from the 1890s is known. They staged a rapid rebound to more than 13,000 pairs by the early 1940s, prompting the temporary enactment of more control measures. Massachusetts breeders were extirpated by the early 1800s, and it wasn't until the 1940s that pairs returned to Boston, Salem, and the Weepecket Islands of Buzzards Bay. The overall New England population reached 15,000 pairs by the 1970s, and cormorants are presently well-established along most of the region's coast and abundant in many areas. They are now known to feed largely on less commercially viable species such as alewives, smelt, and gunnel.

Cormorants owe their ability to recover to their adaptability: they nest in a variety of coastal habitats, including bluffs, level headlands, and small rocky islands, and are also increasingly present at inland lakes, ponds, and reservoirs. They have actually defoliated some small islets, as their waste kills the tall trees they nest in. Because their feathers lack the waterproofing oil glands that are present in other seabirds, cormorants are often seen with their wings spread, using sea breezes to dry off. Most migrate south to warmer climes from November to March (flocks as large as several hundred have been noted), though periodic winter sightings have been documented in Massachusetts since 1976, and they are considered very uncommon along the southern New England coast in general.

SWORDFISH (*Xiphias gladius*)

The sight of a swordfish breaching the open ocean on a high leap or basking on the surface is a thrilling moment treasured by boaters and saltwater anglers alike. Named for their long, thin upper jaw which constitutes fully one-third of their length, swordfish are powerful swimmers and jumpers that put up a ferocious battle when hooked, to the point that some have punctured boat hulls. Other identifying traits include a crescent-shaped tail fin and a large dorsal fin that begins behind the head. Body colors vary among individuals and include shades of brown, yellow, blue, gray, black, and silver; the upper portions are darker.

Swordfish head north from the Gulf Stream to New England's offshore waters during June, where they remain through October, when the ocean temperature drops. They are swift swimmers capable of reaching speeds of 60 miles per hour. They feed on schools of fish during nocturnal forays, using their sharp "sword" to attack and immobilize mackerel, herring, squid, and other prey species. Not surprisingly, individuals that reach adulthood have few predators save for large sharks, whales, and sports fishermen. For the past half century, except for a time during the 1970s when catches were restricted due to mercury contamination, swordfish meat has been an increasingly popular food item.

SAND LANCE (*Ammodytes*)

The inclusion of sand lances in an account of New England's iconic and charismatic fauna may seem curious, but as any marine biologist will attest, these narrow, half-foot-long fish, which are commonly but erroneously referred to as eels, are an especially important piece of the ocean's food chain. They are a staple in the diets of many familiar species, including whales, dolphins, porpoises, seals, sea turtles, puffins and other seabirds, and large fish such as salmon, cod, haddock, and yellowtail flounder. The interrelationship between sand lance populations and their predators has been well demonstrated in recent years at the Monomoy National Wildlife Refuge on Cape Cod. After a powerful storm in 2006 reshaped this chain of barrier islands and caused sand lance concentrations to shift elsewhere, the refuge seal population declined as they followed their prey.

Sand lances are common in a variety of marine habitats throughout the north Atlantic coast., including estuaries and open offshore waters up to 120 feet deep. Places with sandy substrates are especially preferred, as the sand lances burrow into these areas to rest and take cover from predators. They are active by day in schools ranging in size from 10 to thousands of individuals, most of which are one to three years old. Sand lances feed on the eggs of invertebrates, as well as phytoplankton at rich areas such as Stellwagen Bank off Massachusetts. Their color varies by the individual;

many have a silvery appearance, but others are blue-green, brown, or olive. Spawning occurs from November to March, at which time females deposit their eggs throughout the coast, especially in estuarine environments.

Coastal : Beach, Intertidal Zone, Tide Pool

The interface between the ocean and shore encompasses a variety of habitats, including sandy and rocky beaches, salt marshes, eelgrass beds, tide pools, mudflats, tidal creeks, and rocky headlands and bluffs. This is where some of the region's most unusual and distinctive creatures, such as sea horses, hermit crabs, and sea stars, are found.

PIPING PLOVER (*Charadrius melodus*)

Thanks to their endearing appearance and presence along many of New England's most popular beaches, piping plovers are among the region's best-known endangered or threatened species. During the warm-weather breeding season, these tiny, well-camouflaged shorebirds nest at scattered favored sites along the coast. Here the female digs a shallow, precariously exposed nesting scrape, often lined with shell fragments and pebbles, along the beach above the tide line. Piping plovers often share this habitat with colonies of least terns, which are listed as endangered in New Hampshire and Maine and threatened in Connecticut. The ever-increasing popularity of beach tourism in recent decades, which draws millions of human visitors and recreational users to these same sands, has inevitably increased the threats to these birds' long-term prospects.

After declining as a result of market hunting in historic times, piping plovers recovered strongly following the enactment of the Migratory Bird Treaty of 1918, but then declined again when much of the coast was developed during the post–World War II years; one study indicated that 70 percent of their potential habitat in Maine alone was lost during the late twentieth century. They are also vulnerable to conflicts with beach visitors and domestic dogs, over-sand and sports utility vehicles, destruction of nests by storms and high tides, and the increased presence of predators such as gulls, foxes, raccoons, and coyotes, all of which thrive in disturbed areas. Local residents sometimes are unsympathetic to their plight when it results in restrictions and beach closures.

When piping plovers were listed as a threatened species in 1986, surveys indicated a mere 547 breeding pairs along the Atlantic coast from South Carolina to Maine. Since that time landowners and conservation groups have worked diligently to protect habitat, including closing entire beaches during the breeding season and restricting access and motorized-vehicle use; such efforts on one eight-mile area at the Cape Cod National Seashore resulted in a notable increase in plovers in subsequent years. As of 2009 the overall Atlantic population has rebounded but is still estimated at fewer than 2,000 pairs.

NORTHERN LOBSTER (*Homarus americanus*)

It's hard to imagine that lobsters were once considered "poverty food" suitable for children, prisoners, and indentured servants, but so abundant and easy to catch were they in colonial times that servants actually demanded contracts restricting the number of times they could be served lobster each week. In recent times, of course, the perception of lobster has changed to that of a delicacy synonymous with coastal New England, especially Maine, where the trade largely defines and sustains the economy of many of the coastal and island communities. Local fishermen have long established an informal series of marked offshore territories, which they carefully monitor and guard; a recent dispute resulted in several boats being sunk in a central Maine harbor.

The roots of commercial lobster fishing in Maine date back to the mid-1820s, when boats known as "smacks," which were designed specifically to transport live lobsters back to the boats' Massachusetts ports, began arriving in Maine fishing villages, buying lobsters for a penny or two, then reselling them for higher prices in Boston. Several years later, canneries, where lobsters could be prepared and easily transported to more distant markets, began operating along the coast. The inevitable increase in lobster catches led to restrictions during the 1870s that prohibited harvesting egg-bearing females and established a closed season with size limits. By 1885 enough fishermen had joined in the pursuit of lobsters that profit opportunities declined, but the trade nevertheless boomed in subsequent years. After a long period of stable catches, lobster harvests substantially increased toward the close of the twentieth century. Conservation continues to be an ongoing story, as scientists and fishermen have long attempted to find common ground to ensure the long-term viability of the species while not restricting economic opportunities.

After spending daylight hours secluded in sandy burrows and rocky crevices, lobsters become hunters themselves at night, using their antennae to seek out a wide variety of food items such as snails, sea stars, crabs, worms, live and dead fish, grasses and weeds, and even other lobsters. Each claw serves a distinct purpose: one, generally the left, is larger and heavier and used to crush the shells of snails, clams, and mussels, while the other is slightly smaller, lighter, and used primarily to catch and cut fish and vegetation. During summer months, lobsters are found in shallow waters close to the shoreline, and in winter they travel offshore to waters as deep as 2,000 feet.

Only a tiny fraction of the 10,000 eggs a female lays annually survive to maturity; juveniles are especially vulnerable during their first two years and spend the bulk of this time hiding along the ocean floor. Lobsters regularly molt and shed their shells, which allows them to replace injured or missing claws and legs. Those that successfully reach adulthood and are lucky or smart enough to avoid traps may live to be as old as 100 years.

ATLANTIC HORSESHOE CRAB (*Limulus polyphemus*)

Horseshoe crabs are yet another species with a misleading common name, for they are not crabs and are in fact more closely related to spiders and distantly to scorpions. They are among the most conspicuous marine creatures, thanks to the large horseshoe-shaped shell for which they are named. Protruding behind this armor is a long, spiky tail that looks like it is capable of all sorts of mayhem, but is in fact used primarily to assist in turning over (they flip upside-down to swim). Hidden beneath the shell are five pairs of legs, which are used for lifting the shell and pushing forward.

Horseshoe crabs reside in sandy bay bottoms as deep as 75 feet. They spawn year-round in southern regions, but along the middle and north Atlantic coasts they wait until the ocean temperature reaches 56 degrees. During May and June, adult females and males come together to the high tide line to breed and lay eggs on beaches. After two weeks, the hatchlings are washed back to sea, where they burrow into sandy bottoms. Maturation is a slow process; after their first year they are but an inch wide, and it takes 9 to 12 years for them to reach full adulthood. Like many other marine creatures, they are highly vulnerable to predation during their youth, but once they mature, their hard shell and size protect them well from most threats. They have been exploited by humans for fishing bait, livestock feed, and even extracts of their blood, which is used by scientific companies to test for toxins. Their greatest concentrations along the Atlantic coast are found at Delaware Bay, where densities of more than 150,000 crabs per mile are possible. Here their eggs serve as a crucial food resource for migratory shorebirds.

FLAT-CLAWED HERMIT CRAB (*Pagurus pollicaris*)

Hermit crabs have one of the most unusual survival adaptations of any creature. In order to protect their soft and vulnerable abdomens, they slip their bodies into the empty shells of moon and mud snails and periwinkles and use these shells for protection as they travel about their various seashore habitats. It may seem like an uncomfortable process, but their curvy bodies actually are well-shaped to fit the round host shells. Maintaining a suitable home is an ongoing process as individuals mature and age, and they are continually in search of new, better-fitting shells. If a pair of hermit crabs come across the same prospective shell at the same time, they may even stage a duel for the prize.

The flat-clawed hermit crab, which is common throughout the Atlantic coast, resides in estuaries and sandy-bottomed wetlands as deep as 360 feet, as well as tide pools, where there are abundant potential shells. They travel by using three pairs of legs to lift their bodies, while two other pairs propel them forward; the hind legs are used to secure the shell in place. Like other crabs, they possess powerful claws; while feeding they hold prey such as clams with the larger right appendage and use the left for cutting and processing. Mating occurs in late spring on mudflats, when the shells serve another crucial function: females use them to ferry and protect the fertilized eggs around before releasing them to hatch. At roughly an inch long, hermit crabs are slightly larger than sand fiddler crabs and smaller than other relatives such as blue, green, and rock crabs.

LINED SEA HORSE (*Hippocampus erectus*)

Lined sea horses are undeniably among the most distinctive of the many wonderfully unusual creatures that inhabit tidal zones: here we have a true fish with a horse-shaped head, an aardvarklike nose, and a kangaroo-style pouch. Named for the series of white stripes on their bodies, lined sea horses are part of the overall sea horse family that includes 33 other species worldwide and are found throughout the east coast in shallow waters up to 230 feet deep. They feed through their snouts on invertebrates and plankton. The tail has an integral function, as it serves as an anchor that allows these somewhat weak swimmers to maintain a footing in their eelgrass habitats.

Sea horse bodies can appear in various tones of red, brown, yellow, gray, or black; they change color while hunting but also as part of courtship rituals as the males duel for prospective mates. During the breeding process it's the male who carries the eggs of his female partner around in his pouch, before roughly 100 to 250 offspring are hatched.

Sea horse populations suffered significant declines from 1931 through the 1950s after roughly 90 percent of the eelgrass communities along the coasts of both the United States and Europe were devastated by what was believed to be a natural marine fungus; many other species, including lobster, waterfowl, and mussels, were adversely affected by the loss of this habitat. Though these important areas have recovered over the past century, they remain vulnerable to industrial waste and sewage.

SEA STAR (class Asteroidea)

Among the most distinctive of the inhabitants of tidal zones and island slopes and shoals are colorful sea stars (the commonly used term "starfish" is a misnomer, as none are fish), of which New England has several species. These include the blood sea star (5 long, thin arms), northern sea star (5 arms with white spines), smooth sun star (10 or more plump arms), and the flowerlike spiny sun star (12 arms, large circular body). All have a disk-shaped center from which their arms radiate, and with the exception of the small blood sea star are roughly a foot long. Their variable colors include hues of red, orange, purple, pink, brown, and green. Sea stars are capable of regenerating damaged or lost arms, even if much of the disk is injured.

Perhaps the most unusual aspect of sea stars is how they feed. Their tiny, circular mouths and lack of arms or claws make them unable to prepare and process food the way other animals do, so they extrude their stomach and digest captured prey such as mussels and oysters from the outside, then retract the stomach back into the body. Because they are especially effective predators of oysters, oystermen have long sought to control sea stars by various means.

Sea stars, sand dollars, sea urchins, and sea cucumbers are members of an overall group known as echinoderms. Though these species are all quite different, the common characteristic for which they are named is an outer skin composed of bumps that help the organism move and that circulate water and food.

BIBLIOGRAPHY

Adamowicz, Joe. *The New Hiking the Monadnock Region*. Hanover, NH: University Press of New England, 2007.

Alden, Peter, et al. *National Audubon Society Field Guide to New England*. New York: Alfred A. Knopf, 1998.

Anderson, Peter. *In Search of the New England Coyote*. Chester, CT: Globe Pequot Press, 1982.

Auster, P. J., and L. L. Stewart. "Species profiles: life histories and environmental requirements of coastal fishes and invertebrates (North Atlantic) Sand Lance." U.S. Fish and Wildlife Service Biol. Report 82 (11.66), 1986. U.S. Army Corps of Engineers, TR EL 82-4.

Brown, Cindy Kilgore. *Vermont Wildlife Viewing Guide*. Helena, MT: Falcon Press, 1994.

Burk, John S. *AMC Massachusetts Trail Guide*. 9th ed. Boston: Appalachian Mountain Club Books, 2009.

Butcher, Russell. *America's National Wildlife Refuges: A Complete Guide*. New York: Taylor Trade, 2008.

Carroll, David M. *Swampwalker's Journal: A Wetlands Year*. Boston: Mariner Books, 1999.

Conkling, Philip W. *Islands in Time: A Natural and Cultural History of the Islands of the Gulf of Maine*. Camden, ME: Down East Books, 1999.

Copeland, Cynthia, Thomas Lewis, and Emily Kerr. *Best Hikes with Kids: Connecticut, Massachusetts, and Rhode Island*. Seattle: Mountaineers Press, 2007.

Davis, William. *Massachusetts Wildlife Viewing Guide*. Helena, MT: Falcon Press, 1996.

DeGraff, Richard M., and Deborah Rudis. *Amphibians and Reptiles of New England*. Amherst: University of Massachusetts Press, 1983.

Duchesne, Robert S. *Maine Birding Trail*. Camden, ME: Down East Books, 2004.

Ferguson, Gary. *National Geographic Guide to America's Outdoors: New England*. Washington, DC: National Geographic Society, 2000.

Friary, Ned, and Glenda Bendure. *Walks and Rambles on Cape Cod and the Islands*. Woodstock, VT: Backcountry Publications, 1999.

Friedman, K., and J. Kocik. *Status of the Fishery Resources of the Northeastern United States.* Northeast Fisheries Science Center Resource Evaluation and Assessment Division, NOAA Technical Memorandum NMFS-NE, 1998.

Godin, Alfred. *Wild Mammals of New England.* Baltimore: Johns Hopkins University Press, 1977.

Jackson, Scott, and Peter Mirick. *Massachusetts Snakes: A Guide.* Amherst: University of Massachusetts Extension and Massachusetts Division of Fisheries and Wildlife, http://www.umass.edu/nrec/pdf_files/ma_snake_guide.pdf.

Johnson, Charles. *The Nature of Vermont: Introduction and Guide to a New England Environment.* Hanover, NH: University Press of New England, 1998.

Kulik, Stephen, Pete Salmansohn, Matthew Schmidt, and Heidi Welch. *The Audubon Society Field Guide to Natural Places of the Northeast: Inland.* New York: Hilltown Books, 1984.

Lanza, Michael. *New England Hiking: The Complete Guide to More Than 380 Hikes.* 3rd ed. Emeryville, CA: Avalon Travel Publishing, 2002.

Laubach, René. *Audubon Guide to the National Wildlife Refuges: New England.* New York: St. Martin's Griffin, 2000.

Nikula, Blair, Jennifer Loose, and Matthew Burne. *Field Guide to the Dragonflies and Damselflies of Massachusetts.* Westborough, MA: Massachusetts Division of Fisheries and Wildlife Natural Heritage and Endangered Species Program, 2003.

Perry, John, and Jane Greverus. *Sierra Club Guide to the Natural Areas of New England.* San Francisco: Sierra Club Books, 1997.

Petersen, Wayne R., and Roger Burrows. *Birds of New England.* Auburn, WA: Lone Pine Press, 2004.

Raleigh, Lloyd. *The Natural History of Coskata-Coatue Wildlife Refuge.* Beverly, MA: Trustees of Reservations, 1998.

Rezendes, Paul. *Tracking and the Art of Seeing.* 2nd ed. New York: HarperCollins, 1999.

Silliker, Bill. *Maine Moose Watcher's Guide.* South Berwick, ME: R. L. Lemke (undated).

———. *Wild Maine: Discoveries of a Wildlife Photographer.* Camden, ME: Down East Books, 2004.

Silverberg, Judith. *New Hampshire Wildlife Viewing Guide.* Helena, MT: Falcon Press, 1997.

Sinton, John, Elizabeth Farnsworth, and Wendy Sinton. *The Connecticut River Boating Guide: Source to Sea*. Helena, MT: Falcon Press, 2007.

Smith, Steven D. *Ponds and Lakes of the White Mountains: From Wayside to Wilderness*. Woodstock, VT: Backcountry Publications, 1993.

Sterling, Dorothy. *The Outer Lands: A Natural History Guide to Cape Cod, Martha's Vineyard, Nantucket, and Block Island*. New York: W. W. Norton, 1978.

Tougias, Michael J. *New England Wild Places: Journeys through the Back Country*. North Attleboro, MA: Covered Bridge Press, 1997.

Tougias, Robert. *Birding Western Massachusetts: A Habitat Guide to 26 Great Birding Sites from the Berkshires to the Quabbin*. Amherst, MA: New England Cartographics, 2003.

University of Florida Entomology Department. Luna moth fact sheet, http://entomology.ifas.ufl.edu/creatures/misc/moths/luna_moth.htm.

Veit, Richard, and Wayne Petersen. *Birds of Massachusetts*. Lincoln, MA: Massachusetts Audubon Society, 1993.

Vermont Fish and Wildlife. Wildlife and Wildlife Management Area Fact Sheets, http://www.vtfishandwildlife.com.

Weber, Ken. *Weekend Walks in Rhode Island: 40 Trails for Hiking, Birding, and Nature Viewing*. Woodstock, VT: Countryman Press, 2005.

Weidensaul, Scott. *Seasonal Guide to the Natural Year: New England and New York*. Golden, CO: Fulcrum Publishing, 1993.

Wetherell, W. D. *The Smithsonian Guides to Natural America: Northern New England*. Washington, DC: Smithsonian Books, 1995.

Wilson, J. M. 2001. *Beavers in Connecticut: Their Natural History and Management*. Hartford: Connecticut Department of Environmental Protection, Wildlife Division. 18 pp.

INDEX

Page numbers in *italic* denote sites that offer especially reliable viewing opportunities of a particular species ("black bear"), group ("songbirds"), habitat ("beach"), or phenomenon ("raptor migration").

Library of Congress Cataloging-in-Publication Data
Burk, John S.
The wildlife of New England: a viewer's guide / John S. Burk. — 1st ed.
    p. cm.
Includes bibliographical references and index.
ISBN 978-1-58465-834-4 (pbk.: alk. paper)—
ISBN 978-1-61168-009-6 (e-book: alk. paper)
1. Natural areas—New England—Guidebooks. 2. Wilderness
areas—New England—Guidebooks. 3. Natural history—New
England—Guidebooks. 4. New England—Guidebooks. I. Title.
QH76.5.N45B87   2011
508.74—dc22   2010050692